Contested and Shared Places of Memory

The Baltic–Russian debates on the past have become a hot spot of European memory politics. Violent protests and international tensions accompanying the removal of the "Bronze Soldier" monument, which commemorated the Soviet liberation of Tallinn in 1944, from the city centre in April 2007 have demonstrated the political impact that contested sites of memory may still reveal.

In this publication, collective memories that are related to major traits of the 20th century in North Eastern Europe – the Holocaust, Nazi and Soviet occupation and (re-)emerging nationalisms – are examined through a prism of different approaches. They comprise reflections on national templates of collective memory, the political use of history, cultural and political aspects of war memorials, and recent discourses on the Holocaust. Furthermore, places of memory in architecture and urbanism are addressed and lead to the question of which prospects common, transnational forms of memory may unfold.

After decades of frozen forms of commemoration under Soviet hegemony, the Baltic case offers an interesting insight into collective memory and history politics and their linkage to current political and inter-ethnic relationships. The past seems to be remembered differently in the European peripheries than it is in its centre. Europe is diverse and so are its memories.

This book was published as a special issue of the *Journal of Baltic Studies*.

Jörg Hackmann is Alfred Döblin Professor of East European History, University of Szczecin (Poland) and Visiting Scholar at the University of Chicago.

Marko Lehti is Senior Research Fellow at Tampere Peace Research Institute at the University of Tampere and Academic Director of the Baltic Sea Region Studies Master's Programme at the University of Turku.

Contested and Shared Places of Memory

History and Politics in North Eastern Europe

Edited by Jörg Hackmann and Marko Lehti

Routledge
Taylor & Francis Group
LONDON AND NEW YORK

First published 2010 by Routledge
2 Park Square, Milton Park, Abingdon, Oxon, OX14 4RN

Simultaneously published in the USA and Canada
by Routledge
711 Third Avenue, New York, NY 10017

First issued in paperback 2013

Routledge is an imprint of the Taylor & Francis Group, an informa business

Typeset in Perpetua by Value Chain, India

British Library Cataloguing in Publication Data
A catalogue record for this book is available from the British Library

ISBN13: 978-0-415-49456-4
ISBN13: 978-0-415-84677-6

CONTENTS

NOTES ON CONTRIBUTORS

Stuart Burch is a senior lecturer in Museum Studies at Nottingham Trent University's School of Arts & Humanities. His initial academic training was in art history with a specific focus on sculpture. This has expanded into a general interest in what can be termed Public History.

Jörg Hackmann is Alfred Döblin Professor of East European History, University of Szczecin (Poland), and Visiting Scholar at the University of Chicago.

Markku Jokisipilä is a Researcher in Contemporary History in the Universities of Turku and Helsinki. He has written extensively on the history and memory politics of World War II.

Matti Jutila is a PhD student at the department of political science at the University of Helsinki. He works in the Finnish Graduate School for Russian and East European Studies (Aleksanteri Institute) writing his thesis on the transnational governance of minority rights in post-Cold War Europe.

Siobhan Kattago is Associate Professor of Political Philosophy at Tallinn University. She received her PhD from the Graduate Faculty of the New School for Social Research and was a postdoctoral fellow at the Remarque Institute at New York University.

Marko Lehti is a Senior Research Fellow at Tampere Peace Research Institute at the University of Tampere and an Academic Director of the Baltic Sea Region Studies Master's Program at the University of Turku.

David J. Smith is Professor of Baltic History and Politics at the University of Glasgow, UK and the regular Editor of *Journal of Baltic Studies*.

Marek Tamm is a lecturer in cultural theory at the Estonian Institute of Humanities (Tallinn University) and a researcher at the Institute of History (Tallinn University). He is currently preparing his PhD at the Ecole des Hautes Etudes en Sciences Sociales, Paris (EHESS).

Theodore R. Weeks is Professor of History at Southern Illinois University at Carbondale, where he teaches world, western Civilization, and European history. His research centers on nationality, inter-ethnic relations, and anti-Semitism in eastern Europe.

Anton Weiss-Wendt received a PhD in modern Jewish history from Brandeis University. Before joining the Norwegian Holocaust Centre in Oslo he taught Soviet history at Keele University in the UK. His book, *Murder Without Hatred: Estonians and the Holocaust*, has been published in 2009 by Syracuse University Press.

INTRODUCTION: CONTESTED AND SHARED PLACES OF MEMORY. HISTORY AND POLITICS IN NORTH EASTERN EUROPE

The events in Tallinn on the night of 26–27 April 2007 have already been deleted from the short-term memory of the international media, but Estonians (and not least Estonian scholars) have come to regard the removal of the so-called Bronze Soldier and the accompanying riots, as well as the actions of Putin's Russia, as a benchmark for Estonia's future. During the past year several studies scrutinizing the Bronze Soldier case have been published, and more are in progress.[1] The debate has not been free from political interests, which minimize the conflict by explaining and interpreting it away on the one hand, and exaggerate it as an example of ethnic Estonian racism and neo-fascism on the other. For many Estonians the whole incident was in the end a disturbing turn in the success story of EU–Estonia, recalling phenomena that they would rather forget and exclude from public debate.

In this volume we will also contribute to this debate. Our aim is not to explain the conflict away, or to blame Estonians or Russians for the outbreak of aggression. We simply argue that the conflict has broader significance for the whole of Europe. The Baltic–Russian, and in particular the Estonian–Russian, debate on the past has become a 'hot spot' in European memory politics. This ongoing debate clearly reveals that Europe cannot be delimited according to the extended borders of the Schengen space. It also shows that public commemoration, which was ossified for decades in the Soviet hemisphere, has become subject to broad memory discourses. Here discussions about forms of cultural memory and political interests are closely intertwined. Even if the significance of the 'Bronze War' in Estonia should not be overemphasized, it offers an interesting insight into collective memory and history politics and their linkage to current political and inter-ethnic relationships. Furthermore, it is important to point out that at the peripheries of Europe the past seems to be remembered differently than at the center. Europe is not just defined in Paris, London and Berlin, but also in Tallinn and Moscow. Europe is diverse and so are its memories. At this point the Bronze Soldier case has wider importance.

In the light of the recent Georgian–Russian conflict and Russia's recognition of the independence of South Ossetia and Abkhazia, one might interpret the conflicts over memory in Baltic–Russian relations as part of a broader political context. Russia's willingness to flex its muscles towards the EU and the USA indicates the onset of a new era of classic power politics. Even so, disputes over collective memory are more than just an accompaniment to power politics, because Russia's conflicts with former Soviet republics are very much tangled up in the Soviet legacy and issues of national pride.

The events in Tallinn in 2007 and the ensuing scholarly debate raise questions. Why does the Second World War still matter 60 years after its end, and what is its influence and use in the construction of current national identities? In the western part of Europe, it is Europe's own evil pre-1945 past that has long constituted the principal 'Other' in European identity; subsequent processes of European integration are seen as a peace project guaranteeing a brave new future without historical burdens. In this discourse the collective mourning of horrors – and of the Holocaust in particular – has a key role. However, the debate in the Baltics as well as in Poland has followed different paths and a different rhetoric. In this discourse right and wrong, guilty and victim are still sought, and national pride secured. Interestingly this politics of memory has been visualized in traditional monuments which elsewhere have lost their power and become invisible. In the Baltics and East Central Europe, the majority of monuments from the socialist period have been demolished, relegated and disgraced or transposed into theme parks, but some are also cherished and guarded. Besides, new monuments have been erected or are planned, such as the 'Freedom Cross' in Tallinn. Interestingly, public performances played out around old Soviet monuments are not only controlled and influenced by governments, but have also attracted the interest of young people, who combine postmodern elements such as the internet and role playing with ultra-nationalistic narratives.

In saying this, we are not trying to depict the Baltic as some kind of antiquated relic of memory politics. Rather, we would argue that there, at the margin of Europe, modern and postmodern forms of commemorating and cherishing national pride are mixing together and are opening themselves up to strategies that seek to render them politically charged. We should not treat the Baltic states as a backward, undeveloped and ultra-nationalistic backyard of Europe which should follow a western European path, but as a unique corner of Europe with its own particular expressions of national identity and collective memory. We should not aspire to judge, but instead try to understand what is going on, because this conflict over memory is important not just for Estonia and the other Baltic states, but for the whole of Europe. To understand the issues it is not enough to focus solely on the Bronze Soldier – broader theoretical, spatial and temporal perspectives are needed.

Such a broader perspective shapes the contributions to this collection. Thus, Jörg Hackmann outlines scholarly discussions on collective memory and places of memory. Current events in Estonia are discussed in the essays by Marko Lehti, Markku Jutila and Matti Jokisipilä and David J Smith. Siobhan Kattago and Stuart Burch add visual aspects to the analysis, while Anton Weiss-Wendt focuses on the Holocaust discourse in Estonia. Marek Tamm and Theodore R. Weeks have longer historical perspectives. The former unfolds Estonian memory templates and the latter analyses Soviet memory politics in Vilnius.

The contributions to this volume are based on and inspired by two conferences. The first one on 'The Long Shadow of the Bronze Soldier: Politics of Memory and National Bluster' was organized by the Tampere Peace Research Institute in June 2007, the second on 'Places of Commemoration in North Eastern Europe' was organized by the University of Greifswald and Tallinn City Archive in Tallinn in September 2007. We express our gratitude to all speakers and participants in the discussions of both sessions.

Note

1 See, besides the contributions in this volume, for instance: Petersoo & Tamm (2008), Brüggemann and Kasekamp (2008), Wertsch (2008), Burch & Smith (2007). See also *Vikerkaar* 2008, no. 4–5, http://www.vikerkaar.ee/?page=Arhiiv&a_act=content&a_number=225, accessed 5 September 2008.

References

Burch, S. & Smith, D. (2007) 'Empty Spaces and the Value of Symbols: Estonia's 'War of Monuments' from Another Angle', *Europe-Asia Studies*, 59, 6, pp. 913–36.

Brüggemann, K. & Kasekamp, A. (2008) 'The Politics of History and the "War of Monuments" in Estonia', *Nationalities Papers*, 36, 3, pp. 425–48.

Petersoo, P. & Tamm, M. (eds) (2008) *Monumentaalne konflikt. Mälu, poliitika ja identiteet tänapäeva Eestis* (Tallinn, Varrak).

Wertsch, J. V. (2008) 'Collective Memory and Narrative Templates', *Social Research*, 75, 3, pp. 133–56.

Jörg Hackmann, *University of Szczecin, Poland*
Marko Lehti, *University of Tampere, Finland*

COLLECTIVE MEMORIES IN THE BALTIC SEA REGION AND BEYOND: NATIONAL – TRANSNATIONAL – EUROPEAN?[1]

Jörg Hackmann

Since the 1980s there has been a steadily increasing interest in issues of remembrance, memory and commemoration amongst the public and in the media, as well as from professional historians and scholars from neighboring fields: the journal *History and Memory*, founded in 1989, is only one indication of this trend. Dan Diner, director of the Simon Dubnow Institute for Jewish History and Culture in Leipzig, has even launched 'memory' as a new paradigm of historical research which is said to have pushed 'society' onto library shelves (Diner 2007). Such a thesis might, of course, be disputed and refuted, but there is no doubt about a boom in memory-related publications.

Looking at the Baltic Sea Region, it is not by accident that Estonia comes to the fore: the public debates and political disputes about monuments commemorating the dead of the Second World War have attracted the attention of many scholars since the removal of monuments in Lihula and Tallinn in 2004 and 2007, respectively.[2] Besides current debates, for many years memory has been a major issue in various disciplines of social studies in Estonia as, for instance, the various projects collecting post-Soviet Estonian life stories show.[3] As the political dimensions of collective memory in north eastern Europe will be closely analysed in the contributions to this collection, these introductory remarks shall first of all highlight some scholarly aspects related to present interests in collective memory.

Key Issues of Collective Memory

Debates on the theory of collective, social and cultural memory, as well as on its manifestations, have very much broadened over the last three decades. However, scholarly discourses have a longer tradition which goes back to the first half of the twentieth century. Besides Maurice Halbwachs' introduction of the category of collective memory into social research in 1925,[4] Walter Benjamin and Aby Warburg – with his 'Mnemosyne' project, which focused on the recollection of the ancient world in images in European societies since the Renaissance – have been named as further ancestors of memory research.[5] Recent research has spanned sociological and cultural approaches, first of all,[6] and has recently been amended by neurobiological and psychological processes of recollection.[7]

Focusing on recent debates about collective memory in the Baltic Sea Region and Eastern Europe, the following issues may be highlighted: as a starting point in his research on collective memory, Halbwachs has stressed the distinction between memory and history.[8] In that perspective, historians studying memory do not ask about scholarly knowledge, how events 'really' (to use Ranke's term) were, or about explorations of historical 'truth', but how historical events, developments or structures are reconstructed and represented in individual and collective consciousness, and how this representation changes. Social memory in that perspective is not an immutable entity, but dependent on social groups as well as on time (Halbwachs 1992, pp. 46–51). Thus, collective memory cannot be regarded as static or homogenous across an entire society. Today, one may connect this notion to constructivist approaches in history writing focusing on perceptions and narratives, which once again underline Diner's thesis of a new memory paradigm (2007).

Looking more closely at the forms of social memory, the distinction between communicative and cultural memory, which has been elaborated in particular by Jan and Aleida Assmann, has to be emphasized. Cultural memory, according to Jan Assmann (1995, p. 129) 'has its fixed point; its horizon does not change with the passing of time. These fixed points are fateful events of the past, whose memory is maintained through cultural formation (texts, rites, monuments) and institutional communication'. Of particular importance for the formation of cultural memory is, as he has pointed out, the 'floating gap' between individual and communicative memory on the one hand and its cultural objectification on the other, which Assmann locates at a time of approximately 40 years *post factum* (Assmann 2002, p. 51).

Furthermore, there is the distinction between *Erinnerung* (remembrance) and *Gedächtnis* (memory) in German: while *Gedächtnis* may be associated with the social storage of individual (or communicated) memories, *Erinnerung* implies the process of remembering, the activations of elements from the storage of memories (Csáky 2004). Cultural and social memories are therefore objects of performances and negotiations, and they are, of course, related to power, as historical arguments and thus the shaping of memories provide a major source of legitimizing power. This leads to the broad field of past and history politics dealt with in the contributions to this collection.

Memory, however, does not exist without forgetting. Debates on forgetting range from neurobiological to social aspects and philosophical reflection.[9] Niklas Luhmann has even argued that without forgetting, there is no evolution.[10] In philosophical debates, Paul Ricœur (2004) has stressed the connection between passive and active forgetting, between amnesia and amnesty, or forgetting and forgiving. Most important in that context are the moral and political implications of forgetting. Ernest Renan famously underlined that the construction of modern nations is based on forgetting. In the aftermath of the Second World War the German debate has been shaped by Freud's notion of working through the past in writings by Theodor Adorno (1971, pp. 10–28) and Alexander and Margarete Mitscherlich (1975).[11] In the context of the German *Historikerstreit* of the 1980s, Hermann Lübbe launched the thesis that active forgetting was a precondition of the political success of the Federal Republic. This provoked much criticism, yet it also received some consent.[12] With the focus on war crimes, and the Holocaust first of all, the imperative of 'we must never forget' – which comprises a much stronger normative element than 'we will always remember' (Weinrich 2004) – has become dominant in present-day political discourses in Europe and beyond.[13]

Memory, Monuments and Politics

It is not by accident that monuments commemorating the dead of the Second World War have become highly political issues in recent years, and have thus become ever more prominent within public awareness.[14] Looking at the different forms of politics related to such monuments one sees first the erection of new monuments such as the Berlin 'Memorial to the murdered Jews of Europe' as a prominent example of international significance. Besides this, there is also iconoclasm and the translocation of monuments, as in the case of the monument to the 'Soviet Liberators of Tallinn', which reflect modes of memory politics obviously based on conflicting memories. Such 'divided memories', which are not restricted to the former Soviet hemisphere,[15] may also result in the conscious or unconscious neglect of monuments. Even the official German policy of protecting and preserving Soviet war monuments cannot prevent such monuments from becoming invisible – as Robert Musil (1995, p. 87) has stated in his well-known dictum – if they do not attract practices of commemoration. Whereas Marx and Lenin may be transposed into theme parks or become the subject of ironic actions, war memorials are immune to such treatment, as the victims demand mourning. In that respect, the fate of the 'Bronze Soldier' – as the Soviet monument in Tallinn has been renamed in everyday speech – points at debates that will surely arise elsewhere, if they have not already started. The connection of mourning the dead with monumental forms of praising the victory of the Red Army will either become subject to political debates or will fall into oblivion.

Memory and Space

Besides the debates on memory politics and the revived interest in theoretical aspects of collective memory, there is one more important point related to the memory paradigm on which Dan Diner draws: the rise of the memory paradigm goes along with a turn towards rediscovered historic spaces (not least in eastern Europe). Observations that underline such a statement are for instance the widely read essays by the German historian Karl Schlögel (1986, 2003) and those by other authors, such as Robert Traba (2003) and Andrzej Stasiuk from Poland and Yurii Andrukhovyich from Ukraine (Andruchowytsch & Stasiuk 2004). Spatial explorations in Central and Eastern Europe discover 'forgotten' regions and places, which are now conceived as an integral part of (a new) Europe. The success of these essays may be explained by the fact that memories here are connected to specific places, cities, landscapes etc., and evoke a world of a pre-national 'unity in diversity' which is rarely found in the Europe of today after the destruction of the twentieth century. By the same token, these remembered places form a new mental map of a united Europe that differs from its current political boundaries.

This connection between space and memory is not confined to intentionally erected monuments, and it is already well known from antique cultures. As a kind of anthropologic constant, it seems suited for the adaptation to modern societies, as the broad reception of Jan Assmann's publications shows. The most influential connection of memory and space during the last few years has undoubtedly been the French notion of *lieux de mémoire* initiated and developed by Pierre Nora.[16] His idea that the French nation can only be commemorated in single places, but not in a coherent framework of space and time, will not be presented here *in extenso*. It should, however, be mentioned that Nora's notion is not based on a primarily scholarly approach, but focuses on the preservation of (French) collective identity, which can only be achieved by keeping alive fragmented memories connected to national symbols. Nora's primary goal of identity-preserving or -building rests upon the assumption of a crisis in French national identity, against which the 'places of memory' are directed. By the same token, topics that could question the national heritage of France are not represented in these volumes edited by Nora.[17] All in all, the notion of fragmenting the approach towards collective commemoration of the past matches with another element of the memory paradigm highlighted by Dan Diner: according to him, diversity, not homogeneity, is the signature of memory.

The various ways in which Nora's notion was transferred to and adopted by other regions and nations in Europe during the last decade have in turn given rise to a great variety in terminology and definition. This refers to the understanding of '*lieux*', where we also see 'sites' or 'realms',[18] as well as to memory, where we see '*Erinnerung*' versus '*Gedächtnis*' in German, 'memory' versus 'commemoration' in English, while the Polish ('*pamięć*') and Estonian discussions ('*mälu, mälupaik*'), for instance, are less encumbered with the difference between remembering and memory. Although there is little disagreement that 'places' need not necessarily be spatially concrete but may also be conceived in metaphorical terms, the spatial dimension obviously remains pivotal in all of these approaches.

As already indicated, there are some reasons for the success and interest in presenting places of memory. The first one is the economic success of the French and German undertakings. Second, the concept of *lieux de mémoire* is frankly identity-related (much more so than one would admit in 'normal' historiography, at least in Germany) and can thus count on greater public support than predominantly de-constructivist approaches. Third, splitting the collective and cultural memory of a given society into single places enables a piecemeal approach which allows for the application of a wider scope and a quicker production compared to traditional historiography.

So far, there have been – besides the German *Erinnerungsorte* (François & Schulze 2001) – several large projects in Central and Eastern Europe dealing with cultures or places of memory, which primarily focus on modern nations and national identity following the notion developed by Pierre Nora in his *lieux de mémoire* of France.[19] Finally, in the Austrian case, the orientation towards publicity is most visible, as a public opinion poll constituted the point of departure for the selection of the Austrian places of memory.[20]

National and Transnational Perspectives

Two perspectives that shape public debates concerning collective memory shall be discussed here more in detail: the first refers to places of memory that are closely tied to national history, and the second focuses on the transformation of individual and communicative (i.e. fluid) memories of the Second World War into cultural memory.

Concerning the national perspective, one may refer once again to Diner's statement that the memory paradigm is based on diversity, and thus ask whether nation or state constitute the sole – or at least the most important – framework within which cultural memory is objectified. Are they not bound to the perspective of homogeneity and thus to a dominant element of the twentieth century which Charles Maier (2000) has already consigned to history? Indeed, criticism of the national orientation of the projects on places of memory is widespread. It has been argued that the German edition may be understood as a new appropriation of German history after the Holocaust (something which, however, has not been made explicit by the editors).[21] The most elaborated criticism of the nationally biased program of researching collective memories has been formulated by Moritz Csáky (2004) within the Austrian context. He argues that the presentation of *lieux de mémoire* first of all contributes to a nationally coded memory, and thus to the functional construction of a normative collective memory, whereas the multilayered character of those places is systematically left aside.

Nevertheless, there are without doubt good reasons for following such national concepts, be it only because nations (either ethnic or civic) form the most relevant large social groups, which in turn are to a large degree based on common history – not as a matter of pure facts, but as a product of stories, narratives, performances and memory. As Anthony Smith's (1986, p. 192) typology of national myths and Peter Burke's (2000) observations on foundation myths show, these form supratemporal traits of almost any society.

On the other hand, the recent re-emergence and dominance of national issues of collective memory is not self-evident, but may be explained in terms of the second perspective. With regard to the transformation of communicative into cultural memory Jan Assmann (2002, pp. 48–51) has stressed the crucial role of the 'floating gap' between communicative and cultural memory. The observation of a 'critical threshold' of 40 years may be illustrated by reference to many of the contemporary debates, and explained by the loosening of the individual memories of aging eye-witnesses and the interest of social groups in making collective memory endure. Thus it is not by accident that since the mid-1980s public debates on how to cope with the past of the Second World War and how to commemorate war-related crimes and victims have significantly increased in Germany, western and northern Europe, and have spread to eastern Europe, too, after the collapse of Soviet hegemony.

The memory discourses in east central and north eastern Europe in particular invite a closer look at the relations between national and transnational memories. So far, transnational or regional aspects are only partly reflected in projects on memory cultures and places of memory. It is surely not by accident that those projects have been introduced in border regions, as for instance in the German–Danish case or in the Saar–Lor–Lux region.[22] The most recent transnational project is an ambitious German–Polish one.[23]

The Baltic Focus

An attempt to further develop the notion of transnational places of memory was made at a conference at Humboldt University in Berlin in 2006.[24] The presentations there showed that national places of commemoration are only a segment of identity-relevant places of memory in many parts of Europe. This issue, however, seems to be perceived first of all in the eastern and northern parts of the continent. With regard to eastern Europe this may be explained by the fact that here one faces various types of places related to transnational memory. A typology might comprise: first, places of memory with national connotations that are situated beyond contemporary national borders;[25] second, places that refer to an imperial, pre-national past; third, places where shared or divided memories of several groups, nations or societies concur; fourth, places that have been re-interpreted and filled with new contents; and finally, places of memory that compete with each other.

Looking at northern Europe such a transnational perspective on places of memory may be linked to the Scandinavian discussion as to whether shared memory may transcend national borders and contribute to entangled regions of commemoration.[26] In that way, the Swedish realm is addressed as a region of memory but without accompanying ideas of cultural or national hegemony.[27] Transferring such an approach to Szczecin, Gdańsk, Olsztyn, Kaliningrad, Riga or Tallinn, for instance, would imply that they are no longer only perceived as places historically bound to one national group only. In fact, these cities have already become initial points of a multicultural region of commemoration. At this point, Csáky's suggestion (2004) of concentrating on a de-constructivist approach to uncover the ambiguity of central and east European spaces seems to be only the first step. Here, one should add a second step and ask whether the revealing of the historical stratigraphy of such places might foster a post-national cultural memory.[28]

Such a path has been – at least in its beginnings – explored with regard to the presentation of European *lieux de mémoire*. In addition to their national projects, Pierre Nora[29] and Etienne François, co-editor of the German project,[30] have discussed classifications of such European places. Their conclusions, however, are rather critical. Nevertheless, it becomes clear that there is a political impetus towards European identity-building, although one should discuss how deeply it may be rooted in history without running into the danger of being easily dismantled as ideological.

What might be adopted from this discourse, however, is the leading figure of thought of '*e pluribus unum*'.

Against the background of the issues outlined here, the regional framework of the Baltic Sea Region may be regarded as particularly appropriate for discussions on the notion of transnational places of memory. The Baltic rim between Szczecin and Vyborg, for instance, could reveal better than many other regions of Europe that places of memory are not necessarily exclusively nationally shaped, but may in a post-national perspective contribute to the formation of regions. Remembering the multilayered history obviously receives more attention in the northern parts of Europe at the moment, in comparison to its southern regions. The impact of transnational places of memory on the formation of regions seems to become most visible in such places that are spatially concrete, such as for instance architecture, urban structures or monuments.

The contributions to this collection focus on the fields of monuments and cityscapes and they reveal the close connection between changes in the mode of collective memory towards cultural memory on the one hand, and rising public relevance of memory discourses on the other. The theoretical background outlined here may contribute to understanding that we do not face political debates based on inevitable clashes of contested memory cultures, but on the contrary: if we turn Halbwachs' assertion that 'the past is a social construction . . . shaped by the concerns of the present'[31] upside down, we may conclude that new perspectives on the past have an impact on shaping new perspectives on the present.

Notes

1 This text is based on my introductory remarks to the conference '*Places of Commemoration in North Eastern Europe*', Tallinn, September 2007.

2 See the contributions by Marko Lehti *et al*. and David Smith in this collection and also: Brüggemann (2008); Brüggemann and Kasekamp (2008); Wertsch (2008).

3 See, among others, Kõresaar and Anepaio (eds) (2003); Kõresaar (2004); Kirss *et al*. (2004).

4 English editions: Halbwachs (1980, 1992). From the many recent publications on Halbwachs see Krapoth and Laborde (2005).

5 See Confino (1997) and Fowler (2005).

6 A by no means complete list includes: Connerton (1989); Assmann (2002, 2003); Ricœur (2004). Also important is Kula (2004).

7 Singer (2004) and Welzer (2002).

8 Halbwachs (1985, p. 103); cf. Assmann (2002, pp. 29–48).

9 Weinrich (2004); Ricœur (2004). On forgetting in Halbwachs' writings see Fowler (2005).

10 Esposito (2002). I am following Andreas Lawaty's presentation from Tallinn in September 2007. I would like to thank him for access to his manuscript. Luhmann's point might be illustrated by the widespread oblivionism in sciences, see Weinrich (2004).

11 Cf. also Olick (1999, p. 344).

12 Piper (1987); cf. Caplan *et al*. (2006).

13 See the international political debates following the Swedish 'Task Force for International Cooperation on Holocaust Education, Remembrance and Research' of 1997, which culminated in the '*Stockholm International Forum on the Holocaust. A Conference on Education, Remembrance and Research*', 26–28 January 2000. I am dealing with this issue more broadly in a forthcoming article on 'From national victims to transnational bystanders? The changing commemoration of World War II in Central and Eastern Europe', *Constellations*, (2009) 16, 1.
14 Cf. in particular Koselleck (2000, pp. 275–84) on the political cult of the dead.
15 An impressive description of the problem is provided in Judt (2002).
16 Nora (1984–1992), for the English version see Nora (1996); see also Nora (1998).
17 This has been criticized several times in the French discussion. I am following the instructive overview prepared by Kornelia Kończal (2007).
18 See Judt (1998).
19 Brix *et al.* (2004–2005). Selected further publications comprise: Jaworski *et al.* (2003); Csáky and Mannová (1999); Rider *et al.* (2002); Corneließen *et al.* (2005). Besides, a project directed by Robert Traba (Berlin) and Hans-Henning Hahn (Oldenburg) shall focus on German–Polish places of memory, for details see Projekt: Deutsch-polische Erinnerungsorte/Polsko-niemieckie miejsca pami ci Exposé, available at: www.cbh.pan.pl/de/index.php?option=com_content&task =view&id=97&Itemid=0, accessed 25 August 2008.
20 See Straub (2005).
21 See the review by Nolte (2001).
22 Adriansen and Schartl (2006). An insightful presentation on Schleswig as a shared or divided place of memory has been given by Steen Bo Frandsen at the Tallinn conference on '*Places of Commemoration*'. On Saar-Lor-Lux see Hudemann *et al.* (2004).
23 It is explicitly based on the history of mutual German-Polish relations. See www. cbh.pan.pl/de/index.php?option=com_content&task=view&id=97&Itemid=0, accessed 25 August 2008.
24 See my report available at: http://hsozkult.geschichte.hu-berlin.de/tagungsberichte/ id=1372, accessed 1 December 2006. A publication is forthcoming.
25 Cf. the mapping of *lieux de mémoire trans-frontière* by Foucher (1993, p. 69).
26 See for instance www.nordicspaces.eu, accessed 25 August 2008.
27 Although misunderstandings and different emphases cannot be excluded, of course. On Narva see Burch and Smith (2007).
28 I have discussed this with regard to Riga (Hackmann 2006).
29 Nora (1988); cf. Bossuat (1999).
30 François (2006) has expanded the idea of divided places from the German *Erinnerungsorte* (François & Schulze 2001) and suggests here 'common', 'divided' and 'negative' places of memory.
31 Lewis Coser in his introduction to Halbwachs (1992, p. 25).

References

Adorno, T. W. (1971) *Erziehung zur Mündigkeit. Vorträge und Gespräche mit Hellmut Becker 1959–1969* (Frankfurt am Main, Suhrkamp).

Adriansen, I. & Schartl, M. (2006) *Erindringssteder Nord og Syd for Graensen. Erinnerungsorte nördlich und südlich der Grenze* (Sønderborg, Schleswig, Museum Sønderjylland – Sønderborg Slot, Kulturstiftung des Kreises Schleswig-Flensburg).

Andruchowytsch, Yu. & Stasiuk, A. (2004) *Mein Europa: zwei Essays über das sogenannte Mitteleuropa* (Frankfurt am Main, Suhrkamp).

Assmann, A. (2003) *Erinnerungsräume: Formen und Wandlungen des kulturellen Gedächtnisses* (Munich, Beck).

Assmann, J. (1995) 'Collective Memory and Cultural Identity', *New German Critique*, 65, pp. 125–33.

Assmann, J. (2002) *Das kulturelle Gedächtnis: Schrift, Erinnerung und politische Identität in frühen Hochkulturen* (Munich, C.H. Beck).

Bossuat, G. (1999) 'Des lieux de mémoire pour l'Europe unie', *Vingtième Siècle. Revue d'histoire*, 61, pp. 56–69.

Brix, E., Bruckmüller, E. & Stekl, H. (eds) (2004–2005) *Memoria Austriae.* 3 Vols (Vienna, Verlag für Geschichte und Politik).

Brüggemann, K. (2008) 'Denkmäler des Grolls. Estland und die Kriege des 20. Jahrhunderts', *Osteuropa*, 58, 6, pp. 129–46.

Brüggemann, K. & Kasekamp, A. (2008) 'The Politics of History and the "War of Monuments" in Estonia', *Nationalities Papers*, 36, 3, pp. 425–48.

Burch, S. & Smith, D. (2007) 'Empty Spaces and the Value of Symbols: Estonia's "War of Monuments" from Another Angle', *Europe-Asia Studies*, 59, 6, pp. 913–36.

Burke, P. (2000) 'Foundation Myths and Collective Identities in early Modern Europe', in Stråth, B. (ed.) (2000) *Europe and the Other and Europe as the Other* (Brussels, Peter Lang), pp. 113–22.

Caplan, J., Frei, N., Geyer, M., Nolan, M. & Stargardt, N. (2006) 'The Historikerstreit Twenty Years On', *German History*, 24, 4, pp. 587–607.

Confino, A. (1997) 'Collective Memory and Cultural History: Problems of Method', *American Historical Review*, 102, 5, pp. 1386–403.

Connerton, P. (1989) *How Societies Remember* (Cambridge & New York, Cambridge University Press).

Cornelißen, C., Holec, R. & Pešek, J. (eds) (2005) *Diktatur, Krieg, Vertreibung. Erinnerungskulturen in Tschechien, der Slowakei und Deutschland seit 1945* (Essen, Klartext).

Csáky, M. (2004) 'Die Mehrdeutigkeit von Gedächtnis und Erinnerung', *Digitales Handbuch zur Geschichte und Kultur Russlands und Osteuropas*, available at: http://www.vifaost.de/texte-materialien/digitale-reihen/handbuch/handb-mehrdeutigk/, accessed 25 August 2008.

Csáky, M. & Mannová, E. (eds) (1999) *Collective Identities in Central Europe in Modern Times* (Bratislava, Inst. of History of the Slovak Academy of Sciences).

Diner, D. (2007) 'From Society to Memory: Reflections on a Paradigm Shift', in Mendels, D. (ed.) (2007) *On Memory: An Interdisciplinary Approach* (Bern & New York, Lang).

Esposito, E. (2002) *Soziales Vergessen: Formen und Medien des Gedächtnisses der Gesellschaft* (Frankfurt am Main, Suhrkamp).

Foucher, M. (1993) *Fragments d'Europe: Atlas de l'Europe médiane et orientale* (Paris, Fayard).

Fowler, B. (2005) 'Collective Memory and Forgetting', *Theory, Culture & Society*, 22, 6, pp. 53–72.

François, E. (2006) 'Europäische lieux de mémoire', in Budde, G.-F., Conrad, S. & Janz, O. (eds) (2006) *Transnationale Geschichte: Themen, Tendenzen und Theorien* (Göttingen, Vandenhoeck & Ruprecht), pp. 290–303.

François, E. & Schulze, H. (eds) (2001) *Deutsche Erinnerungsorte,* 3 vols (Munich, C.H.Beck).

Hackmann, J. (2006) 'Metamorphosen des Rigaer Rathausplatzes, 1938–2003: Beobachtungen zur Rolle historischer Topographien in Nordosteuropa', in Loew, P. O., Pletzing, C. & Serrier, T. (eds) (2006) *Wiedergewonnene Geschichte. Zur Aneignung von Vergangenheit in den Zwischenräumen Mitteleuropas* (Wiesbaden, Harrasowitz), pp. 118–41.

Halbwachs, M. (1980) *The Collective Memory* (New York, Harper & Row).

Halbwachs, M. (1985) *Das kollektive Gedächtnis* (Frankfurt am Main, Fischer Taschenbuch).

Halbwachs, M. (1992) *On Collective Memory* (Chicago, University of Chicago Press).

Hudemann, R., Hahn, M. & Krebs, G. (eds) (2004) *Stätten grenzüberschreitender Erinnerung – Spuren der Vernetzung des Saar-Lor-Lux-Raumes im 19. und 20. Jahrhundert. Lieux de la mémoire transfrontalière - Traces et réseaux dans l'espace Sarre-Lor-Lux aux 19e et 20e siècles* (Saarbrücken), available at: http://www.memotransfront.uni-saarland.de, accessed 5 September 2008.

Jaworski, R., Kusber, J. & Steindorff, L. (eds) (2003) *Gedächtnisorte in Osteuropa: Vergangenheiten auf dem Prüfstand* (Frankfurt am Main, Lang).

Judt, T. (1998) 'A la Recherche du Temps Perdu. Review of "Realms of Memory: The Construction of the French Past"', edited by Nora Pierre (1998) *The New York Review of Books*, 45, 19.

Judt, T. (2002) 'The Past Is Another Country: Myth and Memory in Postwar Europe', in Müller, J.-W. (ed.) (2002) *Memory and Power in Post-War Europe. Studies in the Presence of the Past* (Cambridge, Cambridge University Press), pp. 157–83.

Kirss, T., Kõresaar, E. & Lauristin, M. (eds) (2004) *She Who Remembers Survives: Interpreting Estonian Women's Post-Soviet Life Stories* (Tartu, Tartu University Press).

Kończal, K. (2007) *Europäische Debatten über 'les lieux de mémoire'* (Berlin, Centrum Badań Historycznych PAN), available at: www.cbh.pan.pl/de/images/stories/pliki/pdf/prezentacja%20KK.pdf, accessed 25 August 2008.

Kõresaar, E. & Anepaio, T. (eds) (2003) *Mälu kui kultuuritegur: etnoloogilisi perspektiive. Ethnological Perspectives On Memory* (Tartu, Tartu Ulikooli Kirjastus).

Kõresaar, E. (2004) *Memory and History in Estonian Post-Soviet Life Stories: Private and Public, Individual and Collective from the Perspective of Biographical Syncretism* (Tartu, Tartu University Press).

Koselleck, R. (2000) *Zeitschichten. Studien zur Historik* (Frankfurt am Main, Suhrkamp).

Krapoth, H. & Laborde, D. (eds) (2005) *Erinnerung und Gesellschaft. Mémoire et Société* (Wiesbaden, VS).

Kula, M. (2004) *Między Przeszłością a Przyszłością: O Pamięci, Zapominaniu i Przewidywaniu* (Poznań, PTPN).

Maier, C. S. (2000) 'Consigning the Twentieth Century to History: Alternative Narratives for the Modern Era', *American Historical Review,* 105, 3, pp. 807–31.

Mitscherlich, A. & Mitscherlich, M. (1975) *The Inability to Mourn: Principles of Collective Behavior* (New York, Grove Press).

Musil, R. (1995) *Posthumous Papers of a Living Author* (London, Penguin).

Nolte, P. (2001) 'Durch den Märchenwald der Geschichte. Das große Projekt der "Deutschen Erinnerungsorte" – oder wie man es nicht macht', *Literaturen*, 5, pp. 92–3.

Nora, P. (ed.) (1984–1992) *Les Lieux de Mémoire* (Paris, Gallimard).

Nora, P. (1988) 'Les "Lieux de mémoire" dans la culture européenne', in Angrémy, J.-P. (ed.) (1988) *Europe sans rivage. Symposium international sur l'identité culturelle européenne, Paris, janvier 1988* (Paris, Albin Michel), pp. 38–42.

Nora, P. (ed.) (1996) *Realms of Memory*, 2 vols (New York, Columbia University Press).

Nora, P. (1998) *Zwischen Geschichte und Gedächtnis* (Frankfurt am Main, Fischer Taschenbuch).

Olick, J. K. (1999) 'Collective Memory: The Two Cultures', *Sociological Theory*, 17, 3, pp. 333–48.

Piper, E. (ed.), (1987) *Historikerstreit. Die Dokumentation der Kontroverse um die Einzigartigkeit der nationalsozialistischen Judenvernichtung* (Munich, Piper).

Ricœur, P. (2004) *Memory, History, Forgetting* (Chicago, University of Chicago Press).

Rider, J. L., Csáky, M. & Sommer, M. (eds) (2002) *Transnationale Gedächtnisorte in Zentraleuropa* (Innsbruck, Vienna, Munich, Bozen, Studienverlag).

Schlögel, K. (1986) *Die Mitte liegt ostwärts. Die Deutschen, der verlorene Osten und Mitteleuropa* (Berlin, Siedler).

Schlögel, K. (2003) *Im Raume lesen wir die Zeit. Über Zivilisationsgeschichte und Geopolitik* (Munich, Hanser).

Singer, W. (2004) 'Perceiving, Remembering, Forgetting', in Iglhaut, S. & Spring, T. (eds) (2004) *Science + Fiction, Between Nanoworlds and Global Culture, Pictures and Texts: Texts and Interviews* (Berlin, jovis), pp. 179–97.

Smith, A. D. (1986) *The Ethnic Origins of Nations* (Oxford, Blackwell).

Straub, W. (2005) 'Schnitzel und Erinnerungsorte', *Der Standard*, Vienna, 21 October.

Traba, R. (2003) *Kraina tysiąca granic: Szkice o historii i pamięci* (Olsztyn, Borussia).

Weinrich, H. (2004) *Lethe: The Art and Critique of Forgetting* (Ithaca, Cornell University Press).

Welzer, H. (2002) *Das kommunikative Gedächtnis: Eine Theorie der Erinnerung* (Munich, C.H. Beck).

Wertsch, J. V. (2008) 'Collective Memory and Narrative Templates', *Social Research*, 75, 3, pp. 133–56.

NEVER-ENDING SECOND WORLD WAR: PUBLIC PERFORMANCES OF NATIONAL DIGNITY AND THE DRAMA OF THE BRONZE SOLDIER

Marko Lehti, Matti Jutila and Markku Jokisipilä

> There is no doubt that the April events concerning the Bronze Soldier will become a benchmark in the contemporary history of the state of Estonia. It is the bifurcation point, the point of division, separating 'before' and 'after'. For Estonian society these events are even more important than joining NATO or European Union. Before April 2007 we lived in one country and now we are getting used to living in another one. [Aleksei Semjonov, director of the Legal Information Centre for Human Rights in Tallinn (LICHR 2007, p. 7)]

On the night of 26–27 April 2007, the removal of the so-called Bronze Soldier, previously known as the Monument to the Liberators of Tallinn, from its original location in the city center triggered violent riots in the streets of Tallinn, diplomatic conflict between Estonia and Russia and an aggressive but theatrical performance organized by the Russian youth organization '*Nashi*'. On 30 April the statue was re-erected at the Estonian Defence Forces cemetery and renamed the Unknown Soldier. The original location at Tõnismägi was restricted for a long time as even the last remnants of the monument were cleared out. In past years the site had witnessed ritualized performances of collective memory, with one group trying to guard their symbols and others aiming to defile them and eventually erase them completely from memory. The above quote reveals the symbolic importance of the site for the local Russian-speaking community. Similarly, the fact that the Estonian media has equated the April 2007 events with the failed 1924 communist coup in Tallinn (Astrov 2008) expresses how high the symbolic value of the so-called 'Bronze War' is for the titular nation and how it is seen as a matter of national survival. The incident that shattered the prevalent image of the peaceful integration of Estonia unveiled the sore spots in Estonian–Russian relations, within Estonian society and in Estonian national discourse.

All parties seem to cling to their fixed views of the Second World War. Current relations and future expectations appear still to be determined by events over half a century ago. The removal of the Bronze Soldier was very much a security policy issue as it symbolizes, or was said to symbolize, something sacred and fundamental to all groups concerned. As challenging the dominant interpretations of the past was presented as a threat and the neighbor as an enemy, the Bronze Solder became securitized.[1] However, the fact that the Estonian authorities intentionally avoided the exacerbation of ethnic division and excessive securitization of the Russian-speaking minority may offer a fresh beginning and a way out of the old rigid attitudes.

The whole incident – removal, riots, protests etc. – can be seen as a drama triangle of Estonians, Russians and Estonian Russian-speakers, as a public performance of national dignity in which being noticed and getting one's message across were far more important than any long-term goals. However, it seems that there are more players involved and that younger generations have not necessarily staunchly imitated the policies of state leaders but have their own forms of presentation and message too. In this article we scrutinize recent public performances and symbolism associated with the Bronze Soldier, the particular site of clashing collective memories, and the Victory Day, the symbolically loaded day of commemoration. As performances associated with memorials and monuments can be interpreted as public theater, it is important to ask: who is the audience, what is the actual play on stage, and are there actually several simultaneous dramas? Also, how has the past been recounted and publicly presented in current debates? We argue that World War II is still an essential source of national dignity in both Estonia and Russia, and that this was the main reason why the incident evoked highly ritualized performances with little room for negotiation and compromise. If anything, the conflict showed the urgent necessity of avoiding further marginalization of the Russian-speaking minority.

Glorification of a Nation

The rhetoric around the Bronze Soldier has mainly dealt with issues dating back to World War II and the immediate postwar years, although few of the debaters have any personal memories of them. The war and its consequences still seem to be significant for many people in Estonia and Russia, regardless of their age and ethnicity. They constitute an essential part of collective memories and provide a temporal anchor for individual identities.

In modern societies and especially in nation-states, collective memory and identity are closely interlinked. As Jens Bartelson (2006, p. 33) writes: 'states and nations could hardly be understood other than as outcomes of long historical processes. Each state or nation had its own temporal trajectory'. In the construction of this trajectory crucial symbols and metaphors are nationalized and presented as particular and exclusive. A national Other, oppression and achieving one's freedom are all essential elements of the trajectory. In the words of Aviel Roshwald (2006, p. 88): 'The memory of what others have done to the nation helps define the meaning and value of liberty and highlights the necessity of shaking off foreign yokes or of fighting to maintain independence and security'. Sometimes, recounting the national trajectory requires travelling over decades or centuries, yet temporal distance is rendered insignificant. Forgetting, or national amnesia, is also an essential part of national drama: ill-fitting elements and unnecessary diversity are simply just deleted (Bartelson 2006; Roshwald 2006, p. 58). The trajectory is presented as a natural, logical and solid narrative.

This trajectory, or a narrative of a nation, constitutes a primary source of legitimacy and it is thus easy to securitize. Narrative brings the nation into being as a unique, particular and privileged entity, thus forming a crucial source of national dignity (Greenfeld 1995, pp. 487–8). Pursuing national destiny is impossible without self-respect, and national dignity is the sacred nucleus of a nation. As Roshwald (2006, p. 122) argues, national dignity is intertwined with security and thus guides political decisions. 'Indeed, perceived threats to collective dignity and national well-being often include both challenges to official myths of violation and overt acts of violation, oppression, or exploitation. The cult of past martyrdoms and the awareness of contemporary dangers to national honour, sovereignty, and/or security are commonly intertwined in a dynamic, ever-changing relationship.' Because sacrifices sanctify the nation they must be continually upheld, remembered and celebrated. The public imagery of national communion includes 'the public ceremonies of celebration and commemoration with which the citizenry could identify and in which they could, eventually, participate' (Smith 2003, p. 223). The most sacred ones are those who have sacrificed their lives for the nation, be they patriotic heroes or unknown victims of war or genocide. They are the glorious dead commemorated in public whose fate and dedication guide the nation. Profaning their memory would desecrate the nation as well.

According to Smith the nationalistic cult of the glorious dead merges the Greco-Roman tradition of dignifying patriotic virtue and the Judeo-Christian-Islamic tradition of dedicating a certain place to the memory of sacred persons. Ritual mourning and glorifying of the dead require a holy place, a monument, which makes the collective commemoration possible (Smith 2003, pp. 219–53). The era of nationalism can thus be called an era of monuments. Visual symbols strengthen collective memories and prevent forgetting. Collective memories underpin individual identities and help to concretize 'a transcendent national experience that bridges awkward historical chasms and lends purpose and meaning to the forward progress of the nation through time' (Roshwald 2006, p. 63). The most loaded meanings are contained in war memorials. They can cherish certain heroes, triumphs and victories, but they can also be more non-specific like the Tomb of the Unknown Soldier, signaling anonymous devotion, honor and sacrifice for the nation (Roshwald 2006, p. 65).

During two centuries of nationalism the styles of monuments as well as the obligation and justification associated with them have changed substantially. The cult of the individual hero was characteristic of nineteenth-century nationalism. Industrialized warfare and the mass killing of the First World War replaced singular and particular heroes with Tombs of the Unknown Soldier emphasizing the randomness of war. After World War II, Auschwitz and Hiroshima even the remnants of the heroic cult were replaced by collective mourning for the suffering of innocent civilians, obligating the survivors to continue to act in the name of the nation. However, the World War II memorials still mixed various messages, symbols and styles (Smith 2003, pp. 243–53).

The close relationship between collective memory and identity, so indispensable to national narratives, constitutes a potential source of political and social upheavals. As Bartelson (2006, pp. 35–6) points out, this closeness amounts to vulnerability if the fundamentals of collective memory are challenged.

> As long as we rely on collective memories as a source of personal identity, we will inevitably face a certain loss of self whenever those collective memories are strategically rearranged to cater to new political concerns. The prospective loss of national identity looks scary indeed yet our sense of personal identity will inevitably remain fragile as long as we seek to derive it from belonging in a community thus constituted.

Unwelcome changes may easily arouse bitterness and frustration as old stories and heroes lose their position. But, as Roshwald (2006, p. 147) points out, 'people may lose their interest in hallowed tales about shedding of their forefathers' blood at the hands of their enemies'.

The national trajectories, myths and martyrdom that constitute collective memories shift and change as part of socio-cultural development. Trajectories connected to World War II and its consequences have also undergone a significant change during the past two decades. A surge of critical discussions about communism and especially its Soviet version date back to the end of the Cold War. Some of the books published, such as the hugely publicized *The Black Book of Communism* (Courtois 1999), compared communist atrocities with Nazi genocide and declared that communism was responsible for a greater number of deaths than any other ideology in history. There were increasing revisionist tendencies in World War II historiography, as some conservative historians and right-wing writers wanted to give Hitler's Germany credit for fighting against the Soviet Union and shielding Europe from communism (Roth 1997, pp. 10–27).

In the countries formerly in the Soviet sphere of influence this revisionism was geared to rehabilitating the domestic allies of Hitler. For example, Romanian, Hungarian and Finnish political mythologies constantly invoke the idea of forming a bulwark of Western civilization against the barbaric East. The main trend of this discussion, heavily influenced by nationalist rhetoric aimed at present-day constituencies, has been to highlight the patriotism and anticommunism of the leaderships of the 1930s and 1940s while downplaying their fascist, National Socialist and authoritarian traits. These tendencies stand in a stark contrast to Western European accounts of the war, which are centered on collective mourning for the

Holocaust and written in a deliberately post-national tone. Not surprisingly, central and Eastern European post-communist revisionism is a constant source of grievance to international Jewish organizations, which see, and in many cases rightly so, that Cold War sufferings are used in these countries as a pretext for distracting attention from their anti-Semitism and active participation in the Holocaust. Across central and Eastern Europe, demonizing socialism and underlining its violent antinationalism have become useful tools for politicians manifesting their break with the past, especially for right-wing nationalist parties (Kuljić 2005, 63–86).

To fully comprehend this revisionist turn, one has to take into account the simultaneous existence of two very different, yet interrelated, understandings of history: history as an academic discipline on the one hand, and history as national consciousness on the other. The new versions of national history formulated during the 1990s belonged predominantly to the realm of the latter. They formed an integral part of a defensive nationalist discourse strategy, designed firstly to reconcile the controversial and contradictory parts of collective memory and secondly to counter external criticism of selective hindsight and evading historical responsibilities. In this discourse the political leaders of the 1930s and 1940s are judged only according to their patriotism and faithfulness to nationalist goals. The consequent ethnocentric narratives of World War II revolved around issues such as military strategy, expressions of patriotism and national destiny, leaving little room for more complicated things such as questions of liability, option of choice, causality, treatment of minorities and so on. The former leaders are seen as national heroes and/or martyrs and the collaboration with National Socialist Germany as a mere instrument for safeguarding the national interest.

New interpretations of the morals of national leaders and politics are not the only forms of change in the commemoration of wars. Old memorials and narratives can also be revised by incorporating new elements into them, for instance by writing new ethnicities or groups into the drama. In the Estonian–Russian case, however, this has not happened. Old unitary stories and meanings have strengthened and World War II still carries weight for various generations and ethnic groups. The war also constitutes a source of exclusion and a mechanism of othering. Despite economic success and EU and NATO membership on the Estonian side, and the collapse of the Soviet Union on the Russian side, World War II still plays a crucial role in defining national dignity in both cases.

Mourning Victims and Commemorating Heroism

The Bronze Soldier was perfectly suited to public performances of national dignity. It was unveiled in September 1947 and dedicated to the Liberators of Tallinn, commemorating the Red Army soldiers who conquered the city three years earlier. The soldier himself is anonymous but has a specific and recognizable uniform. Re-burying of soldiers at the site also made the statue a memorial, and the eternal flame (1964) further added to the sacredness of the place. In the Soviet era the monument legitimized Soviet rule and obligated the citizens to build up the new Soviet Estonia for which these glorious dead had sacrificed their lives.

Soon after regaining independence the Estonian government tried to soften the symbolism of the monument, as its message was completely contradictory to the new narrative of the Soviet era as a cruel occupation. In the early 1990s the measures were still rather cautious. The monument was renamed and the eternal flame put out. In an act of de-Sovietization it was rededicated to all who fell in World War II. However, the soldier still had his distinct uniform and the monument was a central site for the revived Victory Day celebrations of the Russian Estonians.

For the Estonians the statue initially symbolized their national tragedy. Celebrating the memory of a Red Army soldier, the organizer of deportations, a war criminal, a murderer, profaned the Estonian nation, an interpretation still widely held. In the recent debate about the identity of the statue's model Estonian authorities have fiercely concentrated on his de-Estonization. An official investigation was launched to show that the model was not the Estonian Olympic champion wrestler Kristjan Palusalu – a national hero – but merely a carpenter called Albert Adamson. The fact that model, sculptor (Enn Roos) and his supervising architect (Arnold Alas) were all ethnic Estonians is deeply disturbing for the narratives of steadfast Estonian resistance, the alien nature of the Soviet system and Estonian victimization. The statue evidently depicts an Estonian Red Army soldier, urging the Estonians to build up a Soviet society.

But the Bronze Soldier has not been the only disturbing war memorial. The April 2007 incidents were preceded by a series of public performances, a so-called a 'war of monuments' dating back to 2004. In the small town of Lihula, Estonian nationalists together with a group of World War II veterans who had served in the German army erected a stone tablet dedicated to 'Estonian men who fought in 1940–1945 against Bolshevism and for the restoration of Estonian independence' (Burch & Smith, 2007, pp. 913–5). According to the dominant Estonian trajectory these veterans were freedom fighters who had to serve in German uniform since no national army was available. Commemoration of Waffen-SS veterans was strongly criticized by the Russian government as well as Jewish organizations and the European Union. In Europe, public commemoration and cherishing of anything associated with Nazi Germany is intolerable. Under foreign pressure the Estonian government had to remove the monument just two weeks after its unveiling, explaining that the bravery of the people who fought for Estonia should be commemorated in a dignified way, 'not in a uniform forced upon them by someone else'.[2]

The Lihula incident sparked a debate on the ban on the public use of symbols of totalitarian regimes and on the politically more correct alternative ways of commemorating those who fought for a free Estonia. Nazi symbols could not be displayed, because even if individual Estonian soldiers in the German army were not necessarily Nazis, reference to SS or Nazi symbols by default glorifies totalitarianism. Following this antitotalitarian logic, Soviet symbols and cherishing the Soviet past should also be prohibited.

What followed was a series of public performances targeted at several war memorials around Estonia. Many war memorials and cemeteries were desecrated during 2004–2006. In particular, the Red Army Memorial at the heart of Tallinn became a touchy issue after the Lihula incident. The monument was defaced with red paint on the night before Victory Day 2005, but the affair started to intensify around

Victory Day 2006. Veteran organizations laid their usual wreaths at the monument, but critics claimed that paying respect to a soldier of a foreign army in the Estonian nation-state should not be allowed. The international media published a picture of a man carrying an Estonian flag and a banner saying: 'Estonian people – don't forget: this soldier occupied our land and deported our people!'[3] On 20 May groups of Estonian nationalists, neo-Nazis and Russian-speaking people defending the monument gathered at the site. Even though these demonstrations were not legally registered, they took place relatively peacefully. The Russian Ministry of Foreign Affairs warned against any attempts to desecrate or transfer the 'Liberator Soldier Monument': 'In Russia, which paid an incompensable price for the victory over fascism, such actions cannot but evoke condemnation'.[4] While the monument's critics planned new demonstrations, young Russian-speakers organized the so-called 'Night Watch' (*Nochnoi Dozor*) to guard the statue. Their declaration followed the lines of the Russian World War II narrative: the Bronze Soldier 'symbolizes the victory of Europe and the whole world over fascism, and also belongs to the history of our grandfathers and parents'. The 'Night Watch' urged the government to protect the monument from vandalism (Nochnoi Dozor 2006). They did not question the legitimacy and independence of the state as such, but by criticizing the state-sanctioned interpretation of World War II they denounced one of the main pillars of the Estonian national narrative.

The discussion on the Bronze Soldier intensified in both the Estonian and Russian language media. According to a media review commissioned by The Non-Estonians' Integration Foundation the coverage of events in May–July 2006 was heavily influenced by national narratives: 'both in the Estonian and Russian language mediaspace a national consciousness plays a very important role in arguments for or against the transfer of the monument' (cited in Poleshchuk 2007, p. 14).

The Estonian authorities started to draft legislation that would permit them to relocate the monument. In spite of some criticism the legislation came into force in the beginning of 2007 and relocation plans proceeded. The attempt to ban all displays of Soviet symbols, including those commemorating the Great Patriotic War, provoked protests from Russian officials.[5] Events developed rapidly on 26 April, as the Ministry of Defence, invoking the Protection of War Graves Act, started the exhumation of the soldiers buried underneath the monument.[6] A large crowd of mostly Russian-speaking people gathered at Tõnismägi to protest. For reasons still somewhat unclear, the protest turned into vandalism and looting, and the police used harsh measures to bring order to the city center. In an extraordinary session, the government decided at 3:40 a.m. to move the monument, in order to 'avoid further gross disturbances of peace, which would place the property and welfare of the public at real risk'.[7] After a further night of riots the situation calmed down and the protest was reduced to attempts by car drivers to block the traffic in the center by driving too slowly and continually honking their car horns.

Immediately after the Bronze War the Estonian government rather puzzlingly declared 8 May as a day of commemoration for the victims of World War II. On that day a ministerial delegation laid wreaths at the Holocaust memorial at Klooga, the monument to the Unknown Soldier (previously the Bronze Soldier) and Maarjamäe memorial complex.[8] Why were these acts of commemoration suddenly needed?

Was it a gesture of conciliation or a national demonstration, and who were the audience? Paying respects to the relocated and renamed Bronze Soldier was hardly an attempt at reconciliation with Estonian Russian-speakers or Russia, as the choice of 8 May as the day of official festivities was a demonstrative rejection of the Russian/Soviet 9 May Victory Day tradition.[9] According to the Museum of Occupation 'the end of World War Two (May 8 1945) was not a watershed event for Estonia. The period of terror culminated with the mass deportation that was carried out on March 25 1949'.[10] Thus 8 May was an insignificant day for the Estonian drama, but its celebration became important in relation to Russia and Europe. It was simultaneously challenging the previously dominant Russian commemorative traditions and connecting Estonia to Western European values and history.

A year later the same monuments were visited by the authorities, but this time with much lower profile and publicity. Instead of ministers or politicians, wreaths were laid by unnamed representatives of the Ministry of Defence.[11] Seemingly a public performance was no longer needed and the original ceremony was introduced merely for the foreign audience in the aftermath of the Bronze War.

Nationalized Politics of the Bronze Soldier

An analysis of national narratives cannot account for the fluctuations in the intensity of nationalist politics. For this purpose we need to investigate the daily reproduction and transformation of national identities in contemporary politics. Rogers Brubaker, exploring Eastern European developments, has focused on the specific forms 'nationalized' politics takes in different fields (Brubaker 1996, pp. 1–22). The nationalist ideal that the borders of states and nations should be congruent (Gellner 1983, p. 1) creates three basic positions for agents: they can represent the state-owning nation, the national minority, or the kin state of the minority. *Nationalizing nationalisms* involves claims made in the name of a core nation (or state-owning nation), defined in ethno-cultural terms. In a nationalizing state the 'state-owning' nation is conceived of as being in a too weak a position and therefore the ruling elites try to improve or defend the status of the core nation within the state (Brubaker 1996, p. 63). Nationalizing policies are often directed against minorities living within the territory of the nation-state or current and potential migrants. *Minority nationalisms* involve claims made in the name of a minority that is conceived of as ethno-culturally different from the main population. Often the most fundamental issue in a political conflict between the (self-proclaimed) core nation and the minority is whether a group should be considered a 'national minority' (Brubaker 1996, pp. 60–2, 64) – with all the related international normative implications (see for example Kymlicka 2007).

In many cases, especially in Central and Eastern Europe, there is also a third party to the dynamics of nations. The *homeland nationalists* claim that the kin state has a right, or even a duty, to protect its compatriots against the discriminative policies of the nationalizing state (Brubaker 1996, pp. 66–7). The triangle of Estonian elites, Russian-speaking community and Russian Federation constitutes a paradigm example of this (see Pettai 2006). The three fields are closely connected, as the actors of one field monitor the actions of others and describe them in more or less biased ways to justify their own standpoints. This 'triadic nexus' (Brubaker 1996, pp. 67–9) easily turns into a vicious circle where partisan views enhance the narratives of disloyalty, danger and enmity (see Jutila 2006).

How does the Bronze Soldier case relate to Brubaker's triadic nexus? It is easy to see this nexus in action. The Estonian government's decision to remove a symbol of a competing interpretation of World War II history from the nationalized space of the center of the capital city was a move of nationalizing nationalism. Estonia underlined its sovereignty to make decisions without consulting anyone else (see also Astrov 2008). As Prime Minister Ansip explained to the parliament:

> On the night of April 26th we had two choices – whether to take control of the situation, together with all the responsibilities relating to the future, or to allow the control to be taken by those who had come to the streets for rioting. We assumed responsibility and decided the course of events.[12]

The government activities before and on 26–27 April vindicated the Estonian narrative of history and underlined its refusal to enter into a dialogue with people who have different views on the past. Despite the obvious multiple meanings of the monument the opponents, the 'hate-mongers', were presented as acting under foreign influence, and the possibility that the Russian speakers could speak with their own voice about their own concerns was denied.[13] For example, the previously successful presidential roundtable on national minorities – often cited by the government as an example of its multicultural policy – never discussed the issue. As the Russian-speaking community was marginalized from decision-making, skepticism about the government's intentions increased.

Russian-speaking minority nationalists opposed the government. The 'Night Watch' tried to protect the monument symbolizing the victory of their 'grandfathers and parents' over fascism (Nochnoi Dozor 2006), but was unable to influence the decision of the government. Various Russian Federation officials and organizations voiced their concern about the activities of the Estonian government in homeland nationalistic form. The Russian Foreign Minister Sergei Lavrov sent a letter to the 'Western partners of Estonia', where he accused Estonia of rewriting history and downplaying the role of Russia in liberating the world from fascism. Lavrov states that Estonian society is divided, but otherwise he presents the dispute as one between Estonia and Russia.[14] The most visible anti-Estonian protests came from the youth movement '*Nashi*': they arranged a demonstration in front of the 'eSStonian' embassy in Moscow, wearing Red Army uniforms, sleeping in tents, organizing fire performances and collecting signatures to a petition to relocate the embassy from the city center to a more appropriate location. This kind of carnivalized protest is a significant element in the construction of the brand of the movement, and it also served to sustain media interest in the relocation of the monument (see Lassila 2007b).[15] The Estonian government reacted to 'the siege to the Estonian embassy in Moscow' – the participants in which were, according to the government, paid by the Kremlin – by demanding a concerted European response. The government claimed that 'the future of people of Russian nationality in the Republic of Estonia is just a rhetorical pretext for implementing "active measures", and the fellow countrymen are used in a much bigger political game'.[16] Again, the conflict was presented as one between Estonia and Russia and thus as a question of national security. The representatives of both Estonia and Russia used very hard rhetoric, accusing each other of violations of European values. The views of nationalizing nationalists in Estonia and homeland nationalists in Russia were diametrically opposed and mutually reinforcing, as Brubaker's model suggests.

The vicious circle of the triadic nexus did not escalate into a large-scale, long-term 'ethnic conflict'. Within Estonia, the representatives of the majority (state) and minority both made conscious efforts to prevent this from happening. Even though the controversy was presented through national imagery and different interpretations of history were voiced on the basis of national groups, both sides avoided rhetoric that could exacerbate the vicious circle. Already in their May 2006 petition the 'Night Watch' had stated that 'We strongly object to the representation of the following situation as attempts at inciting interethnic enmity, disloyalty to the state and the society. We address to mass-media with the request to show responsibility and be precise and correct while broadcasting the events' (Nochnoi Dozor 2006). After the first night of riots President Ilves also avoided a national interpretation of the events: 'The common denominator of last night's criminals was not their nationality but their desire to riot, vandalize and plunder'.[17] In a statement a couple of days later he kept up the conciliatory tone:

> As Estonians, we must understand that people who came here in the Soviet time and live now in the Republic of Estonia, as well as their children and grandchildren, are our fellow countrymen. I invite my fellow Estonians to see this very clearly. Also, I invite all my fellow countrymen to see Estonia as their country. . . . Other nations living in Estonia must understand and admit that Estonians have their own, very painful, historical experience of life under three consecutive occupying powers in the last century. We must all be able to see and understand the tragedies of others.[18]

Even though the 'other nations' are reminded of the Estonians' national sacrifice during and after World War II, Russians are not presented as the perpetrators and criminals but rather as fellow countrymen who will continue to live in the state.

But why was the Bronze Soldier treated merely as a bilateral, Russo–Estonian question and not as a triangle in both Russia and Estonia? To answer that question it is necessary to scrutinize how the Bronze Soldier became an issue of national dignity, and how the monument was securitized.

The Great Patriotic War and Russian Memory

Moscow's strong reaction against the Estonian government in the Bronze Soldier incident reflects the persistent importance of the Soviet victory in the Great Patriotic War for Russians. Memorials and monuments of World War II were among the most powerful and popular sites for the construction of Soviet national identity, and during the 1990s they were transformed from Soviet symbols into Russian ones (Forest & Johnson 2002, pp. 524–47). Russians saw the treatment of the Bronze Soldier as an attempt to question the significance of their victory, a trend so common in the Baltic states. The Great Patriotic War forms the basic image of Russian national consciousness and collective memory. It is still the most important symbol holding the nation together, a historical event completely beyond comparison. In the Soviet Union it was deliberately and forcefully used by the authorities to whip up national pride and allegiance, and after a brief phase of more pluralist memory culture in the late 1980s and early 1990s it was restored as the defining experience of the Russian nation by the Putin administration.

Up to the early 1950s the glorified official version of the war was still rather far from the individual memories that dealt with poverty, hunger, destruction of normalcy, toil, sorrow and death. During the 1950s the authorities suppressed this universe of individual experience with a continuous flow of official ritualistic representations of war from mass media, education, art and public ceremonies. In a gigantic project of politics of memory the Soviet authorities undertook the task of ideologically processing the experience of a whole population. As the years and decades passed, people gradually absorbed the official version and adapted their own experiences to it. The official version of history achieved the status of absolute reality and general validity (Gudkov 2005).

According to the heroic narrative of the war the Soviet Union rescued European civilization from the scourge of Nazism. After becoming a victim of unprovoked aggression by Hitler and his allies the Soviet Union came back from the brink of destruction and not only defeated the *Wehrmacht* but also liberated occupied Eastern and Central Europe. The Allied victory would not have been possible without the ultimate sacrifices of Soviet soldiers and citizens. The Great Patriotic War gave the world a shining example of the true Russian national character, a character that showed its best qualities under the extreme pressures of crisis, war and catastrophe (Gareev 2005).

In foreign commentaries it has been common to interpret the extraordinary place of the war in Russian historical self-image as the proof of the success of Soviet propaganda and the last visible relic of an otherwise so discredited state. It would be wrong, however, to dismiss the narrative of the Great Patriotic War as a mere state-sponsored version of the national past imposed from above. By outliving communism, the heroic narrative of the Great Patriotic War proved to be bigger than the Soviet Union and at least in part independent of it. The 'holiness' of the war is also deeply and strongly felt among ordinary Russians, and most of them feel genuine personal pride in being a member of the nation that achieved a victory so great and epochal. In a poll conducted in 2003 no less than 87% of the interviewees gave the Great Patriotic War as the answer to the question 'What makes you personally most proud in our history?' It is perfectly possible for an individual Russian to view the war simultaneously as proof of the inhumanity of Stalin's rule but also as a source of national pride and patriotism. The war occupies such an honored and sacred place in Russian memory that it cannot be touched by regime changes, not even by the most dramatic events of 1991, when the very state that fought the war disappeared. Although the narrative may be selective and flawed, its endorsement by the people as the 'true version' of the past is very genuine (Gudkov 2005; Tumarkin 2003).

In addition to being a successful propaganda tool in the hands of the Soviet/Russian authorities, the heroic image of the war has provided ordinary Russians not only with pride but also with comfort, relief and distraction from the grimness of everyday life. It instilled hope in people and made them believe that a better future is possible. Because of this popular support the Great Patriotic War essentially became the founding myth of the postwar Soviet Union, refreshing its legitimacy and imbuing it with a new dynamism that lasted well into the Khrushchev era. In difficult times people invoked its images of past heroism to deal with present adversities, be it the stagnation of the Brezhnev era or the all-encompassing uncertainty of the new post-communist realities of the 1990s.

In the new Russia the pride in Soviet achievements eroded, reforms failed, hopes waned and illusions died, but the symbolic importance of the Great Patriotic War persisted and increased. Thousands of statues of Lenin, Stalin and Marx were torn down and removed, but memorials of World War II were barely touched. People still brought flowers to them and posed for photographs in front of them. In the quest for the building blocks for a new Russian identity the victory of 1945 triumphed over both the imperial heritage of pre-Revolutionary Czarist Russia and the Soviet era. Superpower status had been lost and the country as well as its inhabitants faced enormous difficulties in the new political and economic situation. Shattered national self-confidence was desperately searching for some source of pride and sense of togetherness. The victory of 1945 became an anchor of hope and the only binding positive symbol in a situation where there was little to take pride in (Merridale 2003, pp. 13–28).

The collapse of communism did not reduce pressures against history: again it was used by journalists and politicians to legitimize new governments, to offer consolidation to those whose better days were now permanently over. In Putin's Russia the memory of war has once again been appropriated and monopolized by the state authorities to legitimize centralism and mobilize the nation. Government-owned TV channels air war movies and documentaries on a daily basis and commemorate the heroic battles in Moscow, Stalingrad, Kursk and Leningrad. New Russian nationalism has created its own peculiar version of the national past, where the Great Patriotic War is linked to other suitable events selected from imperial and Soviet histories and to the idea of the self-sufficient sovereignty of Russianness and its rivalry with the often so ignorant and ungrateful 'West'. As the Kievan Rus' shielded Europe from the Tatars and Mongols, so the Soviet Union shielded it from fascism.

Celebrations of Victory Day on 9 May in Russia are very different compared with ceremonies of Victory in Europe Day on 8 May in western parts of the continent. In Russia the ceremonies are not about the mournful commemoration of the dead and the victims of war, the suffering and destruction, but literally about honoring and glorifying the victory, the triumph of the Red Army over Hitler's Nazi troops. This nationalist and militarist spectacle leaves no room for the victims and there is no trace of the universal approach towards the war as a common human tragedy concerning individual people of all nations involved. Victory over Nazism is also the grand narration of how Russia's Europeanness has been defined; contesting the victory is thus tantamount to challenging the position of Russia in Europe. While the EU currently declares its monopoly over defining Europe, Russia has remained, and renewed the older narration of Europe grounded in the legacy of World War II. Still, despite the best efforts of the state authorities, attitudes towards history should not be regarded as monolithic in today's Russia. The entirely different horizons of life make the past strange in the eyes of younger generations, who cannot understand their parents' and grandparents' obsession with a story that was already over when they were born. As Catherine Merridale points out, 'the monochrome of the old world has been replaced by vibrant capitalism' in the landscape of young people (Merridale 2005, pp. 76–82), but sometimes the visual signs and symbols of the Great Patriotic War are used, even if perhaps also carnivalized as in case of '*Nashi*'.

Collective Amnesia

After the collapse of the Soviet Union the ultimate end of World War II in the Baltic states has been declared at least thrice: first with the regaining of independence in 1991, then when the last Russian troops left their soil in 1994, and finally when Estonia, Latvia and Lithuania became members of both NATO and the European Union in 2004. At the same time, a new future-oriented economic heroism was introduced to narrate Estonia into Europe. What has been surprising is that neither the ultimate end of the long Second World War nor the identification of Estonia as a 'tiny Tiger' has been able to eradicate World War II from the Estonian collective memory. Why has the war preserved its fundamental role in the Estonian drama?

One answer to this persistent presence of World War II is obviously the continuous and strengthening challenge of Moscow, but this is only one side of the story. Close analysis of the recent Estonian–Russian debate shows that the challenge from Moscow develops in relation to Estonian narratives and that seemingly World War II is written so deep into the Estonian drama that it is not easy to erase. The commemoration and interpretation of World War II turned out to be the burning issue of Russian–Estonian (and Russian–Baltic) political relations in the late 1990s. The 'Bronze War' was preceded by a heated Russo–Baltic debate over the interpretations of the annexation of the Baltic states to the Soviet Union in 1940 and the subsequent Nazi and Soviet occupations. In 1998 the Russian government sharply criticized the 54th anniversary ceremonies of the battles in Riga honoring the Latvian veterans of the Waffen-SS. As Morozov (2003, pp. 219–26; see also Lehti 2006, pp. 76–8) has pointed out, Russian rhetoric divided Europe into two separate parts, the 'true' and the 'false'. In this discourse Russia, together with other European great powers, is defending European values against barbarism. This argumentation, mostly directed at Berlin, Paris and London on the one hand and at the domestic public on the other, aims to diminish the presumably negative influence of the Baltic states on EU–Russia relations by marginalizing them into insignificance. In Russia Europe is still viewed in terms of individual states, big and small powers, thus also sidelining the EU.

The most striking single event was the celebration of the 60th anniversary of Victory Day on 9 May 2005, which gathered state leaders together in Moscow. Two of the three Baltic heads of state chose to stay away and only the Latvian President, Vaira Vīķe-Freiberga, accepted the invitation, although they knew that with the presence of the leading NATO members this would entail the risk of marginalizing their countries in the eyes of the West and give Moscow a strong argument for presenting them as 'false' Europeans. In the Baltic countries the Victory Day has become too painful a symbol of their national tragedies (Onken 2007, pp. 37–41). Consequently the Western powers expressed their understanding for the special position of the Baltic states, and eventually it was the Russian Foreign Ministry who felt the need to explain its stance on the matter to European audiences:

> The term 'occupation' cannot be used for a legal assessment of the situation in the Baltics in the late 1930s because there was no state of war between USSR and the Baltic states and no military actions were being conducted, and the troops were introduced on the basis of an agreement and with the express consent of the authorities that existed in these republics at the time – whatever one may think of them. In addition, throughout the period when Latvia, Lithuania and Estonia were part of the Soviet Union, there were national bodies of power, with the exception of the time when that part of the USSR territory was occupied by Germany during the Great Patriotic War.[19]

The interpretations of the Second World War have also clashed in the complex controversy over the Russian–Estonian border treaty dating back to the early days of Estonian independence. Even the eventual signing of the treaty on 18 May 2005 did not end the dispute, because the Estonian parliament ratified it only after adding to it references to the 20 August 1991 resolution of the Republic of Estonian Supreme Council 'On the National Independence of Estonia' and the declaration of the *Riigikogu* of 7 October 1992 'On the Restoration of Constitutional Power'. Both of these declarations for their part refer to the Tartu Peace Treaty of 1920 and the illegality of the Soviet Occupation.[20] Russia quickly and harshly refused to accept any alterations to the governmental agreement. It would not ratify the treaty because it argued that amendments could open the door to demands for further border changes and compensations.[21] The issue has once more ended up in deadlock.

Despite the stabilizing effect of NATO and EU membership, the primary interests of Estonian foreign policy, as stated by President Toomas Hendrik Ilves (2005, p. 197), still lie in the East. The reasons for this resilient presence of Russia extend far beyond security politics, to the three core elements of the Estonian national trajectory: the civilizational narrative, ethnic sovereignty and amnesiac denial of the Soviet era. Russia has remained the threatening Other, against which all elements of the Estonian national drama are contrasted. More than military, the threat is cultural or civilizational, and it is directed at the very core of the national narrative.

The founding narrative of the Estonian state is based on two premises: the illegality of Soviet rule in the Baltic countries and the principle of legal continuity. All interpretations challenging these premises are seen as threats to national pride. As Stukuls Eglitis (2002, pp. 70–2) writes, the Soviet era is presented not only as illegal but also as an abnormal state of affairs, while normality is seen to exist in the West. The narrative is also firmly anchored in World War II as a crucial turning point between legal and illegal, natural and abnormal. Estonia has demanded that Russia acknowledge and compensate for Soviet actions during the war and occupation.

The nucleus of the post-Cold War Estonian national drama is formed by the civilizational narrative, defining what Estonia is and what it is not. By emphasizing the country's fundamental differences from Russia, Estonia is placed on the Western side of the civilizational fault line. 'Through the reification of differences, the civilizational narrative generates the notion that Estonia is fundamentally insecure because it is located on a putative civilizational boundary' as Merje Kuus (2007, p. 55) points out. This omnipresent feeling of insecurity is not necessarily linked to the Russian state or the military threat posed by it, but instead 'is framed in terms of Russian identity and culture-Russianness as such' (Kuus 2007, p. 56). Russianness is presented as essentially alien to the West. Individuals or groups supporting integration with the East are seen as a potential fifth column.

Ethnic sovereignty has formed the other central element in the Estonian national narrative: 'the state must nurture the roots of the Estonian nation in Estonian soil. Any erosion of the special relationship between the two poses a security risk to the Estonian state' (Kuus 2007, p. 72). State sovereignty as well as the national trajectory rest on the notions of territorial roots, ethnic homeland and indigenous culture. Unlike the Estonians, whose ancestors have inhabited the Estonian territory from the ancient times, Russian speakers are presented as nomadic and alien: 'Russian speakers are identified as a security problem not because of their actions but because of their lack of roots in Estonia' (Kuus 2007, p. 77). They are seen as a destabilizing force and as a potential fifth column. Estonian officials recognized the risk of the emergence of two separate societies in the late 1990s, as attested by the state program *Integration in Estonian Society* 2000–2007. However, the ethnically exclusive displays of national dignity have so far overridden the more diversified and inclusive perspectives.

The amnesiac denial or collective amnesia of the Soviet era, the third pivotal feature of the Estonian national narrative, means that the whole history of this period is interpreted exclusively in terms of suffering and resistance. A telling example of this is provided by the Museum of Occupation and the Fight for Freedom, founded in Tallinn in 2003 and located just one block from the original site of the Bronze Soldier.[22] The first exhibition sign tells that 'the Museum reflects the struggle between the preservationist responses of the people and destructive impetus of the occupations', i.e. efforts to save the pure Estonian culture from the savage intruders trying to demolish it. The expressions of Estonianness in the Soviet era are reduced simply to people 'yearning for freedom' and 'never losing hope'. In this ethnicized narrative resistance is the only true Estonian virtue and everything else represents alien Russian culture. The active role of ethnic Estonians in politics and culture is silenced, as well as the fact that ethnic Russians too were deported during the first Soviet occupation. Paradoxically, however, while any influence of the Soviet era on Estonian culture is disputed, it is at the same time needed in order to dramatize the national narrative. The very name of the occupation museum articulates both the original drama of oppression and the emerging new heroic epic deifying those who fought for Estonian independence.

However, the Estonian discourse is no longer as unvaried, monolithic and unchallenged as the apparent power and uniformity of the official version seem to suggest. As Kuus (2007, p. 59) points out, 'since the turn of the decade, it has become increasingly possible to argue publicly against Russophobia and for closer contacts with Russia'. There is also an emergent interest in Soviet-era Estonian popular culture. However, the Bronze War seemed to stifle this emergent pluralism, as Estonians almost unanimously blamed Putin's Russia for the riots, demonstrations and web attacks, and saw participants, particularly the '*Nashi*' organization, as mere puppets of the Kremlin. Conflict was interpreted solely in terms of Estonian–Russian relations, with a complete disregard of intrasocietal tensions, making the reaction entirely compatible with the national narrative.

The commemoration of the Second World War has not, however, remained static, for a noticeable transformation and emergence of new myths have followed EU and NATO membership. In the 1990s, the dominating Estonian discourse on the return to Europe emphasized victimhood, as something obligating Western Europeans to accept Estonia into NATO and the EU. In the new millennium, the narrative of victimhood has been challenged by a new heroic narrative of a tiny Tiger whose successful transformation from a Soviet economy to a serious player in the global economy has been completely unparalleled (Lehti 2007, pp. 137–40; Lehti 2006, 82–4). The country is presented as a skilful reformer which, instead of following the Western European model, has already overtaken it, thereby being able to show a new path to old Europeans. After achieving NATO and EU membership a new more active image has replaced the old passive object in Estonian self-identification, yet this active agent has simultaneously been transformed into the collective memories of World War II, too.

In the 1990s collective memory was dominated by the tragic victims of Soviet oppression, but the emerging narrative is replacing them with heroic veterans of World War II and the War of Independence of 1918–1919. The deported have a day of commemoration (14 June), but lack a major public monument. The statue of Linda on Toompea hill, depicting the wife of the epic hero Kalev mourning for the loss of her husband, still serves as a forum of commemoration. In the Soviet era the statue, created in 1880 but erected on Toompea only in 1920, became an unofficial memorial for victims of Stalin's terror, today acknowledged by a plaque bearing the text 'to remember the ones taken away'. Regardless of its political meaning, the statue has remained a site of personal mourning free of state-centric blustering and heroism.

It seems that today's Estonia, a 'tiny Tiger' encouraged by a thriving economy and membership of NATO and the EU, is complementing or perhaps even replacing the previous founding myths of victimization with a new heroic narrative of an active, brave and independent nation. Conquering symbolically important places with monuments has stayed high on the agenda of Estonian statecraft. Narratives of deportation have been superseded by a new cult of soldier heroes, as manifested by new monuments such as the Maarjamäe Memorial Ground or the Statue of Liberty for the War of Independence. Relatively remote Maarjamäe, known for its gigantic Soviet-era war memorial, was recaptured in 2005 with a new monument 'dedicated to those who took part of the defensive battles of 1944. Maarjamäe, therefore, symbolizes the tragic fate of the Estonian soldier in World War II', as declared by the Estonian government.[23]

The simultaneous renaissance of the commemoration of the War of Independence is most striking in the plans to erect a huge cross-shaped monument in the center of Tallinn.[24] On 3 January 2008 Estonian Defence Minister Jaak Aaviksoo urged his listeners at an anniversary ceremony of the War of Independence to 'commemorate those who were and are willing to take up arms to protect Estonia's freedom.... After having exhausted all other means, we are also willing to take up arms to protect our freedom'.[25] Five days later he opened an exhibition for General Johan Laidoner at the Estonian War Museum, emphasizing how 'the heroes of the War of Independence have a fundamental importance today and even more so for the future. Only an individual willing to give up everything in the name of his/her future can be free within the real meaning of the word'.[26]

The Bronze Soldier's inappropriateness has been heightened by the commemorative shift from the deportations of civilian victims to the glorification of Estonian soldiers. Previously the monument symbolized for many the Estonian genocide, but the situation would change drastically if the soldier were to be seen as an Estonian soldier in Soviet uniform. This would fundamentally clash with the new heroic Estonian drama that identifies Estonian patriotism solely with the Estonian soldiers in the German Army and presents the Red Army as an inhuman and markedly non-Estonian occupier. Then, the Bronze Soldier would symbolize a traitor to his nation, and this kind of friction is just not allowed in the simplified national trajectory.

Double or Triple Marginalization

Ritualized and politicized public commemorations diminish the space of private memories and emotions. Putin's Russia has followed its Soviet predecessors in the political exploitation of Victory Day to strengthen the state. Similarly the new ceremonies launched by the Estonian government attest to the fundamentally political nature of public commemorations. Nevertheless, for a large number of Estonian Russians the Bronze Soldier and Victory Day are not so much symbols of Russian/Soviet political and state power as carriers of important communal and particular memories (Burch & Smith 2007, p. 914). Besides official parading, Victory Day has traditionally also been an important family holiday with a strong emphasis on family-level memories of the war. The collective memory of Estonian Russian-speakers has been dramatically shaken by the dissolution of the Soviet Union and the restoration of Estonian independence. Substitute narratives were developed both in Russia and among ethnic Estonians, but Estonian Russian-speakers could not really anchor their private memories in either of these. Although Putin's Russia has eagerly utilized the common roots of the Russian and Estonian Russian narratives as it has played the part of advocate of Russians everywhere, the Bronze Soldier incident must first and foremost be seen as a desperate cry of a minority to be recognized. It remains to be seen whether the incident will become a unifying experience for the minority, strengthening its position within Estonia.

We argue that the Estonian Russian-speaking community is doubly marginalized in this theater; they are marginalized by Russian as well as Estonian discourses. It is also interesting that they should even be needed as an audience of this theater. Perhaps just for a brief moment they were taken seriously after the Bronze War, but they were soon forgotten again. They do not have a role in the play of national pride. With the removal of the monument, perhaps the only public forum for expressing an alternative reading of the Estonian drama within Estonia was taken away. The Estonian drama has been performed for Russia in particular but also recently for Europe, and some parts of it are clearly directed at the local ethnic Estonian audience. The same also goes for Russia, which is also in constant communication with Estonia's partners in the EU and NATO.[27] This supports Eva-Clarita Onken's (2007) interpretation of the treatment of the 60th anniversary of Victory Day in the Baltic states. She divides the fields of memory politics into three spheres: the European Union, the bilateral relations and domestic politics.

Because the bilateral relations with Russia are at a standoff, this field dominates Estonian memory politics. Because of the strong presence of national dignity all comments, performances and accusations are taken very seriously. A need to replace the Estonian tragedy with a heroic epic has kept attention focused on the World War II years. The dynamics of the Russian–Estonian history war also sustain the importance of this era. Simultaneously, Europe has remained an important audience, since one's own interpretation has been tied to European norms, thus justifying one's own Europeanness. All issues are seen through the prism of bilateral and European relations and thus the domestic memory political debate has been neglected. As long as the Soviet era is presented as an abnormality and the Russian-speaking minority as a fifth column and an alien element within Estonia it is not possible to narrate their experiences and memories within the collective memory of the Estonian state. Or, as Roshwald (2007, p. 368) argues, the idealized criterion for civic nationalism is not assimilation but 'the promise of a place of recognition and dignity for each ethnic subculture within the public arena of the nation as a whole'.

Beside the double marginalization of the Estonian Russian community, there is an obvious danger that Russia and Estonia are marginalizing themselves in the European context. Europe's own violent past, meaning in particular the experiences of World War II, was for a long time the grand narrative of the EU and thus the EU's Other was its own past. In this aspect the attitudes have changed remarkably. One of the long-term goals of European integration, both within and outside the European Union, is to create a genuinely common European historical understanding. One of the most prominent academic proponents of postnational European identity, Jürgen Habermas, has suggested that in creating this new identity, Europe should make use of the negative elements of its past. On a general human level it can be argued that it is precisely the memory of atrocities and tragedies that binds postwar Europe together: the two world wars, the destructiveness of nationalism, imperialism, colonialism and, most importantly, the Holocaust (Habermas 2000).

If Russia and Estonia continue on their chosen path of history-based identity politics, they are radically departing from more general European trends. Recently many scholars have argued that the EU is currently defined more in spatial than in temporal terms by naming friends and enemies, neighbors and candidates (Joenniemi 2008). Thus, Estonian or Russian appeals to World War II as part of a quest for recognition of their Europeanness are no longer tenable, because World War II is no longer part of the dominant discourse of an EU–Europe that is aiming to assume the role of global actor.

Epilogue: The Good Soldier Palusalu and His Fortunes in World War II – and After

As has been repeated several times in this article and by other researchers (for example Mälksoo 2007), the Russian epic of the Great Patriotic War and the Estonian tragedy of more than four decades of occupation or the new epic of anti-Soviet resistance cannot be combined in the same narrative: the heroes of one story are the villains of the other. Staging World War II as a drama of unified nations cannot produce new options to commemorate the events together. Each individual is supposed to be tied to the national narrative. Both the common plot structures of international politics, the epic and tragedy, are based on black and white, good or evil characters and the violent final act ends either in victory or catharsis. Different stories are needed.

Emancipation from the straitjacket of World War II narratives would thus be an important step towards a new beginning. That is why we wish to conclude by concentrating on the plot structures of the national World War II narratives. Following Aristotelian poetics, three basic plots are available: epic, tragedy and comedy. In national narratives, tales of victory are often told as heroic epics, but tragic stories of sacrifice are told as powerful, legitimizing narratives. The heroic epic strives to give the community a justified mission, a purpose for which even lives can be sacrificed. It defines and emphasizes the elements of virtue and nobility, endowing the community with a source of dignity. Tragedies, although inevitably headed towards a predestined disaster, may also promote communality and serve as therapeutic and protective narratives. They rationalize past failures and catastrophes and offer emotional release. Both heroic epics and tragedies are inclined to gross simplifications, violent solutions and the rejection of compromise, especially when linked to perceptions of national dignity.

The majority of collective national narratives of World War II fall within one of the two dominant plot structures, the narratives of heroism on the one hand and victimization on the other (Confino 2005). These are obviously closely related to the narrative strategies of heroic epics and tragedies. Heroic narratives, like the Russian Great Patriotic War, the British idea of World War II as 'the good war' or the American notion of the US citizens who fought in the war as 'the Greatest Generation', stress the virtues of perseverance, sacrifice, courage, nobility and vitality. They tell stories of victories or military prowess otherwise displayed on the battlefield, gallantry, bravery and moral superiority. Almost all countries have their own versions of heroic war myths, and these have been especially important in periods of physical and mental reconstruction after the war. The experience and memories of war and the hardships endured during it have been crucial tools in the construction of new postwar national identities (Judt 2000).

Sufferings caused by others form the core of the narratives of victimization: being betrayed and sold out, becoming a target of outside aggression and deliberate measures of physical destruction, even genocide. Victimhood is often also linked to the idea of national martyrdom, the notion that suffering has been caused by the fact that the nation has persistently stood firmly by its beliefs, values and convictions, or that through its sufferings and tribulations it has protected and shielded, possibly even saved other nations. This is evident, for example, in French, Belgian and Dutch accounts of the war, trying to reconcile the need for national pride with humiliating occupation and disturbing evidence of extensive indigenous collaboration with the German aggressors (Lagrou 1999, pp. 262–91).

Although national war histories are usually predominantly built around one of the above-mentioned metanarratives, most of them tend to incorporate elements from both and even combine them in the same myths. Both the heroic and victimized interpretations of the past have been used to avoid historical responsibilities and muffle the discussion of the more problematic parts of national history. Great Britain and the USA have been reluctant to contemplate the moral implications of their strategic bombing campaigns against Germany and Japan, maintaining that the high civilian casualties caused by these raids were not only unavoidable but also militarily necessary. In Japan the collective memory has centered on the devastating bombings of Hiroshima and Nagasaki, and refused to take responsibility for the Nanking massacre, sex slavery and other atrocities of the Imperial army. In countries occupied by Germany, the rich mythologies of resistance have helped to heal the wounds of national humiliation and push away the awkward memories of collaboration. Austrians for their part tried to claim for themselves the status of the first victims of Hitler, and explained the strong local support for National Socialism with historical burdens, economic adversities and German repression. By stressing the overwhelming importance of defeating Nazism and fascism the Western Allies avoided facing the fact that in the immediate postwar situation they effectively surrendered Eastern Europe to the mercies of Stalin (Mosse 1994, pp. 201–26).

The most flammable controversies over history arise from situations where the heroes of one party are considered perpetrators by the other. Actions that are considered brave and heroic and are important sources of national pride in one nation may have or may be perceived to have caused suffering among the members of another nation, either directly or indirectly as 'collateral damage'. This is exactly the case in the row over history between Russia and the Baltic countries (Krzeminski 2005).

What would then be the alternative form of telling? From a more universal point of view wars are always personal catastrophes. Regardless of who wins and how evil the defeated enemy was, millions of people, most of them still in their youth, lose their lives in the general madness. But commemorating universal tragedy is not a way to remember the particular events in which people themselves or their parents and grandparents participated. For this, the third form of Aristotelian poetics, comedy, could be an alternative. Comedies do not necessarily need to be hilarious stories of strange personalities and their comical sidekicks with happy endings, although they often are. Most importantly, from the point of view of national narratives, they question, stir and mix up established patterns of thinking instead of offering simple and absolute explanations together with a morally clear-cut cast of good and evil characters. Comedies combine surprising things with unpredictable ways, dealing out ridicule even-handedly among all actors. In comedies even heroes may fail, misunderstand the intentions of others and opt for unconventional strategies without losing face (Kuusisto 2007). This, according to Carl von Clausewitz,[28] is what war is all about.

Comic plot structures are also evident from the fortunes of the model of the Bronze Soldier in World War II,[29] even though the story is not a happy one. During the first independence Kristjan Palusalu was a national hero, who won two gold medals at the Berlin Olympic Games in 1936. After the first occupation in 1941 Palusalu was deported to Archangel and sentenced to death, but the sentence was changed to military service on the Finnish front. He deserted from the Red Army and walked across the lines to the Finnish side, shouting 'Don't shoot, here are Estonian boys!' He was captured and soon recognized by the regiment doctor Heikki Savolainen, also an Olympic medalist in Berlin. Finland returned Palusalu to Estonia, which was still in German hands, but he was again captured when the Soviet forces 'liberated' the country in the fall of 1944. He was released in 1946 without sentence, at the time when Enn Roos was sculpting the monument. His athletic merits were not publicly celebrated by the Soviet authorities, since the Berlin Olympic Games were not recognized and he was not a real pro-Soviet model citizen. But nevertheless he became the model for the Bronze Soldier. He lived a normal, quiet life in the countryside and also occasionally worked as a wrestling trainer.

Palusalu has been presented as a national hero whose personal history reflects the history of the Estonian nation. But if the storyline were narrated in the form of a comedy not all the Soviet characters would need to be evil; Palusalu was released by some Soviet official even though he had deserted from both a labor camp and a penal battalion, and was later allowed to live on the farm awarded to him after the gold medals. Both of these things should be impossible if the system were inhuman and evil to the core. More complicated stories can thus be told about individual fortunes in wars and under occupation. The history of nations could also be narrated less nationalistically, bringing to the fore the complex events, hidden agendas and switchovers concealed by the unifying narratives of good and evil. This should not be regarded as insulting national dignity, but rather as recognizing that people in the past lived in as complex a world, with no easy solutions, as we do today. Only then can there be an end to the battles over World War II and it can be commemorated together by Estonians and Russians from both sides of the border. In the current trenches of the Russian–Estonian history wars, this seems unlikely. But hopefully they could some day show an example to the rest of the world.

Notes

1 Securitization is a concept developed by Ole Wæver, Barry Buzan and their colleagues at the Copenhagen Peace Research Institute. It refers to the political process in which certain issues are presented as an existential threat to a specified referent object. If successful, securitization legitimizes extraordinary measures that are beyond normal democratic political procedures in order to deal with the threat. See Wæver (1995); Buzan, Wæver & de Wilde (1998). For a debate on securitization of minority issues see Roe (2004, 2006); Jutila (2006).

2 Government Communication Office, 'Monument unlawfully put up in Lihula to be removed', 2 September 2004, available at: www.valitsus.ee, accessed 6 February 2008.

3 'Eesti rahvas—Ära unusta: See Sõdur okupeeris meie riigi ja küüditas meie rahva!'

4 MFA of the Russian Federation 'Statement of the Ministry of Foreign Affairs of the Russian Federation Regarding Desecration in Estonia of the Monument to the Soviet Soldiers Who Fell in the Years of the Great Patriotic War', 23 May 2006, available at: www.mid.ru, accessed 6 February 2008.

5 'Estonia's decision to ban Soviet symbols disgraceful—Lavrov', 1 December 2006, available at: en.rian.ru/world/20061201/56317748.html; 'Russian intelligence justifies Soviet annexation of Baltic states', 23 November 2006, available at: en.rian.ru/russia/20061123/55932837.html; 'Estonia's WWII memorials demolition law immoral—Speaker Mironov', 15 November 2006, available at: en.rian.ru/russia/20061115/55665080.html; all sites accessed 6 February 2008.

6 'Estonian Ministry of Defence commencing preparation work for the identification of the war graves located at the Tõnismägi green area', 26 April 2007, available at: www.valitsus.ee, accessed 6 February 2008.

7 'Government of the Republic of Estonia and crisis management committee hold extraordinary session', 27 April 2007, available at: www.valitsus.ee, accessed 6 February 2008.

8 'Members of the Government commemorated the victims of WWII at Klooga'; 'Government lays a wreath at the monument to the Unknown Soldier'; 'The celebration of the memorial day on 8 May was concluded by laying wreaths at Maarjamäe', Estonian Government, 8 May 2007, all articles available at: www.valitsus.ee, accessed 5 June 2007.

9 Differences between European and Russian dates are just originally a question of time zones; final surrender was accepted at Berlin on 8 May 1945 but because of the time zones it was already 9 May in Moscow.

10 Exhibition tablet at the Museum of Occupation, 29 January 2008.

11 Estonian Ministry of Defence, 'Representatives of the Ministry of Defence place wreaths at the monuments to the victims of World War II', 8 May 2008, available at: www.mod.gov.ee, accessed 12 June 2008.

12 Prime Minister Andrus Ansip's speech in the *Riigikogu*, 2 May 2007, available at: www.valitsus.ee, accessed 6 April 2008.

13 'Declaration of the Minister of Foreign Affairs of the Republic of Estonia', 1 May 2007, available at: www.valitsus.ee, accessed 6 April 2008.

14 The letter was published by *Eesti Päeväleht* on 11 May 2007. 'SERGEI LAVROV: Venemaa kaebekiri Eesti peale', available at: http://www.epl.ee/artikkel/385394, accessed 6 February 2008.

15 For a more general analysis of *Nashi* rhetoric see Lassila (2007a).

16 'Declaration of the Minister of Foreign Affairs of the Republic of Estonia', 1 May 2007, available at: www.valitsus.ee, accessed 6 April 2008.

17 'President Ilves: I invite everyone to exercise level-headed and rational thinking', 27 April 2007, available at: http://www.president.ee/en/, accessed 6 February 2008.

18 'President Ilves: We can agree upon a common future', 2 May 2007, available at: http://www.president.ee/en/, accessed 6 February 2008.

19 'Comments by the Russian Foreign Ministry Information and Press Department in Connection with Remarks by Some European Politicians Regarding the "Occupation" of the Baltic Countries by the Soviet Union and the Need for Russia to Condemn This', 4 May 2005, available at: www.ln.mid.ru/brp_4.nsf/e78a48070f128a7b43256999005bcbb3/3575341bd4842979c3256ff8002f095f?OpenDocument, accessed 21 August 2008.

20 Riigikogu ratifitseeris Eesti-Vene piirilepped (20 June 2005) & Eelinformatsioon 13–19. juunini (10 June 2005), available at: www.riigikogu.ee/index.php?id=36947 and www.riigikogu.ee/index.php?id=31920, accessed 21 August 2008).

21 'Statement by Alexander Yakovenko, the Spokesman of Russia's Ministry of Foreign Affairs, Regarding Estonian Parliament's Ratification of Border Treaties with Russia', 21 June 2005; 'Statement by the Ministry of Foreign Affairs of the Russian Federation Concerning the Ratification of the Border Treaties with Russia by the Estonian Parliament', 22 June 2005, available at: www.ln.mid.ru/brp_4.nsf/e78a48070f128a7b43256999005bcbb3/5400e7d6355b0634c3257028003c7a52?OpenDocument. 'Estonian reaction: Statement by the Estonian Ministry of Foreign Affairs', 22 June 2005 and 27 June 2005, available at: http://www.vm.ee/eng/kat_138/5744.html?arhiiv_kuup=kuup_2005 and http://www.vm.ee/eng/kat_138/5744.html?arhiiv_kuup=kuup_2005, sites accessed 21 August 2008.

22 www.okupatsioon.ee. Interestingly the original name of the museum is the 'Museum of Occupations', with 'Occupations' in the plural, but apparently the word 'occupation' is currently used in the singular.

23 Estonian Government Communication Office, 'Estonia commemorates those perished in World War II', 27 April 2005, available at: www.valitsus.ee, accessed 24 January 2008.

24 Estonian Ministry of Defence, 'The statue of liberty of the War of Independence receives its revamp', 19 December 2007, available at: www.mod.gov.ee, accessed 24 January 2008. See also www.vabadusemonument.ee, accessed 21August 2008.

25 Estonian Ministry of Defence, 'Anniversary of the Estonian War of Independence ceasefire commemorated at Tallinn Reaalkool', 3 January 2008, available at: www.mod.gov.ee, accessed 24 January 2008.

26 Estonian Ministry of Defence, 'General Laidoner exhibition opens at Estonian War Museum', 8 January 2008, available at: www.mod.gov.ee, accessed 24 January 2008.

27 See for example Lavrov's appeal to EU countries after the removal of the Bronze Soldier, *Eesti Päevaleht*, 11 May 2007.

28 On friction and the fog of war, see Clausewitz (1997[1832], book I, ch. VII; book II, ch. II).

29 This story is based on Paloheimo (1997, pp. 124–6), Marttinen (2006, pp. 135–49) and Hakala (2007). The 'historical statement' commissioned by the Ministry of Foreign affairs states that: 'It is unlikely that Roos took a risk and used a "people's enemy" who had just escaped from a prison camp as a model for such a politically sensitive monument' (Kaasik 2006). Helle Palusalu said in an interview in the Finnish daily *Helsingin Sanomat* that her father had told her that he was the model, even though some changes were made to reduce the recognizability of the face (Hakala 2007). The latter statement seems more convincing than the official *reductio ad impossibile*.

References

Astrov, A. (2008) 'Monumentaalne kriis: "natsid", "okupandid" ja teised hinilisted', in Tamm, M. & Petersoo, P. (eds) (2008) *Monumentaalne Konflikt: mälu, poliitika ja identiteet tänapäeva Eestis* (Tallinn, Varrak), pp. 92–111. Paper presented at ISA Annual Convention, San Diego 22–25 March.

Bartelson, J. (2006) 'We Could Remember It for You Wholesale: On the Constitution of National Memories', Paper presented at the ISA Annual Convention, San Diego, USA, 2006.

Brubaker, R. (1996) *Nationalism Reframed: Nationhood and National Question in the New Europe* (Cambridge, Cambridge University Press).

Burch, S. & Smith, D. J. (2007) 'Empty Spaces and the Value of Symbols: Estonia's "War of Monuments" from Another Angle', *Europe-Asia Studies*, 59, 6, pp. 913–936.

Buzan, B., Wæver, O. & de Wilde, J. (1998) *Security: A New Framework for Analysis* (London, Lynne Rinner).

Confino, A. (2005) 'Remembering the Second World War, 1945–1965: Narratives of Victimhood and Genocide', *Cultural Analysis*, 4, pp. 46–65.

Courtois, S., Nicolas Werth, N., Bartošek, K., Panné, J.-L., Margolin, J.-L. & Paczkowski, A. (1999) *The Black Book of Communism: Crimes, Terror, Repression* (Cambridge, MA, Harvard University Press).

Forest, B. & Johnson, J. (2002) 'Unraveling the Threads of History: Soviet-Era Monuments and Post-Soviet National Identity in Moscow', *Annals of the Association of American Geographers*, 92, 3, pp. 524–547.

Gareev, M. A. (2005) 'Lessons of the Great Patriotic War, local wars and prospects of developing modern military science and military art', *Military Thought*, April–June 2005, available at: http://findarticles.com/p/articles/mi_m0JAP/is_2_14/ai_n15622984, accessed 22 August 2008.

Gellner, E. (1983) *Nations and Nationalism* (Oxford, Basil Blackwell).

Greenfeld, L. (1995) *Nationalism: Five Roads to Modernity* (Cambridge, MA, Harvard University Press).

Gudkov, L. (2005) 'The Fetters of Victory: How the War provides Russia with its identity', *Eurozine*, 3 May.

Habermas, J. (2000) *The Postnational Constellation* (Cambridge, Polity Press).

Hakala, P. (2007) 'Painija Palusalu valmistui Pronssisotilaan malliksi' & 'Puna-armeijasta paennut Kristjan antautui Toivolle', *Helsingin Sanomat*, 13 May.

Ilves, T. H. (2005) 'The Pleiades Join the Stars: Transatlanticism and East European Enlargement', *Cambridge Review of International Affairs*, 19, 2, pp. 191–202.

Joenniemi, P. (2008) 'The European Union Is Not What It Used To Be: Once a "Peace Project", And Now a "Force For Good"', Paper presented at BRIT IX conference, Victoria, Canada, 12–15 January.

Judt, T. (2000) 'The Past Is Another Country: Myth and Memory in Postwar Europe', in Deak, I., Gross, J. T. & Judt, T. (eds) (2000) *The Politics of Retribution in Europe: World War II and its Aftermath* (Princeton, NJ, Princeton University Press), pp. 293–324.

Jutila, M. (2006) 'Desecuritizing Minority Rights: Against Determinism', *Security Dialogue*, 37, 2, pp. 167–185.

Kaasik, P. (2006) '*Common grave for and a memorial to Red Army soldiers on Tõnismägi, Tallinn: Historical statement*', available at: http://www.valitsus.ee/brf/doc.php?282742, accessed 16 June 2008.

Krzeminski, A. (2005) 'As many wars as nations. The myths and truths of the World War II', *Signadnsight.com* 6 April, available at: http://www.signandsight.com/features/96.html, accessed 5 February 2008.

Kuljić, T. (2005) 'Revised History and New Identity in East Europe', *Identities – Journal for Politics, Gender, and Culture*, 4, 1/2, Summer/Winter, pp. 63–86.

Kuus, M. (2007) *Geopolitics Reframed. Security and Identity in Europe's Eastern Enlargement* (New York, Palgrave).

Kuusisto, R. (2007) 'Komedia on ratkaisu maailmanpolitiikan konflikteihin', *Kosmopolis*, 37, 3, pp. 5–23.

Kuusisto, R. (forthcoming) 'Comic Plots as Conflict Resolution Strategy', *European Journal of International Relations*.

Kymlicka, W. (2007) *Multicultural Odysseys: Negotiating the New International Politics of Diversity* (Oxford, Oxford University Press).

Lagrou, P. (1999) *The Legacy of Nazi Occupation: Patriotic Memory and National Recovery in Western Europe, 1945–1965* (Cambridge, Cambridge University Press).

Lassila, J. (2007a) 'Commissars on the market: Discursive commodities of the youth movement NASHI', in Vanhala-Aniszewski, M. & Siilin, L. (eds) (2007), pp. 99–136.

Lassila, J. (2007b) 'Paatosta vai brändejä? Fasismi nuorisojärjestö NASHIn retoriikassa', *Kosmopolis*, 37, 3, pp. 73–8.

Lehti, M. (2006) 'Eastern or Western, New or False: Classifying the Balts in the Post-Cold War Era', in Tassinari, F., Joenniemi, P. & Jakobsen, U. (eds) (2006) *Wider Europe: Nordic and Baltic Lessons to post-Enlargement Europe* (Copenhagen, Danish Institute of International Studies), pp. 69–88.

Lehti, M. (2007) 'Protégé or Go-between: The Role of the Baltic States after 9/11 in EU–US Relations', *Journal of Baltic Studies*, 38, 2, pp. 127–51.

LICHR (ed.) (2007) *Bronze Soldier: April Crisis* (Tallinn, Legal Information Centre for Human Rights).

Lipschutz, R. D. (ed.) (1995) *On Security* (New York, Columbia University Press).

Mälksoo, M. (2007) *The fallen 'Bronze Soldier' and the subaltern memory wars in the post-Soviet space*, available at: http://www.casecollective.org/ideas-in-action/read/90, accessed 7 February 2008.

Marttinen, E. (2006) *Heikki Silvennoinen – voimistelun jättiläinen* (Helsinki, WSOY).

Merridale, C. (2003) 'Redesigning history in contemporary Russia', *Journal of Contemporary History*, 38, 1, pp. 13–28.

Merridale, C. (2005) 'Amnesiac Nation', *Index on Censorship*, 34, 2, p. 79.

Morozov, V. (2003) 'The Baltic States in Russian Foreign Policy Discourse: Can Russia Become a Baltic Country', in Lehti, M. & Smith, D. J. (eds) (2003) *Post-Cold War Identity Politics. Northern and Baltic Experiences* (London & Portland, OR, Frank Cass), pp. 219–252.

Mosse, G. L. (1994) *Fallen Soldiers: Reshaping the Memory of the World Wars* (Oxford, Oxford University Press).

Nochnoi Dozor (2006) '*Petition*', 24 May, available at: http://pomnim.com/index_eng.htm, accessed 7 February 2008.

Onken, E.-C. (2007) 'Baltic States and Moscow's 9 May Commemoration: Analysing Memory Politics in Europe', *Europe-Asia Studies*, 59, 1, pp. 23–46.

Paloheimo, P. (1997) *P. Paloheimo, Pispalan Tarmo* (Porvoo, WSOY).

Pettai, V. (2006) 'Explaining ethnic politics in the Baltic States: Reviewing the triadic nexus model', *Journal of Baltic Studies*, 37, 1, pp. 124–36.

Poleshchuk, V. (2007) 'War of the Monuments: A Chronological Review', in LICHR (2007).

Roe, P. (2004) 'Securitization of Minority Rights: Conditions of Desecuritization', *Security Dialogue*, 35, 3, pp. 279–94.

Roe, P. (2006) 'Reconstructing Identities or Managing Minorities? Desecuritizing Minority Rights: A Response to Jutila', *Security Dialogue*, 37, 3, pp. 425–38.

Roshwald, A. (2006) *The Endurance of Nationalism* (Cambridge, Cambridge University Press).

Roshwald, A. (2007) 'Between Balkanization and Banalization: Dilemmas of Ethno-cultural Diversity', *Ethnopolitics*, 6, 3, pp. 365–78.

Roth, K.-H. (1997) 'Revisionistische Tendenzen in der historischen Forschung über den deutschen Faschismus', in Klotz, J. & Schneider, U. (eds) (1997) *Die selbstbewusste Nation und ihr Geschichtsbild – Geschichtslegenden der Neuen Rechten* (Köln, Papy Rossa), pp. 10–27.

Semjonov, A. (2007) 'Preface', in LICHR (2007).

Smith, A. D. (2003) *Chosen Peoples. Sacred Sources of National Identity* (Oxford, Oxford University Press).

Stukuls Eglitis, D. (2002) *Imagining the Nation. History, Modernity, and Revolution in Latvia* (University Park, PA, The Pennsylvania State University Press).

Tumarkin, N. (2003) 'The Great Patriotic War as myth and memory', *European Review*, 11, 4, pp. 595–611.

Vanhala-Aniszewski, M. & Siilin, L. (eds) (2007) *Voices and Values of Young People – Representations in Russian Media*. Aleksanteri Series 6/2007 (Helsinki, Aleksanteri Institute).

Wæver, O. (1995) 'Securitization and Desecuritization', in Lipschutz, R. D. (ed.) (1995) (New York, Columbia University Press) pp. 46–86.

'WOE FROM STONES': COMMEMORATION, IDENTITY POLITICS AND ESTONIA'S 'WAR OF MONUMENTS'

David J. Smith

This year marks the 20th anniversary of the start of Estonia's 'Singing Revolution'. Looking back on these events, one is reminded not least of the important role that the reappearance of Estonian national symbols had in galvanizing the mass movement for independence. Here one thinks particularly of the national flag – so much in evidence during 1988 – but also of the work by the Estonian Heritage Society to restore monuments connected to the founding of the Estonian Republic during 1918–1920. These monuments had been systematically destroyed after 1940, as part of a failed effort to expunge the memory of inter-war independence and transform Estonia into a Soviet place. Restoring them in the 1980s became an essential part of undermining Soviet power and restoring sovereign statehood.

The events of 1987–1991 thus underline the fact that – to quote George Schöpflin – the 'use of flags, monuments and ceremonies is not a superfluous extravagance, but a central component of identity creation and maintenance' (Schöpflin 2000, p. 29). As markers of political space, public monuments have a particular significance for efforts not only to establish and legitimize but also to contest state power. This significance has recently been demonstrated in a wholly new context, as public monuments have become emblematic both of sharpened socio-political divisions within Estonia and of an intensification of long-standing international disputes between Estonia and the Russian Federation. In what follows, I first seek to analyze the origins and nature of the so-called 'War of Monuments' that broke out during 2004–2007, and reached its peak in the April 2007 riots that followed the relocation of the Bronze Soldier.[1] I then conclude by discussing the possible significance of the April 2007 crisis for ongoing processes that seek to construct an integrated 'multicultural democracy' in Estonia.

As John R. Gillis has observed, 'the core meaning of any individual or group identity, namely a sense of sameness over time and space, is sustained by remembering; and what is remembered is defined by the assumed identity' (Gillis 1994, p. 1; see also Halbwachs & Coser 1992; Assmann 1992). In the case of contemporary Estonia, efforts to build an imagined national community embracing all residents of the restored sovereign state have been complicated by the existence within the population of two divergent – one could say diametrically opposed – national collective memories relating to the events of World War II and its aftermath. For the vast majority of Estonians, these years are synonymous first and foremost with suffering at the hands of the Soviet regime: 1940 marked military occupation and forcible annexation, 1944 not liberation but simply the replacement of one occupying regime by another. In both cases, the Soviet takeover was followed by a wave of deportations and killings that left hardly a single family untouched. These mass individual memories of Soviet repression and the popular resistance that they elicited were banished to the private sphere by the Soviet regime, whose subsequent nationalities policy prompted growing fears as to the Estonian nation's continued possibilities for cultural reproduction in the long term.

For most of Estonia's Russian-speaking population, or at least of the immigrant community that developed during Soviet rule, World War II is remembered as a victorious struggle against a Nazi German invader that inflicted immense suffering on the peoples of the USSR. Once again, this struggle was one that touched almost every family. Within this variant of national collective memory, the arrival of the Soviet army in Estonia in September 1944 was understood not as renewed occupation but as part of the liberation of Europe from fascism. Moreover, the official Soviet narrative of history held that the events of 1940 in Estonia did not constitute occupation and annexation, but rather voluntary incorporation into the USSR. The intervening period of Estonian independence was dismissed as an illegitimate 'bourgeois dictatorship' and a line of continuity was drawn back to 1919 and the abortive Estonian Workers Commune that sought to impose Bolshevik rule on Estonia with the aid of the Red Army. The Russian-speaking immigrant community established in Estonia after the war certainly developed a separate 'Baltic' form of identity that distinguished it from Russians living in what is today the Russian Federation. However, many of these Soviet citizens had no sense that they were living in another country – for them, Estonia was another constituent part of the USSR; moreover, Soviet nationalities policy meant that they were able to use Russian freely in all spheres of social existence, and were thus under no obligation to undergo linguistic and cultural integration with the majority population.

To point to divergent collective memories is not to essentialize nationality or to posit the existence of two internally homogenous groups with no points of contact between them. Ultimately, memory is a matter for individuals rather than communities. Estonia's Russian-speaking population – not to speak of the Soviet immigrant population – is far too diverse a group to speak as one, displaying tremendous heterogeneity in terms of ethnicity, descent, degree of integration with

Estonian culture and political outlook. Recent events also testify to the marked divisions that exist amongst ethnic Estonians over how to define Estonian nationhood and over what should and should not be commemorated in an independent Estonia. Nevertheless, it is possible to point to diverging national collective memories in the sense of different frames in which 'nationally-minded individuals place and organize their histories in a wider context of meaning, thus forming collective identity' (Müller 2004, p. 3).

The latent tension between these different frames or fields of identity within Estonia has been exacerbated by the poor state of relations between Estonia and neighboring Russia, a situation which itself rests upon diametrically opposed foundational narratives of nationhood. In this regard, the Russian view of 1991 as a 'year zero' in Estonian–Russian relations clashed headlong with the Estonian doctrine of legal continuity, which saw the 1920 Tartu Treaty as the sole legitimate basis for relations. Whereas most Estonians saw the collapse of the USSR as marking a return to European 'normality', most Russians in the neighboring RSFSR saw it as anything but. The period since 1992 has witnessed an increasing recourse to the traditional Great Power discourse and the use of Soviet past within Russia's own current project of nation-building, including adherence to the Soviet fiction that 1940 was not occupation but voluntary incorporation. These developments, coupled with Moscow's pretensions to speak on behalf of ethnic Russian 'compatriots' in neighboring countries, have fuelled continued perceptions within Estonia of an external Russian threat.

The project of nation-building in the restored Estonian Republic has been first and foremost about rejecting the Soviet past, reclaiming the historic homeland for the titular nationality and reconnecting with the 'Western World' following five decades of enforced isolation (Lauristin *et al.* 1997). Key to realizing both of these aims was the doctrine of legal continuity, upheld by the Western powers throughout the Cold War, which framed the period 1940–1991 as an illegal occupation and traced a direct line of continuity back to the foundation of the Estonian Republic in February 1918. This recourse to legal continuity, however, was inevitably tempered by recognition of post-Soviet realities within a state order that is often characterized as a variant of an ethnic control regime.[2] Thus, the original citizenship law of 1992, while prioritizing the claims of the inter-war citizen polity – and thus the titular nationality – to the homeland, also created a legal mechanism for integrating Soviet-era immigrants and their descendents into the polity. The state also extended fundamental civil rights and social and economic entitlements to all permanent residents, regardless of citizenship, and has continued to fund basic mother-tongue education for all Russian-speaking residents, with a switch to bilingual upper secondary education thereafter. Finally, the creation of a single, overarching societal culture based on the Estonian language has not precluded the continued use of Russian as a second working language of government in those areas of the north-east where Russian-speakers constitute a local majority.

In the symbolic/commemorative sphere, too, the 1990s were marked not by efforts to impose a new unifying national narrative of the past, but rather by the persistence of 'competing myths and dissonant voices' with few points of connection between them.[3] The fact that all permanent residents have the right to vote in local elections, for instance, means that municipal governments in Tallinn and the north-east have had to remain at least partially responsive to the concerns of their Russian-speaking constituents as far as commemoration of the past is concerned. This can be seen perhaps most strikingly in the case of Narva, where Soviet-era monuments continue to sit alongside new or restored ones that commemorate the foundation of the Estonian Republic, the Stalinist deportations of the 1940s and – in the case of the Lion re-erected in 2000 – the historical Swedish 'Golden Age' of the city's development (Burch & Smith 2007). To give one example, the Narva city government appointed in October 1993 promptly removed Estonia's last remaining statue of Lenin from the central Peter's Square. The monument was not, however, definitively banished from the city; instead, the 'father of the proletariat' has been relocated to a quiet corner of the grounds of Narva's German castle, where he stands somewhat incongruously alongside a recently mounted plaque commemorating Finnish fighters who helped to liberate the city from the Bolsheviks in 1919. This kind of approach presents an image of Narva as a borderland with a complex hybrid identity that is neither 'Western' nor 'Eastern', neither Estonian nor Russian, but something in-between. This can be illustrated not least by the fact that Lenin's former plinth on Peter's Square still remains unoccupied. Seen from the standpoint of those who would seek to 'nationalize' political space, this symbolizes the 'empty' space at the heart of the city that still needs to be filled – this, at least, was the view put forward by one local journalist in the fall of 2000 (Solodov 2000).

Elsewhere in Estonia, the most prominent symbols of communist power such as statues of Lenin and other Soviet leaders were quickly removed in the aftermath of independence; however, more than a hundred Soviet-era monuments to the Great Patriotic War were left in place. These monuments had been erected as markers of Soviet power in Estonia, and yet at the same time they served as memorials to the fallen. By leaving them intact, the state implicitly continued to recognize this latter function. This can be seen clearly in the case of the 'Bronze Soldier': previously entitled the 'Monument to the Liberators of Tallinn', this monument had its Soviet-era plaques referring to 'liberation' removed, and was reframed simply as a memorial to 'the fallen of World War II'. The Bronze Soldier, of course, was always going to be particularly contentious, given its central location and its proximity both to the seat of government power and to the country's main Lutheran cathedral. It is perhaps also significant that there has until 2008 been no Estonian Freedom Monument in central Tallinn that might have served as a countervailing symbol of Estonian statehood.[4] Nevertheless, the site continued to function as an unofficial site of memory for those residents of Tallinn who remembered the end of the War as liberation from fascism rather than renewed occupation. Until 2005 the annual gatherings at the monument on 9 May did not form the object of great controversy. Most Estonians, it seemed, had learned to ignore the monument; no doubt many Russians had, too.

Outwardly, at least, the past did not seem to matter that much to most residents of Estonia during the decade or so after independence. This was a period when the Estonian and Russian-speaking communities appeared to converge in many important respects: there was a steady decrease in the number of people without Estonian citizenship, while legislative amendments adopted as part of the EU accession process ensured that citizenship will cease to be an issue altogether in the medium term;

knowledge of the Estonian language amongst Russian-speakers – at least those living in Tallinn – increased enormously; the state, meanwhile, adopted a new strategy for 'multicultural integration' designed to enable residents of non-titular nationality to preserve their own language and aspects of their own distinct culture and heritage whilst integrating into the polity and the Estonian 'common core'. This strategy also recognized that integration was not a one-way process affecting one community, but a matter for society as a whole (Lauristin & Heidmets 2002); finally, *New Baltic Barometer* surveys taken during 1993–2004 showed that despite obvious discontent over the citizenship law and perceptions of discrimination, a growing number of Russian-speakers expressed approval of the economic and also the political performance of the Estonian Republic, suggesting a trend towards pragmatic adaptation to the new state order (Smith, D. 1998; Kolstö 2002; Budryte 2005; Ehin 2007).

Highlighting these trends, however, should not be taken to imply the emergence of an integrated political community within Estonia during this period. In many important respects, Estonian and Russian-speakers have continued to inhabit different social worlds which coexist somewhat uneasily alongside one another. The *New Baltic Barometer* survey data from 2004 found that support for the political community remained ethnically based, with most Russian-speakers in Estonia (and Latvia) declaring immediate locality and Russia as the primary bases for self-identification. Commenting on these results, Piret Ehin (2007, p. 15) notes that this identification with Russia

> should not be regarded as politically alarming *a priori*, provided this attachment is primarily cultural-ethnic in nature. However, this also means that regime allegiance of Baltic Russians depends, to a larger extent, on the Baltic regimes' ability to perform and deliver: there are no bonds of cultural-ethnic loyalty to fall back on when times get tough.

Research carried out by Estonian social scientists since 2004 would seem to suggest that things have indeed been getting tougher in recent times. Research conducted by sociologists from Tartu University over the past two years, for instance, points to a widening socio-economic gap between Estonian and Russian-speakers, with respondents from the latter category expressing higher levels of dissatisfaction with their economic status as well as a perception that they are disadvantaged in terms of access to jobs and education and of participation in political life.[5] In this respect, the events of 2006–2007 testify to the emergence, amongst a *younger* generation of Russian-speakers, of a protest identity that has centered on the symbols of the Soviet past, with the 'Bronze Soldier' becoming a particular focus. This development has challenged previous understandings which emphasized issues of citizenship and language and saw integration as mainly a question of generational replacement in what was fast becoming a dynamic and forward-looking 'tiger economy'. The events of April 2007 in particular suggest that Estonia, beacon of the 'New Europe', is facing the very 'Old European' challenge of how to diminish feelings of exclusion amongst second- and third-generation immigrant youth. This realization was conveyed neatly in a newspaper article by Tartu University Professor Eiki Berg (2007), who stated that: 'What shouldn't have happened has happened: burning kiosks, upturned cars, windows kicked in . . . The images are not from East Jerusalem, Jakarta's "Chinatown" or the Banlieues of Paris, but from the heart of Tallinn . . . in a state that is marketed as the purveyor of innovative solutions'.

The same research has found that most Estonians remain wary of seeing greater participation by Russian-speakers within economic and political life. This testifies to the continued feelings of insecurity (one might say existential anxiety) arising from the experience of Soviet occupation, which have persisted despite Estonia's entry to the European Union and NATO.[6] In some respects, these insecurities may even have increased over the past decade in the face of rapid economic and political change. Jüri Böhm, the self-styled 'Estonian nationalist' whose actions prompted scuffles at the site of the Bronze Soldier on 9 May 2006, stated that his avowed aim was to 'awaken the Estonian people from the dream of well-being where we fell after regaining independence'.[7] As Dovile Budryte (2005, pp. 3–10) has suggested, the ongoing promotion of a minority rights discourse by the EU and its cognate international organizations has also evoked resentment and unease amongst more nationally minded Estonians, who portray external conditionality in this area as something threatening to the political and cultural hegemony of the Estonian nation within the state.

Also relevant in this context has been 'growing international pressure to face up to uncomfortable questions of the past and to research past crimes against humanity also if committed by one's own countrymen' (Onken 2007b, p. 110). The Estonian state has responded to these calls to 'democratize' the discussion of history, most notably through the establishment in 1998 of a Historical Commission charged with researching both totalitarian occupations of Estonia during 1940–1991. However, such pressure has also jarred with a still-dominant Estonian collective memory that emphasizes national victimhood at the hands of the Soviet regime and the heroism of those compatriots who resisted it by force of arms. This could be seen clearly in the Lihula events of 2004, which marked the opening battle in the 'War of Monuments'. In August of that year, veterans' groups and prominent 'dissident' Estonian nationalists erected a stone tablet in the western town of Lihula, dedicated 'to Estonian men who fought in 1940–1945 against Bolshevism and for the restoration of Estonian independence'. In flagrant disregard of the taboo in Western Europe against display of Nazi symbols, the stone carried the image of a soldier, machine pistol aloft, wearing the uniform of the Estonian SS Legion. In the face of predictable international condemnation, the Estonian government of the day ordered the monument to be removed. The ill-conceived police operation to carry out this order on 2 September 2004 provoked clashes with local residents, sparking a political storm that contributed to the fall of Prime Minister Juhan Parts several months later.

The groups behind the Lihula stone can hardly be seen as representative of ethnic Estonian opinion as a whole. For some commentators, the events of September 2004 and their aftermath were occasioned first and foremost by governmental ineptitude and high-handedness in effectuating the removal, and by the broader problematic relationship between state and society.[8] For all this, there was undoubted resentment at the government's perceived alacrity in bowing to external pressure. There was also a predictable response to the official justification given by Prime Minister Parts, who argued that there was no room in Estonia for symbols glorifying totalitarianism. This led critics of the government to argue that the same logic should now be applied to remaining Soviet monuments. The latter – including the Bronze Soldier – were subjected to a wave of attacks following the events at Lihula, which in turn prompted retaliation against monuments to the Estonian independence drive and German military cemeteries within Estonia.

The Lihula episode was, not least, a propaganda gift to official commentators in Russia, who have long made it clear that they will brook no alternative interpretations of the Soviet Union's role in the events of 1939–1945. Estonian efforts to challenge the narrative of Soviet (read Russian) liberation of the Baltic (and the wider Europe) have therefore been characterized as expressions of sympathy for 'fascism', as part of a campaign designed to isolate the Baltic governments within the international political architecture of the new Europe. Although largely unsuccessful, Russia's efforts in this regard simply reinforce continued suspicion and fear of the 'Eastern Neighbor'. These have only grown during the Putin era, which has been synonymous with the reassertion of centralized political control and a renewed international assertiveness on the back of soaring energy revenues. As such, the war of words with Moscow has shown no signs of abating since 2004; indeed, it has actually intensified, and it has begun to focus more and more on the past.

As several commentators have noted in recent times, the victory over Nazism in 1941–1945 has arguably become the main unifying factor within Russian national identity and 'the constitutive story defining the Russian position in Europe' (Lehti 2007, p. 141).[9] In this regard, as Olga Brednikova (2007, p. 62) observes, 'from the whole of Soviet history, only the period of the Great War . . . makes it possible to find "heroes free from doubt"'. As space for public discussion has receded ever further in Russia, we have seen an ever greater sacralization of the Great Patriotic War within Russian political discourse and, correspondingly, a decreasing likelihood that the Russian political elite will ever acknowledge the repression that the Soviet Union perpetrated against the peoples of the Baltic states and the other central and east European countries during and after World War II. The contemporaneous entry of the Baltic states to NATO and the EU has led some sections of the political elite in these countries to 'abandon their diffidence' (Bult 2006, p. 165) towards Russia and challenge the dominant Western 'memory regime', by insisting more loudly that the crimes of the Soviet regime in eastern Europe should be placed on a par with those committed by the Nazis (Onken 2007a).

Pointing to the links between the defenders of Soviet monuments in Estonia and Russia-based forces such as the pro-Putin youth group *Nashi*, many Estonian commentators have argued that external manipulation lay at the root of what happened in April 2007. Whatever view one takes on the origin of these events, the increasingly bitter discursive conflict between Estonia and Russia from 2004 could hardly fail to have affected inter-communal relations within Estonia. One obvious factor in this regard has been the lack of a common media space linking Estonian and Russian-speakers; while the overwhelming majority of Estonia's Russian-speakers have not developed an active political affiliation with Russia during the post-Soviet era, many nevertheless continue to receive most of their news from Russia. One key event linking the external and internal spheres was the controversy surrounding the 9 May 2005 commemoration in Moscow, which led to heightened public discussion – though not necessarily constructive debate – over the events of World War II (Onken 2007a). Not least for the purposes of the present discussion, the anniversary focused attention on the 'Bronze Soldier' – already firmly in the public eye following the Lihula events – as a continued locus for commemoration in Tallinn. In the changed socio-political context of 2005–2006, this monument in the heart of Tallinn was 're-Sovietized': it ceased to be a simple memorial to the dead and was again politicized as a symbol of occupation/liberation.[10]

The 'War of Monuments', however, began as a series of small-scale public demonstrations by what could rightly be termed radical fringe groups. Polls undertaken during the 12 months prior to April 2007 showed that public opinion more broadly was far from ethnically polarized over the question of the Bronze Soldier: the overwhelming majority of Russian-speakers wanted the monument left *in situ*; the ethnic Estonian majority, however, was almost evenly divided over whether it should stay or it should go. The fact that the dispute culminated in a large-scale riot and an international incident can be attributed partly to external interventions by Russia in the dispute, but also in no small measure to the Estonian electoral campaign of 2006–2007. In this context, those voices calling for a calm and constructive debate over the past were drowned out by those of the main parties, who were determined to use the issue for political ends. In this regard, the Reform Party (*Reformierakond*) vied with a revived Fatherland League (*Isamaaliit*) to present itself as the embodiment of national coherence and order in the face of a purported external threat. The Centre Party (*Keskerakond*), meanwhile, sought to exploit Russian-speakers' sensibilities over the issue. Opinion polls during the campaign showed that most voters did not see the monument as a burning issue; however, by the time the election was settled, the new government had painted itself into a corner over this question.

The crisis that broke in late April 2007 briefly turned the eyes of the world upon Estonia. Attentions, however, quickly shifted to Moscow. The Kremlin's heated response to the crisis and the many misrepresentations of events by the state-controlled Russian media further exacerbated tensions in Estonia around the Bronze Soldier issue. However, the blockade of the Estonian Embassy and the attacks on Estonian (and Swedish) diplomatic representatives ensured that the controversy was framed more as an issue in EU–Russia relations than a domestic affair of Estonia as such. If the British press coverage of the issue is anything to go by, the international media showed far greater understanding for the Estonian position than it did for the Russian.

The international fallout for Estonia was thus far less dramatic than some had predicted. The longer-term ramifications of the crisis for Estonian society, however, remain to be seen. In domestic terms, the immediate effect of the April events was to polarize public opinion along ethnic lines, but there have since been indications that the profound sense of shock engendered by the nights of violence in April 2007 has served to engender a more meaningful public debate over how to resolve the continued challenges of 'multicultural integration'. Yet the question remains as to how best within this context to tackle the issue of divergent collective memories and commemorative practices. Logically, a multicultural approach to society-building would not seek to achieve 'some elusive thick social consensus in which one narrative of the past is enthroned', but rather a state of 'negotiated memory' based on mutual critical engagement with the past and greater tolerance of different viewpoints (Müller 2004, p. 33).

In the course of the 1990s and again during the long maturation of the Bronze Soldier crisis during 2006–2007, a number of Estonian commentators – including the current President Toomas Hendrik Ilves – argued that rather than removing the statue, the surrounding space should be reconfigured and transformed into a site of memory where anyone – Russian or Estonian – could go to commemorate the events of World War II. Such proposals would seem to represent the kind of 'innovative approach' of which Eiki Berg (2007) has spoken and which has indeed been applied in the case of the Maarjamäe memorial complex, now transformed into a multi-layered site of memory.[11] Although the setting of the Bronze Soldier was very different, the failure to consider something comparable in the case of this monument strikes one as an opportunity lost as far as fostering a more constructive approach to the past is concerned. In the event, the degree of contention that came to surround the monument during 2006–2007 was such as to render relocation the only viable option.

The removal of the Bronze Soldier has not depoliticized the former site of the statue on Tõnismägi in central Tallinn. However, the statue itself – now reconfigured as a more nonspecific monument to the Unknown Soldier – appears to have quietly re-attained its status as a memorial to the fallen within its new setting of the Armed Forces Cemetery, where it stands amidst the graves of a multiplicity of different combatants, reflecting Estonia's complicated history. The wreath-laying by the Estonian Prime Minister and Defence Minister at the newly relocated Bronze Soldier on 8 May 2007 appeared at the time to be an important symbolic gesture of reconciliation. This gesture was repeated in 2008, albeit with a lower degree of public visibility. In the meantime, public monuments and commemorative practices have provided the focus for an ongoing war of words between the Estonian government and the numerous social scientists who criticized the removal of the monument in April 2007. The latter – whose arguments the government characterizes as unpatriotic and detrimental to state security – have now focused their ire on the 20-meter-high 'Freedom Cross' that will be erected on Tallinn's main square in November 2008 to mark the 90th anniversary of the start of Estonia's War of Independence against Soviet Russia. The inauguration of this monument will enshrine a heroic narrative of Estonian nationhood, while also symbolically marking the shift in power in the Estonian capital after 1991.

The state and the political elite have a considerable responsibility and a key role to play in terms of fostering an open and critical discussion of the past. Such a process, however, would also logically seek to engage a wide range of societal actors and individuals. As sociologists from Tartu University have asserted over the past year and a half, negotiation of the past needs to be embedded within broader measures to prevent ethnic segregation, foster tolerance, dialogue and interaction between communities and promote civil society development more generally. No-one can pretend that this will be an easy process. It is made all the more complicated by the international dimension to the 'memory politics' equation, which, as this essay has sought to demonstrate, locks the Estonian state and its constituent nationalities into a dynamic interrelationship with the Russian Federation and Estonia's new Western partners within the EU and NATO.[12] However, only by adopting this approach will it become possible to focus attention away from the divided past towards the common future of which Estonia's leaders have spoken on a number of occasions since April 2007.

Acknowledgement

Part of the work towards this article was supported by British Academy small research grant ref. SG-39197, entitled 'Public Monuments, Commemoration and the Renegotiation of Collective Identities: Estonia, Sweden and the "Baltic World"'.

Notes

1 The title of this essay is a translation of the title of a *Postimees* editorial from 3 August 2007 entitled 'Häda kivide pärast'. This is a play on 'Häda mõistete pärast', which the Estonian title of Aleksandr Griboyedov's 1820s satirical comedy '*Gore ot uma*', known in English as 'Woe from Wit'.

2 On the relationship between legal continuity and post-Soviet realities, see Smith, D. J. (2001). With regard to the Supreme Council declaration of 20 August 1991 that paved the way for international recognition of independence, Marju Lauristin (1996, p. 81) has spoken of a compromise 'third way' that guaranteed the legal continuity of statehood and yet allowed for the possibility of radical renewal according to the democratic principles of the late twentieth century. Subsequent accounts (Smith, G. 1994; Pettai & Hallik 2002) have pointed to continued practices of ethnic control during the ensuing decade and a half, although Western governments and international organizations have been instrumental in the adoption on new measures designed to facilitate the legal-political and linguistic integration of the large non-citizen population.

3 This phrase is taken from a more general discussion of identities across the FSU in Smith, G. *et al.* (1998, p. 26).

4 This offers a further illustration of how the form and context (physical, temporal, political) of a monument is intrinsic to its ascribed meaning: for instance, it is interesting that the more abstract and far more peripheral Soviet monument at Maarjamäe on the outskirts of Tallinn has not aroused a similar degree of contention, despite being far larger than the Bronze Soldier. In this regard, one might say the same about the immense Soviet war memorial in Riga, which is quite far removed from the historic center of the Latvian capital. To extend this analogy further, it is perhaps also significant that central Riga retained the inter-war Freedom Monument as a symbol of Latvian statehood and national liberation.

5 This conclusion is based on data from the 2005 *MeeMa* survey, and subsequent survey data from 2006 and 2007, provided by Professor Marju Lauristin of Tartu University. See also Triin Vihalemm and Veronika Kalmus, 'Conflict, Citizenship and Civil Society' and Külliki Korts 'Post-Communist social transformation and changes in the attitudes among ethnic Estonians and Russians', both papers presented at the 8th Annual Conference of the European Sociological Association, Glasgow, 3–6 September 2007.

6 Vihalemm & Kalmus, 'Conflict, Citizenship and Civil Society'.

7 From an interview on the DVD of the Estonian *Kanal 2* documentary film 'Pronksöö: vene mass Tallinnas', 2007.

8 For a full discussion of the Lihula events and their link to debates over the Bronze Soldier, see Feest (2007).

9 See also 'Politoloog Andres Kasekamp: Eesti on praegu väga haavatav', *Postimees*, 27 April 2007.

10 Prime Minister Andrus Ansip stated this quite explicitly during the run-up to the election. As was noted in a the 3 August *Postimees* editorial, one of the saddest features of the 'War on Monuments' was that war memorials had lost their function of commemorating the dead and become objects of contestation. 'Juhtkiri: häda kivide pärast', *Postimees*, 3 August 2007.

11 The Soviet memorial at Maarjamäe commemorates the Soviet army units that took Tallinn in 1944, and was constructed around the 50th anniversary of the 1917 Bolshevik revolution. Alongside it one now finds memorials to the Estonians who defended Tallinn against Soviet forces in 1944, and a restored cemetery that contains the graves of Germans and Estonians who perished during 1939–1945 but which is dedicated to the 'victims of all wars', as well as the soldiers in question. The neighboring Estonian History Museum complex will also soon become home to a new sculpture park that displays previously dismantled Soviet monuments, along the lines of Lithuania's *Grūto Parkas* and an analogous museum in Hungary.

12 A number of scholars have explored this relationship in recent times. See, for instance: Smith, D. J. (2002) and the review of more recent work by Pettai (2006). For the best exploration of 'memory politics' within this framework, see Onken (2007a).

References

Assmann, J. (1992) *Das kulturelle Gedächtnis: Schrift, Erinnerung und politische Identität in frühen Hochkulturen* (Munich, C.H. Beck).

Berg, E. (2007) 'Killud, mis ei too õnne', *Postimees*, 30 April.

Brednikova, O. (2007) '"Windows" Project *Ad Marginem* or a "Divided History" of Divided Cities? A Case Study of the Russian–Estonian Borderland', in Darieva, T. & Kaschuba, W. (eds) (2007), pp. 43–64.

Budryte, D. (2005) *Taming Nationalism? Political Community Building in the Post-Soviet Baltic States* (Aldershot, Ashgate).

Bult, J. (2006) 'Everyday Tensions surrounded by Ghosts from the Past: Baltic-Russian Relations since 1991', in Tiirmaa-Klaar, H. & Marques, T. (eds) (2006) *Global and Regional Security Challenges: a Baltic Outlook* (Tallinn, Tallinn University Press), pp. 127–65.

Burch, S. & Smith, D. J. (2007) 'Empty Spaces and the Value of Symbols: Estonia's "War on Monuments" from another Angle', *Europe-Asia Studies*, 59, 6, pp. 913–36.

Darieva, T. & Kaschuba, W. (eds) (2007) *Representations on the Margins of Europe* (Frankfurt & New York, Campus Verlag).

Ehin, P. (2007) 'Political Support in the Baltic States, 1993–2004', *Journal of Baltic Studies*, 38, 1, pp. 1–20.

Feest, D. (2007) 'Histories of Violence. National Identity and Public Memory of Occupation and Terror in Estonia', in Darieva, T. & Kaschuba, W. (eds) (2007), pp. 132–50.

Gillis, J. R. (1994) 'Memory and Identity: The History of a Relationship', in Gillis, J. R. (ed.) (1994) *Commemorations: The Politics of National Identity* (Princeton, Princeton University Press).

Halbwachs, M. & Coser, L. A. (1992) *On Collective Memory* (Chicago, University of Chicago Press).

Kolstö, P. (ed.) (2002) *National Integration and Violent Conflict in Post-Soviet Societies: the Cases of Estonia and Moldova* (London, Rowman and Littlefield).

Lauristin, M. (1996) 'Kommentaarid', in Riigikogu Kantselei (ed.) (1996) *Kaks otsustavat paeva Toompeal (19–20 August 1991)* (Tallinn, Eesti Entsüklopeediakirjastus), pp. 81–2.

Lauristin, M. & Heidmets, M. (2002) *The Challenge of the Russian Minority: Emerging Multicultural Democracy in Estonia* (Tartu, University of Tartu Press).

Lauristin, M., Vihalemm, P., Rosengren, K.-E. & Weibull, L. (1997) *Return to the Western World. Cultural and Political Perspectives on the Estonian Post-Communist Transition* (Tartu, Tartu University Press).

Lehti, M. (2007) 'Protégé or Go-between? The Role of the Baltic States after 9/11 in EU–US Relations', *Journal of Baltic Studies*, 38, 2, pp. 127–52.

Müller, J.-W. (2004) 'Introduction: The Power of Memory, the Memory of Power and the Power over Memory', in Müller, J.-W. (ed.) (2004) *Memory and Power in Post-War Europe* (Cambridge, Cambridge University Press).

Onken, E.-C. (2007a) 'The Baltic States and Moscow's May 9th Commemoration: Analysing Memory Politics in Europe', *Europe-Asia Studies*, 59, 1, pp. 23–46.

Onken, E.-C. (2007b) 'The Politics of Finding Historical Truth: Reviewing Baltic History Commissions and their Work', *Journal of Baltic Studies*, 38, 1, pp. 109–16.

Pettai, V. (2006) 'Explaining Ethnic Politics in the Baltic States: Reviewing the Triadic Nexus Model', *Journal of Baltic Studies*, 37, 1, pp. 124–36.

Pettai, V. & Hallik, K. (2002) 'Understanding Processes of Ethnic Control: Segmentation, Dependency and Co-optation in Post-communist Estonia', *Nations and Nationalism*, 8, 4, pp. 505–29.

Schöpflin, G. (2000) *Nations, Identity, Power: the New Politics of Europe* (London, Hurst & Co).

Smith, D. J. (1998) 'Russia, Estonia and the Search for a Stable Ethnopolitics', *Journal of Baltic Studies*, 29, 1, pp. 3–18.

Smith, D. J. (2001) *Estonia: Independence and European Integration* (London, Routledge).

Smith, D. J. (2002) 'Framing the National Question in Central and Eastern Europe. A Quadratic Nexus?', *Ethnopolitics*, 2, 1, pp 3–16.

Smith, G. (ed.) (1994) *The Baltic States: the Self-determination of Estonia, Latvia and Lithuania* (London, Macmillan).

Smith, G., Aasland, A. & Mole, R. (1994) 'Statehood, Ethnic Relations and Citizenship', in Smith, G. (ed.) (1994), pp. 181–205.

Smith, G., Law, V., Wilson, A., Bohr, A. & Allworth, E. (1998) *Nation-building in the Post-Soviet Borderlands. The Politics of National Identities* (Cambridge, Cambridge University Press).

Solodov, A. (2000) 'Svyato mesto pusto ne byvaet', *Narvskaya Gazeta*, 25 November.

COMMEMORATING LIBERATION AND OCCUPATION: WAR MEMORIALS ALONG THE ROAD TO NARVA[1]

Siobhan Kattago

> When the time is right, an era of the past may serve as a screen on which new generations can project their contradictions, controversies, and conflicts in an objectified form. (Krzysztof Pomian, quoted in Rousso 1991, p. 5)

The side-road from the resort town of Narva-Jõesuu to the city of Narva offers a compressed glimpse into the different interpretations of recent Estonian history. The war memorials dotted along the Narva River between Estonia and Russia are testament to the different layers of Estonian history: Swedish, Tsarist Russian, Estonian Republic, Nazi and Soviet occupations. The Soviet war memorials and German military cemetery remind one of how Estonia was caught within the ideological struggle between Nazi Germany and the Soviet Union. Given the context of the conflict over the Lihula monument in 2004 commemorating Estonian soldiers who fought on the Nazi German side against the Soviet Regime, the debate over the 60th commemoration of Soviet Victory Day in 2005 (Onken 2007) and the relocation of the Soviet 'Bronze Soldier' from the center of Tallinn to a military cemetery (2007), different narratives have emerged: return to history, occupation versus liberation, victim versus perpetrator, and the unsettled end of World War II as 8 or 9 May.

Are the Soviet war memorials merely outdated and antiquarian pieces of stone or does the ideological version of history which they represent potentially block the integration of Russian postwar emigrants into modern-day Estonia? Why do some Soviet war memorials to fallen Red Army soldiers such as the Bronze Soldier in

Tallinn inspire conflict, while others such as the Soviet tank outside Narva remain invisible? After the Bronze Soldier riots in April 2007, Estonians seem to have one memory of World War II (1939–1945) and communism (1940–1941 and 1944–1991) emphasizing victimhood, occupation, deportation and national suffering at the hands of two dictatorships and Russians another, emphasizing the Great Patriotic War (1941–1945) liberation, victory and national suffering at the hands of Nazi fascists. This essay will argue that the conflict over war memorials is not simply a domestic issue for Estonia, but is part of a politicization of the past in contemporary Europe about how to come to terms with two different, but interconnected aspects of the recent past: the role of the Red Army in World War II and the criminal nature of the Soviet regime. Conflicts over Soviet war memorials thus become screens in which many of the blank spots of 20th century history are sharply contested.

Narva: A City Scarred by War and Socialist Planning

During World War II, Narva's vulnerable location caused it to become a military target for the Soviet Regime and Nazi Germans. German military authorities ordered the civilian evacuation of Narva between 25 January and 3 February 1944. Although damaged by land combat in 1941 and smaller air raids throughout the war, Narva was still relatively intact until February 1944 (Tannberg 2000, p. 276). The Soviet Army heavily bombarded Narva on 6 and 7 March 1944 and destroyed most of the baroque town. By the air raids of 25 July 1944, 98% of Narva had been destroyed, and only the Kreenholm factory remained relatively intact. The ruins of the city were taken by the Red Army on 26 July 1944. In the 1950s the Soviet Regime decided not to reconstruct the baroque old town of Narva, but to rebuild it as a modern 'socialist city' (Brüggemann 2004). Similar to Königsberg/Kaliningrad, the original residents of Narva were not allowed the right to return to their native city. Likewise, Narva and the rest of northeastern Estonia underwent a rapid industrialization process and immigration of Russian-speaking workers from other parts of the USSR (Burch & Smith 2007, p. 922; Mertelsmann 2004). Narva was thus forcibly tranformed into a Russian-speaking town. From a population of roughly 70,000 only 3,000 are Estonians, with the majority of contemporary Narva composed of first- and second-generation Russian-speaking immigrants.

From 1945 to 1989, the percentage of ethnic Estonians in Estonia dropped from 94% to 61% due to the Soviet policy of mass immigration of industrial workers from Russia, Ukraine and Belarus, who then predominantly settled in places where large industry developed – in northeastern Estonia and Tallinn. Death due to war, the Stalinist mass deportations of Estonians in 1941 and 1949, along with the emigration of Estonians to Western countries such as Sweden, the United States and Canada also contributed to the dramatic population drop of titular Estonians. As a result of these large demographic changes, ethnic Russian-speakers now constitute about 26% of the entire population in Estonia (Lagerspetz 2005, pp. 8–9).

The demographic changes in contemporary Estonia are most visible in the border town of Narva. In 1934, Estonians accounted for 79.1% of the population of northeastern Estonia (Ida-Virumaa) and 54% of the population of Narva

TABLE 1 Ethnic composition of Narva, 2006

Estonians	4.02%
Russians	79.76%
Ukrainians	2.62%
Belorussians	2.26%
Finns	0.81%
Tatars	0.53%
Others	10.00%

(Population Registration Office of Narva City government, Narva in Figures 2006)

(Rand 2004, pp. 369–70). Today the city of Narva is overwhelmingly Russian-speaking, with only 4% of the population made up of ethnic Estonians (Table 1).

Estonia, like other former communist countries, is rewriting its history to reflect its 'return to Europe' and 'return to the West' after 50 years of Soviet occupation (Lagerspetz 1999; Vihalemm & Lauristin 1997). While Estonia is returning to its democratic independence, the narrative of return is a longer and more complicated process than initially anticipated. After re-independence in 1991, Estonian citizenship was granted to those residents who could trace their ancestors back to the first Republic of Estonia. All others could become citizens after taking a citizenship test, passing an Estonian language test and fulfilling the five-year residency requirement. In Narva, 44% of the city residents have Estonian citizenship, 33.4% have Russian citizenship, 21.64% have grey 'Alien's passports' and the rest have other national passports (Narva in Figures 2006).

War Memorials and Representations of the Past

Historical places of commemoration and sites of historical events are the living topography of the nation. National spaces become sacred and symbolic, imbued with mythic reverence and piety. 'Landscape is central to nationalism, since territory becomes inscribed with history and temporality' (Outhwaite & Ray 2005). Landscape and monuments become as Bakhtin notes, 'chronotypes' – or fusions of time and space (Bakhtin 1981). Some monuments are fiercely remembered, while others fade into the background – forgotten and overgrown.

Given Estonia's complicated history through the different occupations, memorials tend to chronicle the history of Estonia through the eye of the occupier. One could simply pass by the memorials as outdated remnants of another time, but somehow it is difficult not to notice them because they are so numerous and large. As the Austrian writer Robert Musil has noted, monuments have a dual ability to attract and repel at the same time. Musil in his short essay reflects on the inadequacy of monuments to represent the complexity of history. They are too one-sided and flat. Instead of inspiring memory, they often engender forgetfulness. They fade into the background and become part of the local landscape.

> Monuments are so conspicuously inconspicuous. There is nothing in this world as invisible as a monument. They are no doubt erected to be seen – indeed, to

attract attention. But at the same time they are impregnated with something that repels attention, causing the glance to roll right off, like water droplets off an oilcloth, without even pausing for a moment. (Musil 1987, p. 61)

War memorials represent a particular type of memorial because they commemorate military loss in the name of the nation. As Anthony Smith argues, war memorials refer to the sacred origins of the nation. Memorials to 'the Glorious Dead' are part of the symbolic landscape of the modern nation (Smith 2003, pp. 218–53). Offering more than concrete factual information – dates, places of battles, names of soldiers killed – war memorials offer a reason *why* these particular soldiers and/or civilians were killed (Koselleck & Jeismann 1994). Military cemeteries and memorials do not only honor individual death, but are sacred places of national honor and mourning. Whether the war memorials commemorate victory or defeat – the emphasis is on a national narrative. Without a coherent story, the numerous graves become overwhelming and senseless. In response to the question: 'why did so many soldiers die on this day?' War memorials provide a single answer: 'for our nation'. The memorials present a certain version of history that often borders on national mythology. War memorials, particularly Tombs of the Unknown Soldier, are symbolic places of national identity and collective memory.

Although war memorials have existed since the days of ancient Greece, they were built in great numbers after World War I. In particular, Tombs to the Unknown Soldier were created after World War I and served as quasi-religious sites to honor the dead of particular nations (Inglis 1993, pp. 150–71). As the historian Eric Hobsbawm has pointed out, it is not accidental that the proliferation of war memorials after 1918 coincided with the independence of many European nations during the interwar period – Estonia among them. National monuments are firmly rooted in the identity and self-understanding of the modern nation (Hobsbawm 1992).

War memorials become important places of memory or *lieux de mémoire* for families of lost soldiers and war veterans (Nora 1996). Whether in large military cemeteries such as Verdun or Arlington, or smaller national cemeteries throughout Estonia – cemeteries have a highly symbolic presence. War memorials often become surrogate gravesites for those families whose relatives are buried elsewhere. The memorials can be traditional sculptures of a soldier or non-traditional monuments to national loss such as the Vietnam Veterans Memorial in Washington, DC. Traditional memorials emphasize national cohesion and a seamless national narrative. Non-traditional monuments such as the Vietnam Veterans Memorial separate individual death from governmental policy and the ideological reasons of war (Wagner-Pacifici & Schwarz 1991).

Because the creation and re-creation of memorials is often more about *how* the present society wishes to remember itself than about what really happened, war memorials take on an important cultural dimension. They become cultural reminders of how the past is linked to the present. As the French sociologist Maurice Halbwachs noted in the 1940s, collective memory is malleable and often based more on the needs of the present than on the facticity of the past.

Society from time to time obligates people not just to reproduce in thought previous events of their lives, but also to touch them up, to shorten them, or

> to complete them so that, however convinced we are that our memories are exact, we give them a prestige that reality did not possess. (Halbwachs 1992, p. 51)

War memorials are made by the survivors in memory of the dead. As Koselleck thoughtfully notes,

> The only identity that endures clandestinely in all war memorials is the identity of the dead with themselves. All political and social identification that try to visually capture and permanently fix the 'dying for . . .' vanish in the course of time. For this reason, the message that was to have been established by a memorial changes. (Koselleck 2002, p. 289)

Soviet War Memorials to the Second World War: Antifascism as Foundational Ideology

Like other war memorials, Soviet memorials serve as places of collective memory, social cohesion and national identity. However memorials to the Great Patriotic War in the Soviet Union represented not only the enormous loss of life from the Soviet side, but, more importantly, mythologized the very existence of the Soviet Union. Moreover, the Great Patriotic War (1941–1945) serves as the foundational mythology for the legitimate expansion of the Soviet Union. War memorials did not valorize a national hero, but the Soviet hero or *Homo Sovieticus* – a person linked through class rather than through the traditional bonds of nation, language, religion and culture. Just as the Soviet Union was an empire rather than a nation, common bonds had to be forcibly created from above by Soviet elites. National, cultural and linguistic ties were broken, while a new social bond was created.

In socialist Estonia, as in other communist countries, antifascism was one of the many ideological justifications for the existence of the Soviet Union. As Antonia Grunenberg outlines, antifascism is a binary that divides the world into two camps: fascist and antifascist (Grunenberg 1993, pp. 120–44). Antifascist mythology was heavily used for the ideological justification and superiority of both East Germany and the Soviet Union. Antifascism operates on the level of mythology. Roland Barthes' theoretical conception of myth captures the way in which antifascism was ideologically used: 'Myth hides nothing: its function is to distort, not to make disappear' (Barthes 1957/1972, p. 121). Myths simplify and distort the complexities of a historical moment. Particularly within the complex relationship between the USSR and Nazi Germany, myth simplifies the changing of alliances and the actions of soldiers during the Great Patriotic War.

> In passing from history to nature, myth acts economically: it abolishes the complexity of human acts, it gives them the simplicity of essences, it does away with all dialectics, with any going back beyond what is immediately visible, it organizes a world which is without contradiction because it is without depth, a world wide open and wallowing in the evident, it establishes a blissful clarity: things appear to mean something by themselves. (Barthes 1957/1972, p. 143)

In many ways, war memorials are more about how the present society remembers and understands itself. They are symbolic representations of the past. Soviet war memorials represented the needs of Soviet elites to mythologize the glorious foundation of the Soviet Union. The valor of Soviet heroes against fascism was emphasized for the new collective identity of the Soviet citizen. The Soviet memorials replaced the deliberately forgotten annexation and occupation of Estonia with the central memory of Soviet martyrdom to fascist aggression.

The memory of 'victim' is particularly difficult in Soviet war memorials because the soldiers were also 'victims' of fascist aggression and of their own ruling elites. Conscripts on both sides of the ideological battle can be viewed as victims of the period in which they lived. But 'victimhood' is too singular and one-sided because it does not allow for the victimhood of Estonians under Soviet occupation. Either one has a hierarchy of victimhood or a leveling of victimhood in which all victims of war are memorialized together.

The contentious debate surrounding the redesigning of the *Neue Wache* in Berlin in 1993 into the central German memorial highlighted many of the problems of victimhood. As historians such as Koselleck carefully pointed out, the label of victimhood erases the horrible complexity of German society during National Socialism (Koselleck 1993, pp. 200–3). To honor a Nazi soldier next to a concentration camp victim and civilian is problematic, as the debates which raged in German newspapers demonstrated. Likewise in Estonia, the label of 'victim' blurs the important historical distinction between Soviet occupation and liberation from Nazi Germany. The final variant of the German national memorial in Berlin (*Neue Wache*) represented German victimhood with an enlarged pieta of a mother mourning her dead son. Modeled on Käthe Kollwitz's sculpture of the artist mourning her own son killed in World War I, the private pieta became a national symbol of German national mourning. However, the plaques on the side of the memorial listed the different 'victims' of Nazi aggression who were mourned. The intention was to maintain the complexity of German history and respectfully mourn those who died in the name of the German nation (Stölzl 1993).

Because some Soviet war memorials in Estonia serve as places for Russian-speaking families to honor their dead, it is difficult to alter or remove them – particularly in areas with a Russian majority, such as Narva. The commemoration of World War II in contemporary Estonia is an example of a 'moral trauma' or 'negative event' that has conflicting and multiple meanings. As Wagner-Pacifici and Schwarz argued in reference to the Vietnam Veterans Memorial in the United States:

> negative events are moral traumas: they not only result in loss or failure but also evoke disagreement and inspire censure. But these traumas cannot always be ignored without denying their noble side, without forgetting commitments and sacrifices that would be considered heroic in the service of other ends. (Wagner-Pacifici & Schwarz 1991, p. 384)

Both Russians and Estonians link monuments to national identity and national loss: the Estonians to Estonian national identity and the Russian minority to Russian and, at times, Soviet identity.

Topography of Memory: War Memorials Along the Narva River

The commemorative road driving south from Narva-Jõesuu to Narva (Figure 1) begins with a Soviet military T-34 tank posed with its gun towards inland Estonia. Similar to other Soviet military memorials in the region, a carefully tended path of red stones leads the visitor to the well-preserved monument. The inscription remains unchanged since Soviet days:

> On 25–26 June 1944 the Leningrad front advanced into this region of the Narva River, broke through the fascist German defense and liberated the city of Narva.
>
> *25–26 juunil 1944 a. forsseerisid Leningradi rinde väed selles rajoonis Narva Jõe, murdsid fašistliku-Saksamaa vägede kaitse ja vabastasid Narva linna.*

The Soviet tank (Figure 2) is without graffiti and adorned with red carnations. Unlike the large Soviet military monument in the Maarjamäe suburb of Tallinn, with its extinguished eternal flame, the Narva war monuments are active memorials adorned with fresh flowers and well preserved. On the one hand, the tank is an actual piece of history and a fossil from the old Soviet empire. Unlike the Bronze Soldier monument in Tallinn, it is not a site of conflicted or politicized memory between Estonian- and Russian-speakers. Although the memorial represents Soviet military

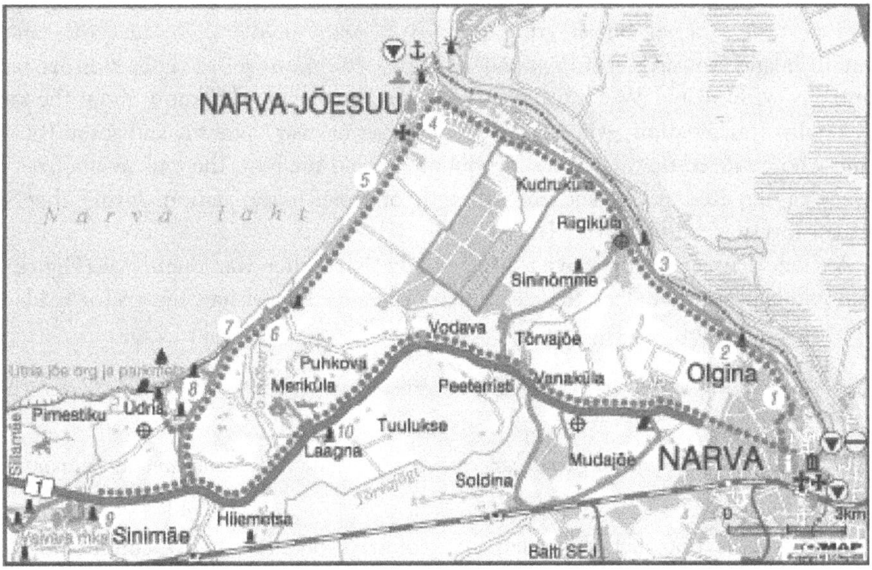

FIGURE 1 War memorials along the Narva River.

(1) German Military Cemetery; (2) Monument to the Northern War. The Estonian Military Cemetery to the War of Independence is adjacent and across the street; (3) Soviet T-34 Tank about 4 kilometers from Narva, with the Soviet memorial to fallen soldier Grafov, nearby towards Narva.

Map: Eesti matkarajad. Narva jalgrattamatk, available at: http://matkarajad.maaturism.ee/index.php?pg=object&id=148, accessed 3 September 2008.

FIGURE 2 Soviet tank (Photograph by Meelik Kattago).

victory, there has not been any discussion in Estonia about removing it. It serves as a commemorative place for the glorification of the Red Army, a place for newlyweds to tie their ribbons around the gun and a place for honoring military death. Likewise it preserves how the battle for the city of Narva was officially represented during Soviet Estonia: as liberation from fascism and legitimation of Soviet power. Unlike the Red Army tanks in central Berlin at the *Sowjetisches Ehrenmal* in Tiergarten, the Narva tank is not part of a larger burial ground for Red Army soldiers. Because the tank is pointed inland towards Estonia and Europe, its message of liberation remains hauntingly within Cold War hostilities. For those Estonians who know about the tank, it symbolizes occupation, while for Russian-speaking war veterans and some Russian young who come to tie their wedding ribbon around the gun, the tank symbolizes the bravery of the Red Army and the strength of the Russian nation during the Nazi German invasion of the Soviet Union.

A short drive from the Soviet tank, one finds another war memorial (Figure 3). Again with red stones before the clean memorial and the red star, the visitor reads the following inscription:

> In this place on 22.2.1944, a Hero of the Soviet Union, Lieutenant Igor Grafov committed his heroic act.

> *Siin sooritas 22.2.1944 a. oma kangelasteo nõukogude liidu kangelane n. Leitnant Igor Grafov.*

The issue is not that this particular soldier's death is being commemorated, but the way in which his death is mythologized in the name of the Soviet Union. The soldier's death not only memorializes military loss of life, but specifically commemorates death for the greater good of the Soviet Union. The soldier is valorized as a hero for the Soviet Union during the battles to capture Narva from Nazi Germans and Estonians. The term 'hero' (*kangelane*) is problematic due to the two Soviet occupations of Estonia: first in 1940–1941 and later in 1944–1991. Numerous accounts portray the 'liberation' of Europe by the Red Army with looting, killing

FIGURE 3 Memorial to Igor Grafov (Photograph by Meelik Kattago).

and mass rape (Beevor 2002; Naimark 1995). Unlike the Bronze Soldier in Tallinn, this grave to a fallen Red Army soldier does not have a wider meaning beyond this individual soldier's death. It fades into the background as a memorial gravesite representing the period in which it was constructed. It commemorates individual mourning as well as victory.

Continuing another few minutes along the road to Narva, against the background of the Narva River and Russia, one sees a monument commemorating Russian defeat in the battle between Swedes and Russians during the Great Northern War for the city of Narva in 1700 (Figure 4). The monument was built in 1900 to commemorate Russian loss of life as well as the victorious recapturing of Narva in 1704 (Mälestise koond, Monument Põhjasõjas 1700, 1995). 'The Monument to the Northern War 1700' was restored after the Second World War and has been officially listed under heritage protection since 1995.

After seeing the Soviet 'liberation' tank and the monument to the Soviet hero, this monument continues the narrative of Narva as a part of Russia – whether in its Tsarist or Soviet incarnation. The monument commemorating Russian defeat to Sweden emphasizes military death and loss in the name of the Russian nation.

Almost across the street from the Northern War monument, one sees an Estonian military cemetery dedicated to those Estonian soldiers killed during the War of Independence (1918–1920) (Figure 5). The individual crosses have been crudely knocked off the gravestones, which stand destroyed and maimed. In the center of the cemetery is a classical memorial sculpture restored in 1995 with an inscription commemorating the soldiers buried in this cemetery.

> To the memory of brave defenders of the Fatherland who died in the War of Estonian Independence 1918–1920 at the Narva Front. With gratitude, Narva, September 1921.
> *Eesti vabadussõjas 1918–1920 Narva väerinnal langenud vapratele kodumaakaitsjatele. Tänulik Narva september 1921.*

FIGURE 4 Monument to Fallen Soldiers killed in the Northern War, 1700 (Photograph by Meelik Kattago).

FIGURE 5 Narva Garison cemetery, memorial to those killed in the War of Independence (Photographs by Meelik Kattago).

However, only when the visitor walks around the monument can one find a small plaque narrating the important history of this military cemetery. The cemetery was dedicated in October 1919 and the memorial was added in 1921. During the fall of 1940 the memorial was blown up by the Soviet Regime, the crosses were crudely knocked off and given over to a metal scrapheap in the 1960s. In the 1970s the cemetery was cordoned off and the first rows of the graves were grown over with weeds. In 1995 the restored foundation of the destroyed memorial was erected along with a plaque explaining the history of the monument and graveyard. By 1996, the cemetery was restored to its current status (Mälestise koond, Narva Garnisoni kalmistu, 2006). The cemetery is one of many throughout Estonia in which the physical memory of the War of Independence was destroyed by the Soviet Regime with the intention to erase the event of Estonian independence from history. The cemetery in Narva is not unique but part of a systemic policy of the monumental destruction of the Estonian nation during which numerous monuments to Estonian independence were destroyed and crosses removed from military graves (Erelt 2007).

The desecration of the gravesites is made even more visible because a Russian cemetery with well-preserved Orthodox crosses is directly adjacent to the Estonian military cemetery. The brutal destruction of Estonian gravesites along with the blown-up memorial to Estonian independence by Soviet Regime hauntingly recalls George Orwell's famous quotation that 'Whoever controls the past, controls the future'. In its current form, the Estonian military cemetery to the War of Independence demonstrates the depth of Soviet occupation over Estonia.

The Estonian military cemetery is starkly contrasted with the final memorial on the road to Narva; that of the Nazi German soldiers cemetery (Figure 6). Abstract and simple, the cemetery honors the death of German soldiers killed, without mention of communism or fascism. The cemetery commemorates the death of German World War II soldiers with the inscription: '*Narva Deutscher Soldatenfriedhof* 1939–1945'. Originally built in 1943 as a cemetery for the *Wehrmacht*, the site became a central cemetery for German soldiers killed on the Narva Front. The major reconstruction of the cemetery and the addition of granite crosses and names were completed in 1999 by the Organization of German Gravetakers (*Volksbund Deutsche Kriegsgräberfürsorge*). Groups of three stone crosses stand together commemorating military death. Granite slabs are engraved with the names of 4,000 soldiers who are buried in the cemetery. The central symbol of the cemetery is a cross 4.5 meters high overlooking Russia and the Narva River.[2]

Individual death is remembered, without glorifying the ideological cause of fascism and without the linkage to heroism. Instead the cemetery signifies the

FIGURE 6 Narva German military cemetery (Photograph by Meelik Kattago).

historical context of German military loss with the historical dates of World War II. The German cemetery in many ways reflects the larger debate in unified German society as to how to commemorate German military death without praising fascism or making German soldiers into national martyrs. By simple mention of dates and subsequent plaques with the names, birth and death of each soldier, the visitor is given the chance to reflect on the magnitude of loss during the Second World War. The soldiers are not described as heroes, liberators, aggressors or occupiers, but remembered as German individuals, who died for their country. The cemetery seeks to avoid monumentalizing history and instead offers a minimalistic reflection on World War II. One might question whether the dates 1939–1945 will be sufficient for future generations. However, the aim of the cemetery is to honor German soldiers who were killed in the battle for Narva during the war. The emphasis is on mourning and loss without grandeur or heroism.

Past Politics: Coming to Terms with Communism in a Changing Estonia and Europe

Attempts to cast European memory within a single grand narrative silence the many different experiences of World War II and the Cold War which divided the continent. Indeed as Tony Judt has elegantly argued, postwar Europe is full of shifting myths and mismemories (Judt 2002, pp. 157–83; Judt 2005) Since the break-up of the Soviet Union, debates about war memorials and the narration of recent Estonian history have been part of a reassessment of the many meanings of World War II and communism. The recent past is politicized and linked to contemporary identity formation in rapidly changing societies. Past politics in north-eastern Europe after 1989 tends to focus on three overlapping points: the blank spots of history, victims versus perpetrators and the relevance of national history in contemporary society (Hackmann 2003, pp. 82–9).

The debates in Estonia surrounding the Lihula monument (2004) and the Bronze Soldier monument in Tallinn (2007) were screens onto which many of the blank spots of twentieth-century history were projected. While the Lihula monument demonstrated that it is politically incorrect for an Estonian soldier to be remembered wearing a German military uniform, the Bronze Soldier monument demonstrated that an Estonian soldier can be remembered wearing a Red Army uniform. The German military uniform is taboo because it symbolizes Nazi aggression, whereas the Red Army uniform is polysemic, symbolizing liberation, aggression and occupation. The Lihula monument was removed by the Estonian government and relocated to a private museum outside Tallinn. The intention of the monument was to honor those Estonian soldiers who fought on the side of Nazi Germany against the Soviet Union. The Soviet Bronze Soldier monument in Tallinn was also removed by the government during contentious riots in April 2007, but relocated to a military cemetery outside Tallinn city center.

Contemporary Estonian debates surrounding monuments to World War II raise similar questions to those of the West German Historians' debate in the 1980s:

- Whether communism can and should be compared with National Socialism, or whether the two ideologies are *sui generis* different and utterly incomparable.

- The criminal nature of the communist regimes in Eastern Europe and the Soviet Union.
- Distinctions between victim and perpetrator.
- The different interpretations of the role of the Red Army during World War II and communism.

Given the context of the growing importance of the Great Patriotic War in contemporary Russia, the rehabilitation of the Soviet melody for the Russian national anthem, Putin's claim that the break-up of the Soviet Union was the greatest mistake of the twentieth century, and the *Nashi* nationalist youth movement in Russia, different historical narratives about World War II are emerging which reveal dramatically different understandings of the recent past. All of the narratives though share similar Manichean distinctions between good and evil.

In the Western narrative, National Socialism is represented as the main evil. Since the 1960s, one could argue that the Holocaust is viewed as the primary trauma and victim of Nazi aggression. The 8th of May marks the end of World War II, and the defeat and eventual division of Germany. Communism, while also viewed as negative through the prism of the Cold War, cannot be compared to the inherent criminal nature of National Socialism. Moreover the Holocaust is a unique defining feature of National Socialism.

In the Soviet-Russian narrative, encouraged by Putin's government, fascism (National Socialism) is the main evil and the Russian people are the primary victim of Nazi aggression, rather than the Jews. The Red Army soldier is the hero and liberator of Europe. 'The war' is not World War II, but the Great Patriotic War (1941–1945) whereby the years when Stalin and Hitler were allied, namely 1939–1941, are downplayed and even arguably forgotten. Finally, 9 May marks the end of the war as Victory Day, not 8 May.

In the post-communist, post-Soviet narrative that one finds in countries such as Estonia, both National Socialism and communism are considered evil; however, communism is *the* main evil. Estonian national victimhood is the primary trauma, not Jewish. The Red Army soldier is an occupier, not liberator of eastern Europe. The end of the war is more concretely seen in the re-establishment of national independence and the withdrawal of Soviet troops. Narratives of return to history, Europe and the West dominate the national narrative.

The Holocaust is not interpreted as a central part of Estonian memory; rather, it is seen as peripheral and more of a German or European problem than an Estonian one. Estonian politicians tend to draw attention to the forgotten suffering of Estonians during the Soviet deportations as well as the secret Molotov–Ribbentrop pact of 1939 when Estonia was occupied by the USSR. Whereas one might argue that the genocide of European Jewry has been internalized into a Western narrative about the Second World War, for the Soviet-Russian and post-communist Estonian perspective, the Holocaust is seen as external to their central narratives of the same period: 1939–1945.

The different narratives about the Nazi and communist pasts are related to a generational change which affects what is remembered. As many of the survivors and veterans who experienced the war are dying out, most people learn about it second-hand in a form of what Jan Assmann calls 'cultural memory'. Thus, media images, photography, film and docudramas, as well as history books are the dominant sources of how the recent past is represented and remembered (Assmann 1995).

'Islands of the Past'

In his reflections on history, Nietzsche described different ways of remembering the past. Keenly aware of the power of historical interpretation, Nietzsche emphasized three different types of historicization. Monumental history is the most common. Great leaders and events are mythologized in the name of the nation. History is recalled via the Napoleons and Bismarcks – via the different wars and historical epochs. But this version of history is limited and leaves out the complexity of the past.

> Thus, whenever the monumental vision of the past *rules* over the other ways of looking at the past, I mean the antiquarian and the critical, the past itself suffers *damage*: very great portions of the past are forgotten and despised, and flow away like a grey uninterrupted flood, and only single embellished facts stand out as islands . . . . (Nietzsche 1980, p. 17, italics in original)

Soviet war memorials in their glorification of the Great Patriotic War and of Soviet military liberation of Narva indeed damage the past by not acknowledging the other interpretation of history, namely, the Soviet occupation of Estonia and Eastern Europe. Thus with the monuments, 'only single embellished facts stand out as islands' (Nietzsche 1980, p. 17).

Antiquarian history preserves and reveres the past with a certain piety and respect, without questioning whether past traditions should be continued. For Nietzsche, antiquarian history becomes excessive when the past dwarfs the present. 'Thus it hinders the powerful resolve for new life, thus it paralyzes the man of action who, as man of action, will and must always injure some piety or other' (Nietzsche 1980, p. 21). The monuments on the way to Narva contain aspects of both a monumental and antiquarian sense of history. The past is revered and mythologized in the tank as a relic of history and the gravesite of a Red Army soldier.

Critical history, on the other hand, is the condemnation of the past and the severing of past from present. From time to time, a critical view of history is necessary for individuals to be able to live fully in the present.

> Here it becomes clear how badly man needs, often enough, in addition to the monumental and the antiquarian ways of seeing the past, a *third* kind, the *critical*: and this again in the service of life as well. He must have the strength, and use it from time to time, to shatter and dissolve something to enable him to live: this he achieves by dragging it to the bar of judgment, interrogating it meticulously and finally condemning it: every past, however, is worth condemning – for that is how matters happen to stand with human affairs: human violence and weakness have always contributed strongly to shaping them. (Nietzsche 1980, pp. 21–2)

In its extreme form, critical history severs the link between past and present without acknowledging their intrinsic connection. As Nietzsche emphasizes, whether we like it or not, we are always linked to the actions of previous generations. 'If we condemn those aberrations and think ourselves exempt from them, the fact that we are descended from them is not eliminated' (Nietzsche 1980, p. 22).

For Nietzsche, all three different types of historical reflection, monumental, antiquarian and critical, are necessary – not for the sake of the past – but for the sake of the present. History is in the service of present and future generations. Historical reflection should not burden one to the past but provide meaning for present and future generations. In his terse reflections on history, Nietzsche emphasizes the need for a balance between the historical and unhistorical, between memory and forgetting: 'the unhistorical and the historical are equally necessary for the health of an individual, a people and a culture' (Nietzsche 1980, p. 10).

'The Past in the Present'

In many ways, the restoration of the Swedish Lion monument in 2000 commemorating the Swedish victory over Russia for the city of Narva in 1700 was an example of antiquarian history. As Stuart Burch and David J. Smith argue, the commemoration recalling Russian loss of empire in an overwhelming Russian-speaking city could only be peaceful because the events were seen within the context of Narva's 'Golden Age' as a baroque jewel of the East (Burch & Smith 2007, pp. 920–1). The Swedish Lion commemoration downplayed national politics and instead emphasized the wider context of shared cultural links in the city of Narva. Since the Great Northern War was perceived by the majority of Narva residents as the distant past, it avoided the conflicts surrounding commemorations which referred back to World War II or the Soviet era. '. . . [U]nlike the events of 1940s, the Great Northern War is *the past* rather than – as Michael Ignatieff puts it – the "past in the present"'(Burch & Smith 2007, p. 932).

The Soviet memorials surrounding Narva are examples of both antiquarian and monumental understandings of history. As relics of the Soviet empire, they represent Narva within a Soviet narrative and thus reflect the period in which they were built. As national monuments, they are mostly invisible because they are located in the periphery, not in the center of the Estonian nation. Are they simply examples of invisible monuments to a bygone age that have faded into the local landscape, or does the ideological version of history that they represent block a more nuanced understanding of Estonia's recent past? The fact that there is not any discussion about removing the Soviet tank testifies to its curious invisibility. While an actual piece of recent history, the meaning is less about mournful loss than defiant victory. The Bronze Soldier in Tallinn, on the other hand, was more of an example of monumental history because of the sharp conflict between liberation and occupation that the statue inspired. Once moved to a military cemetery, the meaning of the memorial charged from monumental to antiquarian and reverential.

Although the restoration of Estonian independence in 1991 means the juridical continuity of the Republic of Estonia, one cannot go back in time to the first Republic. Due to Nazi and Soviet occupations, the newly restored Estonia is territorially, demographically and socially different from the first Republic of 1918. The reassessment of war memorials is part of the rewriting of Estonia's complex and multi-layered history. One vitally important step towards social integration in restored Estonia, particularly in Narva, is a common understanding of twentieth-century history. Such an understanding would be less Manichean and more open to the complexity of the past. Acknowledgement of the criminal nature of the Soviet regime also entails a more nuanced appraisal of the Red Army. The fact that Russia refuses to acknowledge the Soviet occupation of the Baltic states only perpetuates the different interpretations of history within Estonia. As Mart Laar, historian and former Prime Minister of Estonia, wrote:

> During recent years Estonia alongside the other Baltic republics has repeatedly raised the issue of the necessity to condemn communist crimes on an international level. Regrettably, Russia has stuck to the concept formulated already in the time of the Soviet Union, according to which Estonia was not occupied, but it voluntarily joined the Soviet Union – consequently, neither the Soviet Union nor its legal successor Russia can be responsible for the crimes against humanity which were committed in Estonia. (Laar 2005, p. 47)

For Estonians and ethnic Russians living in contemporary Estonia, World War II is a moral trauma and negative event symbolizing *both* liberation and occupation. The future lies in memorials which can aesthetically and visually represent the complexity of Estonian history. Rather than emphasizing World War II as either liberation or occupation, contemporary monuments face the challenge of representing the liberation of Europe from Nazi Germany by the Soviet Union *and* the occupation of Eastern Europe by the Soviet Union.

Notes

1 A shorter version of this essay was presented at a conference in Tallinn, Estonia 'Places of Memory in Northeastern Europe: National – Transnational – European?', 21 September 2007. The author is grateful for reviewer comments and criticism, as well as those by Jörg Hackmann and Johanna Söderholm.

2 'Deutsche Kriegsgräberstätten von Ägypten bis Usbekistan', available at: http://www.volksbund.de/kgs/stadt.asp?stadt=1903, accessed 29 March 2008. 'Narva Deutscher Soldatenfriedhof 1939–1945', available at: http://vana.narva-plan.ee/vananarva/soldatenfriedhof/indexd.htm, accessed 29 March 2008.

References

Assmann, J. (1995) 'Collective Memory and Cultural Identity', *New German Critique*, 65, Spring–Summer, pp. 125–33 [translated by John Czaplicka].

Bakhtin, M. (1981) 'Forms of Time and the Chronotype in the Novel', in Holquist, M. (ed.) (1981) *The Dialogic Imagination* (Austin, University of Texas Press).

Barthes, R. (1957/1972) *Mythologies* (New York, Hill & Wang) [translated by Annette Lavers].

Beevor, A. (2002) *Berlin: the Downfall 1945* (London & New York, Penguin Books).

Brüggemann, K. (2004) 'Der Wiederaufbau Narvas nach 1944 und die Utopie der "sozialistischen Stadt"', in Brüggeman, K. (ed.) (2004) *Narva und die Ostseeregion. Narva and the Baltic Sea Region* (Narva, TÜ Narva Kolledž), pp. 81–103.

Burch, S. & Smith, D. J. (2007) 'Empty Spaces and the Value of Symbols: Estonia's "War of Monuments" from Another Angle', *Europe-Asia Studies*, 59, 6, pp. 913–36.

Erelt, P. (2007) 'Kui monumente teisaldati dünamiidiga', *Eesti Ekspress*, 30 January, available at: www.ekspress.ee/print/266851090B9FC7C2257273003A71EA, accessed 15 March.

Grunenberg, A. (1993) 'Antifaschismus als Staatsdoktrin: die DDR', *Antifaschismus: ein deutscher Mythos* (Hamburg, Rowohlt), pp. 120–44.

Hackmann, J. (2003) 'Past Politics in North-Eastern Europe: The Role of History in Post-Cold War Identity Politics', in Lehti, M. & Smith, D. J. (eds) (2003) *Post-Cold War Identity Politics. Northern and Baltic Experiences* (London, Frank Cass Publishers), pp. 78–100.

Halbwachs, M. (1992) *On Collective Memory* (Chicago, University of Chicago Press).

Hobsbawm, E. (1992) *The Invention of Tradition* (Cambridge, Cambridge University Press).

Inglis, K. (1993) 'Grabmäler für Unbekannte Soldaten', in Stözl, C. (ed.) (1993) *Die Neue Wache Unter den Linden: ein Deutsches Denkmal im Wandel der Geschichte* (Berlin, Koehler & Amelang).

Judt, T. (2002) 'The Past is Another Country: Myth and Memory in Post-War Europe', in Müller, J.-W. (ed.) (2002) *Memory and Power in Post-War Europe* (London, Cambridge University Press), pp. 157–83.

Judt, T. (2005) *Postwar: A History of Europe since 1945* (New York, Penguin Press).

Kattago, S. (1998) 'Representing German Victimhood and Guilt: The Neue Wache and Unified German Memory', *German Politics and Society*, 16, 3, pp. 86–104.

Koselleck, R. (1993) 'Bilderverbot', in Stölzl, C. (ed.) (1993), pp. 200–3.

Koselleck, R. (2002) 'War Memorials: Identity Formations of the Survivors', in *The Practice of Conceptual History. Timing History, Spacing Concepts* (Stanford, Stanford University Press).

Koselleck, R. & Jeismann, M. (eds) (1994) *Der politische Totenkult: Kriegerdenkmäler in der Moderne* (Munich, Wilhelm Fink Verlag).

Laar, M. (2005) *Red Terror: Repressions of the Soviet Occupation Authorities in Estonia* [translated by Tiina Mällo] (Tallinn, Grenader).

Lagerspetz, M. (1999) 'Postsocialism as a Return: Notes on a Discursive Strategy', *East European Politics and Societies*, 13, 2, pp. 377–90.

Lagerspetz, M. (2005) 'Active Civic Participation of Immigrants in Estonia', Country Report for POLIS, Oldenberg, available at: www.uni-oldenburg.di/politics-europe.

Mälestise koond (1995) 'Monument Põhjasõjas 1700. a.langenud vene sõjaväelastele', available at: http://register.muinas.ee/pdetail01.asp?mo_id=48, accessed 26 March 2008.

Mälestise koond (2006) 'Narva Garnisoni kalmistu, Vabadussõjas hukkunute matmispaik mälestussambaga'. 20 September, available at: http://register.muinas.ee/pdetail01.asp?mo_id=24777, accessed 26 March 2008.

Mertelsmann, O. (2004) 'Die Herausbildung des Sonderstatus der Nordostregion innerhalb der Estnischen SSR', in Brüggeman, K. (ed.) (2004) *Narva und die Ostseeregion. Narva and the Baltic Sea Region* (Narva, TÜ Narva Kolledž), pp. 105–21.

Musil, R. (1987) 'Monuments' *Posthumous Papers of a Living Author* [translated by Peter Wortsman] (London & New York, Penguin Books).

Naimark, N. M. (1995) *The Russians in Germany: The History of the Soviet Zone of Occupation 1945–1949* (Cambridge, MA, Harvard University Press).

Narva in Figures (2006) available at: www.narva_arvudes_2006_eesti_ja_inglise_k[1].pdf, accessed 28 March 2008.

Nietzsche, F. (1980) *On the Advantage and Disadvantage of History for Life* [translated by Peter Preuss] (Indianapolis, Hackett Publishing Company).

Nora, P. (1996) *Realms of Memory: The Construction of the French Past* [translated by Arthur Goldhammer] (New York, Columbia University Press).

Onken, E.-C. (2007) 'The Baltic States and Moscow's 9 May Commemoration: Analysing Memory Politics in Europe', *Europe-Asia Studies*, 59, 1, pp. 23–46.

Outhwaite, W. & Ray, L. (2005) 'Modernity, Memory and Postcommunism', in Outhwaite, W. & Ray, L. (eds) (2005) *Social Theory and Postcommunism* (London, Blackwell Publishing), pp. 176–96.

Rand, S. (2004) 'Die Rolle der Grenze in der regionalen Identitätsbildung aus Sicht der Regionalelite im Südosten und Nordosten Estlands (Setumaa und Ida-Virumaa)', in Brüggeman, K. (ed.) (2004) *Narva und die Ostseeregion. Narva and the Baltic Sea Region* (Narva, TÜ Narva Kolledž), pp. 365–87.

Rousso, H. (1991) *The Vichy Syndrome: History and Memory in France since 1944* [translated by Arthur Goldhammer] (Cambridge, MA, Harvard University Press).

Smith, A. D. (2003) *Chosen Peoples: Sacred Sources of National Identity* (Oxford, Oxford University Press).

Stölzl, C. (ed.) (1993) *Die Neue Wache Unter den Linden. Ein Deutsches Denkmal im Wandel der Geschichte* (Berlin, Koehler & Amelang).

Tannberg, T., Mäesalu, A., Lukas, T., Laur, M. & Pajur, A. (2000) *History of Estonia* [translated by Anu Õunapuu, Leelo Linask, Kristjan Teder & Ester Roosmaa] (Tallinn, Avita Press).

Vihalemm, T. & Lauristin, M. (1997) 'Cultural Adjustment to the Changing Societal Environment: The Case of Russians in Estonia', in Vihalemm, T. & Lauristin, M. (eds) [with K.E. Rosengren & L. Weibull] (1997) *Return to the Western World: Cultural and Political Perspectives on the Estonian Post-Communist Transition* (Tartu, Tartu University Press), pp. 279–97.

Wagner-Pacifici, R. & Schwartz, B. (1991) 'The Vietnam Veterans Memorial: Commemorating a Difficult Past', *American Journal of Sociology*, 97, September, pp. 376–420.

AN UNFOLDING SIGNIFIER: LONDON'S BALTIC EXCHANGE IN TALLINN

Stuart Burch

The ostensible subject of this essay is the building known as the Baltic Exchange. It was erected in London at the start of the twentieth century and blown up by the Irish Republican Army (IRA) in 1992. The salvaged remains were recently bought by two Estonian businessmen with the intention of reconstructing the building in Tallinn. The structure is now in Estonia, although construction work had not yet begun at the time of writing.

This essay capitalizes on this liminal moment to explain how and why the Baltic Exchange building has ended up in the Estonian capital – and what consequences its presence might have there. It explores various issues raised by this nomadic monument. The first half of the essay, which seeks to establish the history of the building leading up to its removal to Estonia, focuses on the heritage debates that took place in London over whether to rebuild, remove or replace the damaged building. By bringing this 'external' case study to bear on the Baltic region it is hoped that light will be cast on the most important focus of this essay: namely the contested landscape of contemporary Tallinn.

As was the case with several other contributions to this collection, this essay found its origin in the conference 'Places of Commemoration in North-Eastern Europe: National – Transnational – European?' My contribution was to provide a concluding comment on the issues that had been raised by the preceding speakers. It sought to draw parallels between the conference's main themes through recourse to a comparative example: the Baltic Exchange. The wide-ranging and open-ended nature of my presentation extends to this written version. It needs to be read in conjunction with the two essays published here that deal with the 'Bronze Soldier' war memorial in Tallinn. For, whilst my text does not address this monument directly, it has in fact provided the essay's principal motivation. The violent response to its removal revealed with shocking clarity the vital importance of urban symbolism. The riots in Tallinn of April 2007 place an onus on the academic community to investigate why a sign such as the Bronze Soldier is so contentious, explain what factors led to such violent protests, and draw far-reaching conclusions from these findings.

The opening section of this essay seeks to aid this endeavor by providing a theoretical framework for analysing material culture. It focuses on the work of French social theorist Roland Barthes, in part because his prophetic words were spoken exactly 40 years before the upheaval surrounding the Bronze Soldier. Such anniversal moments are always significant. They serve to thrust the past into the present, reframing the latter and revealing again and again how history is a contemporary, constructed phenomenon.[1]

Some readers will object to this hackneyed focus on Barthes. I, however, concur with the view that Barthes remains a 'crucial figure in modern literary and cultural theory' (Allen 2003, p. 1). One preeminent instance of his enduring appeal is James S. Duncan's brilliant book *The City as Text* (1990). Duncan's study takes up Barthes' recommendation to 'read the city' in a manner that embraces a diverse range of 'voices' (Duncan 1990, p. 17). It shows the enormous benefits that can be reaped when cultural landscapes are construed as entities capable of being read in a myriad of multiple ways.

This, however, can only be achieved by taking into consideration competing 'accounts' (Duncan 1990, pp. 17–19). Thus the approach adopted here is deliberately expansive and overtly non-hierarchical. It espouses the notion that cities are constituted by an overlapping and competing amalgam of different interlocutors – from the theorist to the politician, the heritage professional to the interested resident. They identify different aspects of the landscape and reference other times and places to support their point of view. Cities are emphatically *not* read in a linear, chronological fashion by a prescribed number of commentators. They are as much a product of contest as they are of consensus. The proposed insertion of London's Baltic Exchange in Tallinn enunciates this in a particularly striking fashion.

This essay responds with alacrity to Roland Barthes' call to make cities 'sing'. It ends on a polemical note. For the Baltic Exchange provides a means of thinking about heritage as a creative, future-driven phenomenon. This, I seek to argue, needs to be a central component of Tallinn's plans for 2011, the year when the Estonian capital will serve as a European City of Culture. The Baltic Exchange can and should play a central role in this event. In so doing it will provide one means of escaping from the otherwise interminable morass opened up by the Bronze Soldier debacle.

This essay is therefore addressed as much to the academic community as it is the organizers of the 2011 celebration and those with an interest in the built environment of Tallinn and other capital cities in the Baltic region. It aims to impart a theoretically informed contribution to current events by providing a novel and unusual contribution to the scholarly understanding of an important aspect of the Baltic Sea Region's political and cultural life.

Urban Symbols and Unfolding Signifiers

There is 'a growing awareness of the functions of symbols in urban space'. So said the French social theorist Roland Barthes (1997a, p. 167) in a speech given at the University of Naples in May 1967. Events in Tallinn exactly 40 years later suggest that such attention is more intense than ever. This essay seeks to demonstrate that, despite the passing of four decades, Barthes' comments on symbols and urban space remain both highly topical and instructive today.

Barthes (1915–1980) was a 'semiologist' or 'specialist in signs' (Barthes 1997a, p. 166). His extensive publications combined a passion for written language with a broader interest in 'the way in which objects can signify in the contemporary world' (Barthes 1988, p. 180). His studies confirm that material culture can be 'read' like a written text (Tilley *et al.* 2005, p. 7). Indeed, tangible objects constitute a readily accessible introduction to semiology (also known as semiotics).[2]

In 1916, Ferdinand Saussure (1966, p. 16) defined semiology as a 'science that studies the life of signs within society'. A sign is made up of a signifier and a signified. The former is the material aspect of the sign – a sound, a written mark or an actual object. The signified is the mental concept that it generates. In his Naples talk, Barthes (1997a, pp. 168–9) argued forcefully that it was wrong to assume 'a regular correspondence between signifiers and signifieds' and discounted any notion 'of a one-to-one symbolism'.

He made these comments whilst advocating the notion that urban space is in fact a 'discourse' or 'language'. Rather than embarking on a misguided search for the ultimate meaning of an urban symbol, he argued, one ought instead to acknowledge that the city structure is 'a play of signs' that can only be understood by being left open (Barthes 1997a, p. 172). A 'semantic approach to the city' should therefore seek to 'unfold the signifier'.

Barthes (1997a, p. 171) continued that, because cities are not read in a conventional manner, steps should be taken 'to multiply the readings of the city'. Like his compatriot Michel de Certeau (1984), he felt that cities were written as they were read. It is the reader – 'the user of the city (what we all are)' (Barthes 1997a, p. 170) – who actualizes it. Metaphorically speaking, the city is, as a result, less like a single book and more akin to a whole library. And Barthes (1988, p. 186) similarly cautioned that, whilst the individual components of an urban landscape – such as its monuments – might *seem* like individual words written on the pages of the city, 'that would be an inexact comparison, for the isolated object is already a sentence'.

For Barthes all texts – including *city-texts* – are 'worked out in a perpetual interweaving' (Barthes 1990, p. 64). An additional term he deployed to characterize this 'interweaving' was 'texture', a word also used by another of his compatriots, Henri Lefebvre.[3] At one point in *The Production of Space* Lefebvre (1974/1997, p. 222) defines 'texture' as a 'large space' (such as an urban landscape) articulated by a network of 'strong points' (monuments for example). This accords with Barthes' (1997a, pp. 167–8) view that cities are made up of a rhythm of strong/marked and neutral/unmarked signifiers. Like Barthes, Lefebvre (1997, p. 222) discounted the idea that monumental works have definite signifieds, but asserted rather that they operate across a 'horizon of meaning'. Another similarity is Lefebvre's assertion that monumental works are 'acted' rather than 'read' (cf. Burch 2005, pp. 211–212).

To recap, then:

> [T]he signifieds of objects depend a great deal not on the emitter of the message, but on the receiver, *i.e.*, on the reader of the object . . . [T]he object is polysemous *i.e.*, it readily offers itself to several readings of meaning; in the presence of an object, there are almost always several readings possible, and this not only between one reader and the next, but also, sometimes, within one and the same reader. (Barthes 1988, p. 188)

We can now begin to appreciate how the import of urban symbols differs over time and between users/readers. Take, for example, a signifier such as an imaginary commemorative monument. It will signify different things to different users/readers across a 'horizon of meaning' stretching from the sacred to the profane. Within that scale will be some users/readers for whom the monument was never more than a simple landmark, a neutral signifier – a mere 'stone in the landscape' (cf. Young 1993, pp. 2–3). In addition, a once strong/marked symbol such as a flower-strewn memorial, a memorial to a politically contentious event or a statue of a politician who polarized opinion, could, in time, become a neutral/unmarked signifier – a neglected lump of stone whose commemorative association has been dimmed or broken.

Similarly, alterations to even non-commemorative monuments such as buildings trigger symbolic as well as spatial changes in the city texture. The demolition of one utilitarian monument and its substitution by an alternative building in a different scale, style or material impacts on those vestiges of the past that still feature on the urban scene. The latter might not have materially changed but its advancing age, sudden rarity, increasingly unusual appearance or progressively more anachronistic technologies transforms it into a signifier of 'heritage'. This in turn prompts certain users/readers to vociferously demand its protection and preservation in the face of the development lobby. The endless battle to shore-up ancient monuments against the ravages of time provides eloquent proof that 'use never does anything but shelter meaning' (Barthes 1997b, p. 174). Thus, whilst an object 'serves some purpose, it also serves to communicate information . . . [because] there is always a meaning which overflows the object's use' (Barthes 1988, p. 182).

Monuments are invariably built out of materials that are meant to endure such as metal and stone. But this contrasts markedly with what they signify. For, as Barthes (1997a, p. 169) reminds us, to interpret a monument 'is only to be a kind of witness to a specific state of the distribution of signification'. Monuments cannot therefore be 'read' in isolation: 'meaning is born not from an object, but from an intelligible assemblage of objects: meaning is in some sense extended' (Barthes 1988, p. 186): extended not only across space, but through time as well.

For Barthes (1997a, p. 169), then, what is signified by an object has less to do with its content and more to do with its 'correlative position'. This led him to conclude that 'there is no object which escapes meaning' (Barthes 1988, p. 182). Even an unremarkable fast-food kiosk, in certain 'correlative positions', is well able to signify – as will shortly become clear. And this is why it is incorrect to say that a neglected monument, shifted to some obscure park, covered in graffiti and with its inscription obscured, is devoid of all meaning and has ceased to signify. Rather, the abandoned, vandalized statue on a pedestal 'signifies itself as non-signifying' (Barthes 1988, p. 188). It reveals that a change has taken place in society or in the perceived merits of the person or event that was once deemed worthy of commemoration.

This theory is played out in practice in the monuments which populate the town of Narva in eastern Estonia (Burch & Smith 2007). One such – a statue of Lenin – has been awkwardly left in the corner of the castle courtyard following its removal from a pedestal in the main square.[4] Nevertheless, it is *still* a signifier and it *still* signifies, albeit in a way scarcely imagined by its original proponents. Ironically enough it might well be argued that the displacement of the statue has had the paradoxical effect of rendering it *more* visible than if it were in its 'proper' or 'obvious' place. In this the Narva statue of Lenin serves to elucidate an important point well appreciated by Barthes (1988, p. 184), namely 'the obstacle of the obvious'. What objects 'mean' is seemingly self-evident – they just simply *are*.

An excellent illustration of this is apparent when it comes to landscapes as a whole. In the introduction to their edited volume *Landscapes of Defence*, Gold and Revill (2000, p. 13) draw on the work of Stephen Daniels to address what they term 'the process of naturalization'. This refers to a landscape's 'ability to separate the sign from the practices that produce signification'. Gold and Revill elucidate this apparently complex idea by combining it with Don Mitchell's attempt to theorize the role the state plays in landscape production. Mitchell (cited in Gold & Revill 2000, p. 13) suggests that:

> Landscape is best understood . . . as a certain kind of produced, lived, and represented space constructed out of the struggles, compromises, and temporally settled relations of competing and cooperating social actors: it is both a thing and a social 'process', at once solidly material and ever-changing. Like a commodity, however, the evident (that is temporarily stabilized) form of landscape often masks the facts of production.

This is rendered doubly problematic when it comes to one particular feature of many urban landscapes: commemorative monuments such as statues or plaques. If they *are* noticed their very often protracted and contested genesis is invariably hidden. And anyway, all too often even their 'temporarily stabilized form' is overlooked. They are, as Robert Musil (1995, p. 61) put it, 'conspicuously inconspicuous. There is nothing in this world as invisible as a monument'. Their apparent immutability and formulaic appearance means that they are habitually ignored.

That said, however, even the most unremarkable statue, one that 'stand[s] around quietly, accepting occasional glances' (Musil 1995, p. 63), is a latent signifier waiting for the right correlation of events at which point it will reveal itself capable of becoming a focus for attention or even a catalyst for insurrection. This final scenario affirms the fact that contemporary events alter the legacy of monumental signifiers from previous eras. This is most apparent during a sudden or violent change of political regime – and explains why effigies are toppled from their pedestals whenever a dictator is ousted from power.

Barthes (1988, p. 184) was therefore surely correct to recommend that the user/reader who wishes to study such objects ought to 'resort to an order of representations in which the object is presented in a simultaneously spectacular, rhetorical, and intentional fashion'. Such methods are deployed in the following analysis of the Baltic Exchange, an inadvertently commemorative monument that seems peculiarly well suited to an investigation of this kind. For, as Barthes (1988, p. 184) observed, 'if we are to study the meaning of objects, we must give ourselves a sort of shock of detachment'. When it comes to the Baltic Exchange building in the City of London, this 'shock of detachment' occurred in the most dramatic of fashions: a terrorist bombing.

A Brief History of the Baltic Exchange

The origin of the name 'Baltic Exchange' can be traced back to the Virginia and Baltick coffee house on London's Threadneedle Street.[5] The venue was given this title in 1744, prompted by the merchants and naval officers who met there to discuss trade with the North American colonies and, later, the Baltic region. Goods from that area included tallows, oils, flax, hemp and seeds. In 1823 this gathering place became a subscription-based organization known as the 'Baltic Coffee House' or 'the Baltic Club'. Later, in 1892, a rival organization – the London Shipping Exchange – opened. The two merged in 1900, at which point a new company was incorporated: the Baltic Mercantile and Shipping Exchange Limited. Further takeovers occurred before, in 1903, the company moved to the purpose-built Baltic Exchange, designed by the architects T. H. Smith and William Wimble.

This grandiose classical building was situated on St. Mary Axe in the City of London. Its symmetrical façade featured giant order columns surmounted by a triangular pediment filled with allegorical sculpture (Figure 1). The principal feature was, however, the interior's large marble hall where the trading took place (Figure 2).

These international transactions were inevitably disrupted by the First World War. German members were banned and 62 people affiliated to the Exchange died in the conflict. Marble panels listing the names of the dead were inaugurated in 1920. Two years later an elaborate series of stained-glass memorial windows were inserted above the staircase in the main hall.

The Baltic Exchange declined in importance after the First World War. The shift to the transportation of goods by airplane led to it becoming an air freight exchange in 1949, at which point the Baltic Airbrokers Association was formed. Post-war government controls on the shipping market were relaxed in 1952 and both membership and the building expanded: the foundation stone of an extension to the building was laid by Winston Churchill in 1955, with Queen Elizabeth II formally opening it the following year.

Even so, changes in technology such as improved communications lessened the need for face-to-face dealing. The trading hall became something of an anachronism and the organization began to consider moving operations to a different site (Powell 2006, p. 20). Matters were taken out of their hands at 9:20pm on Friday 10 April 1992. This was the moment when a van, parked outside the Exchange and carrying a 100-pound Semtex bomb wrapped in a ton of fertilizer, exploded.

FIGURE 1 Baltic Exchange façade.

10 April 1992 and After: Terrorism

This event had far-reaching consequences, the most immediate and devastating of which were the injuries inflicted on those unfortunate enough to be in the vicinity. Three people died as a result of the bomb attack. Their deaths serve as a reminder of the devastation wrought by years of conflict over the status of Northern Ireland.[6]

The group responsible for this and many other such attacks was the Provisional Irish Republican Army – the IRA. Members of the same organization planted another device in the adjacent Bishopsgate in April of the following year, again causing enormous damage and destruction but no loss of life. However, whilst the Baltic Exchange had been damaged but not destroyed, the same could not be said for the church of St. Ethelburga on Bishopsgate. This tiny medieval building had escaped the Great Fire of London and the aerial bombing of the Second World War. It did not survive the IRA.

FIGURE 2 Baltic Exchange trading hall with J.D. Forsyth's stained-glass windows *in situ*.

These two actions ushered in strict security measures and led to a so-called 'ring of steel' around the City of London. This is outlined in Jon Coaffee's contribution to the aforementioned book *Landscapes of Defence*. Coaffee (2000, p. 118) lists some of the motivations behind the IRA's actions. Their main aim was to undermine the City of London as a financial capital. They also sought media attention for their cause – something that could be realized by attacking 'prestigious landmark buildings' such as the Baltic Exchange.

The attack therefore had symbolic implications. It struck at what was once 'the commercial heart of the . . . British Empire' especially given that shipping was crucial to the idea of Britain once 'ruling the waves'.[7] This is vividly underscored by a visit to the 'Baltic Glass' display at the National Maritime Museum at Greenwich.[8] There one can see the painstakingly restored memorial windows from the Baltic Exchange. Designed by John Dudley Forsyth (1874–1926), they center on a scene in a Roman temple where centurions welcome the winged figure of Victory as she steps ashore. The symbolism of the image and the fact that the temple is decorated with symbols of British territories overseas shows that a clear analogy is being drawn between the modern era and antiquity: London is the new Rome. Some Irish nationalists are of the opinion that the problems on the island of Ireland are a direct legacy of colonial occupation. Seen in this light the shattered glass of the Baltic Exchange acted as a powerful signifier of the conflict.

This example reveals the uncomfortable fact that iconoclasts – including terrorists – conduct their own readings of the urban environment.[9] The Baltic

Exchange was primarily a functional utilitarian building, not a commemorative memorial. But, as Barthes reminds us, use always hides meaning – and sometimes meaning is only made clear at the moment something is destroyed.

This is an undeniable truth in the wake of the attack on the World Trade Center in New York. This, even more than the Baltic Exchange, was a symbol of trade and economic dominance. The terrorists 'read' this landscape and deliberately chose this building for the media attention it would bring. The first plane hitting one of the towers was a media magnet, ensuring that the second plane's approach would be captured on film. At the moment of its annihilation it became 'a pure signifier': 'the [Twin] Tower[s] attracts meaning the way a lightning rod attracts thunderbolts'.[10] The attack realized the iconicity of the building – and unfolded its signification in the most brutal of fashions.

At the precise moment that one iconic monument was being toppled another was being put up. This was *30 St. Mary Axe* by Foster and Partners, a 180-meter tall skyscraper that became an iconic 'symbol of London' almost as soon as it was completed in 2004 (Powell 2006, p. 195). Its designer – Norman Foster, Lord Foster of Thames Bank – describes it as 'a tremendous act of faith and confidence in the future' (cited in Powell 2006, p. 11). This was not only because the client kept their nerve to erect such a vivid landmark post-9/11, but also because this 40-storey structure was itself a product of a terrorist outrage. For *30 St. Mary Axe* is positioned on the very site of the wrecked Baltic Exchange. The heritage of the past was sacrificed for the heritage of the future when English Heritage (the British government's statutory adviser on the historic environment) concluded that the skyscraper was 'of such exceptional architectural interest that it would be a justifiable replacement for the Baltic Exchange' (Powell 2006, p. 16). However, as the following section shows, this decision was neither inevitable nor without controversy.

10 April 1992 and After: Heritage

The building of *30 St. Mary Axe* would not have been possible without the bombing of 1992. This was because the Baltic Exchange was inscribed on a statutory list of buildings of 'special architectural or historic interest'.[11] 'Listing' is a legal safeguard which, according to English Heritage, is 'not intended to fossilize a building' but to ensure that material changes that impact on the building are 'carefully considered before . . . [being] agreed'. Such deliberations were not considered by the IRA in 1992.

Prior to that the Baltic Exchange had been listed, first in 1972 at Grade II and then at Grade II* in 1987. This latter category is reserved for 'particularly important buildings of more than special interest'. This was merited mostly on account of the interior. Indeed, the façade has been described as 'unexceptional' (Powell 2006, p. 15), whilst a survey of Victorian architecture published in 1987 described it as 'a grand classical building with a feebly small pediment' (Orbach 1987, p. 209). It is fair to say that the Baltic Exchange only rose to eminence because so many of the City of London's more significant Victorian and Edwardian buildings had been demolished in the 1960s and 1980s (Powell 2006, p. 15–7).

Nonetheless a pressing question prevailed: what should be done with the damaged remains of the building? One possible solution was to follow the precedent set by the church of St. Ethelburga. This casualty of the 1993 blast was re-erected using those pieces of stonework, carpentry and stained glass which could be salvaged from the bomb site (Figure 3).[12] A similar approach was taken elsewhere in the environs of this protected 'conservation area' where many façades have 'been subject to extensive repair and rebuilding in replica, thereby ensuring that its architectural character is maintained' (Rees 2000, p. 14).

However, the cost of such an undertaking when it came to the Baltic Exchange was prohibitive. In addition, no obvious use suggested itself for the outmoded building. The ensuing heritage debate has been extensively documented elsewhere (see e.g. Powell 2006).[13] However, it suffices to say here that it took eight years from 1992 until 2000 for the matter to be resolved and a further four until the replacement was complete. The protracted affair involved an array of interested parties – ranging from the original owners, property developers, the City of London Corporation,

FIGURE 3 St. Ethelburga's Centre for Reconciliation and Peace plus *30 St. Mary Axe* – 'the Gherkin' – in the background.

the Mayor of London, the Deputy Prime Minister, English Heritage, the campaigning group SAVE Britain's Heritage and the media – before the ultimate developer Swiss Re succeeded in commissioning Foster and Partners to build their opulent new headquarters.

One aspect of the controversy centered on the perceived impact that this skyscraper would have on the London skyline. Its opponents feared – quite correctly – that it would set a precedent for high-rise building in the capital. Those that are currently being constructed or planned include *122 Leadenhall Street* by Richard Rogers (224 m), *Heron Tower* (242 m), *Bishopsgate Tower* (288 m) and *The Shard* (310 m). The last of these – 'The Shard of Glass' – by the Italian architect Renzo Piano will rise alongside London Bridge station. Its soubriquet and shape shows that it strives to be more than just a monolith on the landscape and that it craves the same sort of iconic status as that won by Norman Foster's 'gherkin', so-called on account of its unusual form.

What helped pave the way for these skyscrapers was the decision to allow the building of *30 St. Mary Axe*. It undoubtedly marked 'a watershed for new development in London' (Powell 2006, p. 47). A legacy of this is the recent decision to narrow the so-called 'Protected Vista Directions'. These are intended to safeguard the views towards such iconic structures such as St. Paul's cathedral and the Houses of Parliament.[14] The introduction to the policy document setting out the alterations to these vistas (written by Ken Livingstone, the then Mayor of London) encapsulates the balance that needs to be struck between change and the status quo:

> For London to remain a competitive world city, it must respond to the drivers of growth and continue to develop in a dynamic, organic manner without inappropriate restraints. At the same time, London is valued because of its first class heritage and historic landmarks that are cherished by Londoners and visitors to this great city.[15]

One person who believes that Britain's heritage is being decidedly undervalued is Prince Charles. In January 2008 he addressed the 'New Buildings in Old Places' conference to lament the 'desecration' of Britain's UNESCO World Heritage Sites by buildings such as *30 St. Mary Axe* which 'pockmark [the] skyline'.[16]

The site of the Baltic Exchange was so important precisely because it was situated at the crux of this divide. It marked an important chapter in the long, open-ended record of London's conservation and eloquently confirms that any heritage is a result of 'the negotiation of diverse, conflicting interests and attitudes'. Heritage is always a 'highly contingent' affair shot through with politics (Hunter 1996, p. 16; Earl 1996). This is as true of London as it is Tallinn – the city to which our attention will now turn.

Cultural Salvage

Well before the construction of *30 St. Mary Axe* the stricken Baltic Exchange had been carefully dismantled, with each piece being numbered and photographed before being taken from the site and offered for sale as a 'rich man's set of building blocks'.[17]

It thus became a remarkable, although not exceptional, type of commodity. The preservation and reuse of old buildings is carried out in a number of ways and for a variety of reasons. One of these has already been illustrated, namely the rebuilding of St. Ethelburga's church. There need not, however, be a direct correlation between the old and new structure. In Tallinn, for example, Ernst Kühnert's reconstruction of *Oleviste (the Black Heads') Guildhall* (1919–1921) includes window jambs from a sixteenth-century building that once stood on another part of Pikk street in the Old Town (Hallas 2000, p. 30). The adoption of older elements as a fascia for a new building can even extend to the retention of a whole façade. This point will be developed in the following section, but it suffices to say here that the decision to retain the original elevation is often driven by the desire to maintain a sense of place in sensitive conservation areas. This was the motivation behind the recreation of the Bishopsgate street scene following the bombing of 1993.

Even if old buildings are not re-erected *in situ*, they can be put up elsewhere. That the 'phenomenon of traveling salvages is not confined to recent times' is richly illustrated by John Harris (2007, p. 2) in his study into the widespread export of architectural salvage from Britain to the USA. In a similar vein, the concern to preserve representative examples of disappearing heritage can lead to the relocation of entire buildings. This was a pattern established by the Swede Artur Hazelius, who founded Skansen in 1891 and paved the way for similar open-air museums across Europe, including that which opened in Estonia in 1957.[18]

What might be termed 'cultural salvage' (Connerton 2005, p. 316) has political drivers as well, as when artifacts are taken as signifiers of imperial or economic power. This explains why London, Paris and New York are all furnished with ancient Egyptian obelisks. They evoke the same sort of comparison between ancient and modern imperialism as that suggested by the stained glass memorial windows of the Baltic Exchange.

It was an act of financial imperialism that ultimately determined the fate of the displaced Baltic Exchange. This became apparent as soon as it was reported that the building was to be relocated to Tallinn. When interviewed about this, Sander Pullerits, project manager for the scheme, reflected that: 'The French once brought massive monuments over from Egypt. We're doing something similar. We are bringing a part of the Baltic Sea history back to Tallinn'. He was also reported as saying that 'the building would stand as an icon of Tallinn's maritime history and its renewed economic success' (Alas 2007).

Pullerits could have gone on to add that the relocation of the Baltic Exchange also says a great deal about the changed geopolitical position of Estonia. A frequent refrain among many influential Estonians is that Estonia is at last 'back on the European map'. This is a phrase that features prominently in the booklet produced in support of Tallinn's successful bid to be a European Capital of Culture in 2011. This publication features a map of Europe in which Russia is occluded entirely. The Baltic Exchange, coming as it does from London, underscores the Western orientation of this new EU member state.

But what of the Estonian backers of the scheme? What might motivate them to spend £800,000 on acquiring the remains of the Baltic Exchange? The purchasers were two wealthy businessmen in their forties involved in the oil and shipping industries: Heiti Hääl and Eerik-Niiles Kross. The latter is the son of the late writer Jaan Kross. Thornton Kay, a partner in the salvage company that sold the Baltic Exchange, speculated that Hääl and Kross:

> see the rebuilding of the Baltic Exchange in Tallinn as a kind of bricks-and-mortar political statement, establishing a feature building that not only creates another dimension to the architecture of Tallinn, much of which is Soviet, but also pointedly brings a physical part of the financial culture of the West bang up against the Russian border.[19]

Hääl and Kross intend to integrate the salvaged building into a new structure housing a restaurant, ballroom and offices. It has also been reported that they wish to collaborate with the Estonian Maritime Museum on an exhibition about the sea and trade.

This latter point indicates an awareness of the signifying potential of the Baltic Exchange. It also gives an insight into the ways in which the utilitarian functions of the building merge into its symbolic connotations. This affirms the truth of Barthes' (1988, p. 182) assertion that 'there is always a meaning which overflows the object's use'. Barthes chose to use the humble telephone to illustrate this point. Variations in color, design and age mean that there are telephones that connote 'luxury' or 'femininity'; 'there are bureaucratic telephones, there are old-fashioned telephones which transmit the notion of a certain period . . . ; in short, the telephone itself is susceptible of belonging to a system of objects-as-signs' (Barthes 1988, p. 182). This provides the perfect explanation as to why two businessmen should have invested in the salvaged remains of a century-old building. For one of the fixtures included in the sale was the Baltic Exchange's ornate telephone booths. One hundred years later in a digital and wireless Estonia these kiosks will surely be superfluous in purely utilitarian terms – but that does not mean they have ceased to carry meaning. Indeed, their unusual, anachronistic form and function indicate that meaning really has 'overflowed the object's use'. They promise to encapsulate the exotic appeal of the Baltic Exchange: it has the potential to offer something 'authentically' different.

The Tallinn Palimpsest

In August 2007 it was reported that the Baltic Exchange would be built 'close to the port terminals' on a site that had apparently been chosen 'with the full support of Tallinn city' (Drayton 2007). This disguises the fact that the desired location was clearly a matter of some dispute.

The site favored by Hääl and Kross had been named in an article published in *Eesti Ekspress* in June, the same month that the building began to arrive in Estonia (Tänavsuu 2007). The plot lay just outside the Old Town on an arterial road called *Estonia puiestee*. This is currently occupied by a modest single-storey florist shop and a 24-hour fast-food kiosk. Of more architectural interest is the building facing it on the other side of the road. This would make the perfect foil to the London building. It dates from 1912–1916 and is constructed in a Neo-Baroque style according to the designs of Aleksander Rosenberg, an engineer from St. Petersburg. The central portion of the main façade is articulated by six giant order pilasters surmounted by a triangular pediment. This leads in to a double height hall. These similarities with the Baltic Exchange extend even to the function it serves: in 1996 it was converted into an English college (Hallas 2000, p. 42).

The aforementioned *Eesti Ekspress* feature was accompanied by a computer-generated montage of the proposed building showing the recycled façade of the Baltic Exchange with a much larger glass structure rising above it. Again this would chime with its surroundings: the building next door – designed by Henno Sillaste and dating from 1997–1998 – is a wedge-shaped, seven-storey office block (Hallas 2000, p. 42). Its ground-plan is dictated by the awkward triangular plot delineated by two thoroughfares. The elevation facing one of these is in granite, the other is an undulating wall of tinted glass.

Interestingly enough, the form of the Baltic Exchange as suggested in the *Eesti Ekspress* image carries echoes of one of the early proposals for the original site in London. When it looked as though the building was to be 'restored', the architectural practice GMW drew up an unrealized design for a 'groundscraper' dominating the 1903 façade (Powell 2006, p. 20).

This (albeit unrealized) scheme is just one further example of the ways in which traces of earlier buildings can sometimes remain in evidence even if a site has been comprehensively redeveloped. A clear instance of this occurs in relation to one of the most famous works of contemporary architecture: Richard Rogers' postmodern Lloyd's of London building on Lime Street (1981–1986) not far from the site of the Baltic Exchange. The retention of the entrance to Sir Edwin Cooper's 1928 building on Leadenhall Street sets up a decidedly uncanny juxtaposition: a closer examination of the stone portal reveals that it is simply a screen through which can be seen the metal tubes of Rogers's iconic design.

The final architectural plan for the Tallinn version of the Baltic Exchange has not, as yet, been decided. Its ultimate appearance will, of course, play a large role in the meanings that can be drawn from it. This is important if one thinks back to what Barthes said about the interpretation of a sign. He said that 'the signifieds of objects *depend a great deal* not on the emitter of the message, but on the receiver'. The form and location underscore that, whilst meanings shift, they are rooted in specific contexts. To follow Barthes' approach means adopting a more rigorous, self-questioning approach than that which presupposes there to be one 'truth' to be uncovered.

It is fitting therefore that this signifier will continue to unfold once the form has been decided and realized. This sense of unfurling will be especially apparent should the Baltic Exchange be built on the site suggested by *Eesti Ekspress*. This is because it would be in the environs of Freedom Square (*Vabaduse väljak*), an architecturally and symbolically sensitive area. And it is for exactly these reasons that planning permission might have been denied.

The importance of Freedom Square promises only to increase in the years leading up to 2011, the date when Tallinn will serve as a European City of Culture. Some €44.6m is earmarked for the redevelopment of what is 'Tallinn's central square and the venue for national parade events'. This quotation is taken from the above-mentioned brochure setting out the city's vision for 2011. It goes on to say that a new 'monument and memorial complex to commemorate the Estonian War of Independence' will be built there in 2008. The site will also be converted into 'an active leisure area' and transformed into 'an organic element of the "green belt" of the Old Town of Tallinn' (Haagensen 2007, p. 33).

Whether or not the Baltic Exchange merits being included on the fringes of this development will be determined through a process of negotiation between elected representatives, architects, big business, the heritage lobby and other spokespersons (cf. Hallas 2000, p. 19). Such a debate will bring the Baltic Exchange story full circle.

The fate of the Baltic Exchange will, then, in part at least, be determined by the current and future features of the cityscape. At present the whole southern side of Freedom Square leading to the proposed site for the Baltic Exchange is lined with buildings that are marked with plaques indicating that they are national monuments ('*kultuurimälestis*') together with individual registration numbers and the logo of the national heritage body.

As we have seen, being inscribed in this way is supposed to afford some protection from change. Processes of drawing up legislation for the preservation of the built heritage develop at a national level and at various speeds (Hunter 1996, pp. 9, 114). This local scale is also overlaid with transnational protection, such as that bestowed by UNESCO via its designated World Heritage Sites. Tallinn was included on this list in 1998. This places the Estonian capital under international scrutiny, something that became painfully clear following the critical comments made by Giorgio Piccinato, a representative of the UNESCO World Heritage Committee who visited Tallinn in December 2005.[20] He used the recent high-rise extension to the Viru Center to illustrate the necessity for 'an integral picture' which took into consideration the wider urban context. This, he argued, had not been heeded when it came to the Viru Center, which he criticized for its adverse impact on 'the historical city's silhouette'.[21]

The importance of such a skyline when it comes to heritage is evident from the aforementioned brochure promoting Tallinn as a future European cultural capital (Haagensen 2007, pp. 4–5). Inside, a double-page photograph shows the Old Town with its highly recognizable profile of church spires and eclectic low-rise monuments. This visualizes the symbolic potency – and economic importance – of its heritage. But, just as in London, this is always in conflict with demands for change and development – a perennial fight to maintain traditional appeal whilst also enabling growth and development.

Whilst there are, as again in London, laws intended to protect the historically sensitive core from high-rise development, Tallinn faces some real challenges. A report in *The Baltic Times* in September 2007 cited the city's chief architect, Endrik Mand, as saying that 'there are no controls over building aesthetics' and that 'the council had little power to encourage or direct development, but relied on developers to drive the city's future' (Alas 2007b).

A perfect illustration of this is provided by the recent fate of the *Sakala Center.* This complex on a prime location near the Estonia Theatre is praised in the guidebook to *20th Century Architecture in Tallinn* (Hallas 2000, p. 57). It notes the intriguing irony between its form and function: its ground-plan resembled that of a church, yet it served as the Political Education Center for the Estonian Communist Party. Its walls were built of rusticated limestone, which, the guide says, can be seen as in keeping with the city's Gothic churches. Meanwhile the interior decoration by Aulo Padar and Kristi Laanemaa ('the most stylish examples of Postmodernism in Estonia') was coupled with stained glass by Rait Prääts showing the 'apotheosis of socialism'. It also notes an abortive plan to surmount the building's tower with a globe on which nation states were colored black or red according to whether they were capitalist or communist.

Despite being tainted by its Soviet associations this was clearly a signifier that could be praised for its aesthetic and historical qualities. Nevertheless, and despite the fact that it had found a new use as a cultural center, it was demolished shortly after the parliamentary elections in March 2007 (Kindlam 2007). Three months later contracts were signed to rebuild a new leisure complex at a cost of over 828 million kroons.[22]

This controversial event led many people to voice their criticism of the inadequate measures to protect the built heritage and a widespread perception that 'current development trends in Tallinn . . . allow anybody with money to buy their way past demolition controls and planning schemes'. This was a conclusion reached in an interesting newspaper article entitled 'Tallinn rediscovers Karp legacy' (Alas 2007c). Its subject was 'the most loved and loathed architect in Estonia', Raine Karp. He was responsible for the *Sakala Center* and other iconic late Soviet-era buildings such as *Tallinn City Hall* (1976–1980), the *National Library* (1984–1992) and the *Central Post Office* (1975–1980). The article suggests that a resurgence of interest in these monumental structures is connected to a popular 'rejection of the recent inner-city building boom, which has seen a forest of skyscrapers spring up in the central business district'. They are criticized by the architectural historian Andres Kurg on the grounds that these 'anonymous international style . . . glass and steel buildings' represent a threat to 'the identity of the city' (Kurg cited in Alas 2007c).

The discussion raised by the Sakala controversy serves as a reminder not to make easy assumptions about what is worthy of preserving and what is not. The very last Soviet tower block left standing – even should it be a much maligned serial type such as 'Soviet standard 1-464' – would become 'heritage'. Certain groups would demand its preservation in exactly the same sort of way as people protested at the removal of the Baltic Exchange and the building of *30 St. Mary Axe*.

This confirms Barthes' observation that everything can be meaningful and what matters is determined by a sign's 'correlative position'. Again, it is by unfolding the signifier that is the Baltic Exchange that this becomes clear. Take, for example, my photograph of the site in Tallinn proposed for the building (Figure 4). It depicts a decidedly unremarkable place. And yet, should this view make way for the Baltic Exchange, it would instantly become 'heritage' and worthy of being in an archive. And, even if the Baltic Exchange is *not* erected there, the image will continue to signify as a sign of a path not taken. It will be but one of the potential visions of Tallinn that were proposed but not realized. Investigating why it did not transpire will reveal something of the contested nature of the built environment.

The insertion of the Baltic Exchange will therefore alter the 'readings' of whatever part of the city in which it appears. This was apparent from an on-line discussion in July 2007 prompted by the prospect of the redevelopment and which led to an interesting debate about the site.[23] One of the participants opined: '[T]hat burger-place

FIGURE 4 Proposed site in Tallinn for the Baltic Exchange.

is a real godsend at 5 am after clubbing! Any burger-place is: (a) food (b) drink (c) last resort for scoring girls!' But he and his fellow discussants made such flippant remarks only after making a series of balanced and informed arguments for and against the siting of the Baltic Exchange on *Estonia puiestee*, its potential interaction with the adjacent English College, and the role of the National Heritage Board (*Muinsuskaitseamet*).

This exchange captures the lived sense of the city and its multitude of unrecorded narratives. Its users/readers were aware of planning issues and the history of the building, debating whether it would harmonize or jar with the existing streetscape. This was a working example of the 'rhythms' of the city texture as expounded by Barthes and Lefebvre.

The new Baltic Exchange will, then, provide a fresh layer in the palimpsest that makes up the history of Tallinn. With this in mind, some sense of disjuncture between the façade, the rest of the building and its surroundings is desirable. This will make it apparent that a fusion has taken place, prompting the city's users/readers to ponder why and thereby acknowledge, however unconsciously, that something interesting has occurred. This is likely to continue long after the origins of the building have been consigned to the history books.

Before turning to the final section, it is worth reiterating that the *Sakala Center* controversy and the realization that a burger bar or an undistinguished shop selling flowers can become signifiers in urban space underline that care does indeed need to be taken to avoid assuming what is and what is not of value or meaning. In the case of a country such as Estonia this is a particularly pressing issue given its heritage of Soviet-era monuments. They raise many questions. What do they signify? Should they be preserved? Do they 'belong'?

Wars of Monuments

Some of the flowers purchased from the florist on *Estonia puiestee* might well have been reverentially laid at 13 *Kaarli puiestee*, Tõnismägi. From September 1947 until April 2007 a 'Bronze Soldier' stood on this very spot. It is this sign which like no other addresses 'the functions of symbols in urban space'. It is the epitome of a signifier with multiple signifieds: to some it connotes liberation from fascism; for others it denotes Soviet occupation. It is able to signify more than one thing precisely because signifiers have multiple signifieds and because 'meaning' is cultural rather than given or 'natural' (Allen 2003, p. 119).

Moreover, the relocation of the Bronze Soldier confirms Barthes' point about the importance of context – or 'correlative position' – to any given signifier. In April 2007 it was situated in a prominent location in the city center. The following month it had been moved to the more peripheral setting of a military cemetery. Although it appears unchanged it is *not* the same signifier. This is because '[a]ll we need to do is change the focus of a remark, of a performance, of a body, in order to reverse altogether . . . the meaning we might have given it' (Barthes 1977, p. 66). This gets to the heart of what Barthes (1977, p. 67) meant by 'signification' or the 'degrees of language'. Beyond the literal, 'first-order meaning' of a sign are other, perhaps less obvious but frequently more revealing 'second-order meanings'. However, even if the latter is acknowledged, 'the original, first-order meaning is not completely forgotten' (Allen 2003, p. 44). This is useful to an understanding of both the Baltic Exchange and the Bronze Soldier: their relocations give rise to second-order meanings, but what they signified before has not been erased.

Both the protesters who gathered around the Bronze Soldier prior to its removal and the mourners who paid homage to it in its new setting are the embodiment of this fact. They took up Barthes' (1997a, pp. 170, 172) call for them to make the city 'sing' rather actualizing their readings 'in secret'. Of course, the conjunction of singing and revolution has particular resonance for Estonians. A revolution of sorts took place in the streets of Tallinn on 27 and 28 April 2007. The protestors radically realized the reality of the built environment as they tore bits from the crumbling walls of Raine Karp's nearby National Library and used them as missiles to rain down on the police. Again, this realized something that Barthes well understood:

> The city, essentially and semantically, is the place of our meeting with the *other*, and it is for this reason that the centre is the gathering place in every city . . . [T]he city centre is always felt as the space where subversive forces, forces of rupture, ludic forces act and meet. (Barthes 1997a, p. 171)

Is the rupture in Estonian society exposed by the Bronze Soldier destined to last forever? Well, this is where the Baltic Exchange comes in as a positive symbol. Barthes said that each time he needed to 'test' or 'demystify' a message he 'subject[ed] it to some external instance' (Barthes 1977, p. 67). This is the motivation behind the essay you have been reading. I have taken advantage of the fact that the Baltic Exchange is currently in limbo between its old and new homes as an opportunity to use it as a lens through which to examine a range of Estonian issues associated to 'the functions of symbols in urban space'.

The Baltic Exchange offers the first glimpse of a way out of the Bronze Soldier dilemma. This is because it will be a quiet reminder that a 'war of monuments' is not unique to Estonia. The IRA has taken lives and they are also iconoclasts – targeting signifiers for their own purposes. The clearest example of the latter was provided by *Nelson's Pillar* in Dublin. This unfolding signifier was erected in the nineteenth century and blown up by the IRA in 1966 as a way of marking the fiftieth anniversary of the Easter Rising. Nelson's decapitated head is today in Dublin Civic Museum. The trace of this absent signifier is forever felt in the Irish capital, especially now that its site is occupied by the monumental abstract form known as the *Spire of Dublin*.

Similarly, the Baltic Exchange in Estonia will thus constitute a distant legacy of another sectarian conflict that has lulled but not been resolved. Two recent incidents testify to the fact that the Irish past – like the Estonian – is still contested. The first was the decision to move memorials to soldiers killed in Ulster from their sites at former military bases 'to more secure locations within the province and the British mainland' for fear that they would be defaced once the bases were decommissioned. The second example concerns proposals to redefine the 'Ulster Troubles' as a 'war' (Rayment 2007; Peterkin 2008). The terminology used to describe it, when it started, why and for what reasons are all highly disputed. Such is the way with all struggles of liberation and occupation. They give rise to conflicts that continue to be waged by subsequent generations in the form of 'history wars' (Dean & Rider 2005, p. 44). The Bronze Soldier debacle is one manifestation of this schism, a legacy of a divided heritage between what in Western Europe is known as the Second World War of 1939–1945, and in Russia is still today termed the 'Great Patriotic War' of 1941–1945.

Meanwhile, another of the signifiers damaged in the Anglo-Irish 'war of monuments' – the tiny medieval church on Bishopsgate in the City of London – has been converted into the *St. Ethelburga's Centre for Reconciliation and Peace*, an institution 'devoted to promoting understanding of the relationship between faith and conflict'.[24] Might the Baltic Exchange serve some similar function? Well, it could start to do just this in 2011. In so doing it would resolve a problem identified by the chair of the Selection Panel for the European Capitals of Culture, Sir Robert Scott. In the fall of 2007 he publicly criticized Tallinn's proposed program for 2011, declaring that it 'was "unclear in its European dimension", lacked involvement from "new Estonians," and did not show any new examples of culture'. Others were critical of what they saw as an exclusive focus on the medieval Old Town (Alas 2007d).

What better way of addressing these complaints than by launching the 2011 celebrations in the former trading hall of the Baltic Exchange? This re-erected monument could be promoted as a potent metaphor for *heritage*: that dynamic fusion of the past *and* the present. London's Baltic Exchange in Tallinn as an amalgam of old and new has the capacity to encapsulate the creative potential of heritage. It has, moreover, the wherewithal to demonstrate that something from the outside can be incorporated into – and enrich – the local milieu. And, finally, it goes without saying that the Baltic Exchange signifies across a decidedly *European dimension*.

Notes

1 A very clear instance of this is Onken (2007, pp. 23–46).

2 What follows in this section is a very partial, superficial account that is skewed by the aims of this essay. The interested reader who is unfamiliar with the concept of semiology/semiotics might like to consult one of the many books outlining this 'valuable buzzword' (Cobley & Jansz 2004, p. 3).

3 'Texture' suggests touch – and Lefebvre was keen to promote the idea that the world should be understood by all the senses, not just sight (see Leach 1997, p. 164).

4 Olav Männi's statue of Lenin was originally placed on a pedestal designed by the architect Ilmar Bork. Erected in 1957, it was moved from the main square in 1993.

5 Information on the history of the Baltic Exchange is derived from: 'History – The early years', available at: www.balticexchange.com/default.asp?action=article&ID=388, accessed 6 February 2008; and from the 'Baltic Glass' exhibition at London's National Maritime Museum (available at: www.nmm.ac.uk/server/show/ConWebDoc.20025, accessed 6 February 2008).

6 The people who died in the bombing of 10 April 1992 were Paul Butt, aged 29 and a securities dealer; Thomas Casey, a 49-year-old doorman at the Baltic Exchange; and Danielle Carter, a 15-year-old schoolgirl. The devastation wrought by every death is summed up by the fact that one of the ambulance workers who arrived at the scene of the Baltic Exchange bombing never recovered from his experience. He shot his girlfriend five months later and tried to commit suicide. He is now in a secure psychiatric unit (Beck 2000).

7 Source: 'History – The early years'.

8 Information on this is from Powell 2006, pp. 50–1 and 'Stained glass from the Baltic Exchange', available at: www.nmm.ac.uk/server/show/ConWebDoc.20025, accessed 6 February 2008.

9 This is not to overlook the fact that one of the main aims of the IRA and other terrorist organizations was to cause chaos and carnage, with little care or understanding for life or property. Those responsible for the attack of April 1992 passed on misleading information to the police, indicating that the device was outside the Bank of England. This could have been a deliberate deception, or it might have been an indication that they were so poorly informed that they could not properly identify the buildings they were seeking to destroy.

10 This deliberately skewed quotation is adapted from Barthes' brilliant article 'The Eiffel Tower' (Barthes 1964/1997).

11 Information on listing is taken from www.english-heritage.org.uk/server/show/nav.1374, accessed 6 February 2008.

12 The fact that two-thirds of the tower on the main west front facing Bishopsgate survived the bombing made restoration feasible. Much of the rest, however, needed to be built anew. See www.stethelburgas.org/ourhistory.htm, accessed 6 February 2008.

13 SAVE Britain's Heritage, 2000, *The Baltic Exchange*, available at: http://www.savebritainsheritage.org/baltic.htm, accessed 6 February 2008.

14 See www.london.gov.uk/mayor/strategies/sds/spg-views.jsp, accessed 6 February 2008.

15 See www.london.gov.uk/mayor/strategies/sds/docs/spg-views-final-all.pdf, accessed 6 February 2008.

16 'A speech by HRH The Prince of Wales at the New Buildings in Old Places Conference, St. James's Palace, London', 31 January 2008, available at: www.princeofwales.gov.uk/speechesandarticles/a_speech_by_hrh_the_prince_of_wales_at_the_new_buildings_in__604060620.html, accessed 6 February 2008.

17 Pavilions of Splendour: 'The [dismantled] Baltic Exchange', available at: www.heritage.co.uk/apavilions/baltic.html, accessed 6 February 2008.

18 For an account of this within the wider context of Estonian ethnography, see Elle Vunder, 'Ethnography at the University of Tartu', available at: www.erm.ee/?node=130, accessed 29 May 2008.

19 Cited in T. K. Salvo, 'Baltic Exchange sold to Estonia for £800,000 through an ad on SalvoWEB.com', 23 June 2007, available at: http://salvonews.blogspot.com/2007/06/major-uk-architectural-salvage-deal.html (accessed 31 August 2007). An article in *The Baltic Times* dated 9 August 2001 described Kross – who represented Estonia at NATO membership negotiations – as 'a former coordinator of the work of the national security service with the State Chancellery'. It also named him in connection with a controversial real estate deal involving the then mayor of Tallinn, Tõnis Palts. See Kurm (2001).

20 'UNESCO decries Viru Center', *The Baltic Times*, 7 December 2005, available at: www.baltictimes.com/news/articles/14172, accessed 6 February 2008.

21 'Tallinn officials to provide UNESCO with explanation', *The Baltic Times*, 7 April 2006, available at: www.baltictimes.com/news/articles/15104, accessed 6 February 2008.

22 Source: www.merkoehitus.ee/?id=290 (accessed 6 February 2008).

23 See www.skyscrapercity.com/showthread.php?t=494989 (accessed 6 February 2008). The on-line discussion was triggered by the posting of a news story about the Baltic Exchange from the BBC's website (Lane 2007).

24 'St. Ethelburga's Centre for Reconciliation and Peace', available at: http://www.stethelburgas.org, accessed 6 February 2008.

References

Alas, J. (2007a) 'Historic London building to be reassembled in central Tallinn', *The Baltic Times*, June 13, available at: www.baltictimes.com/news/articles/18054, accessed 6 February 2008.

Alas, J. (2007b) 'Tallinn's planning problems revealed', *The Baltic Times*, 26 September, available at: www.baltictimes.com/news/articles/18891, accessed 6 February 2008.

Alas, J. (2007c) 'Tallinn rediscovers Karp legacy', *The Baltic Times*, 31 January, available at: www.baltictimes.com/news/articles/17229, accessed 6 February 2008.

Alas, J. (2007d) 'Tallinn "not ready" to be culture capital', *The Baltic Times*, 5 September, available at: www.baltictimes.com/news/articles/18704, accessed 6 February 2008.

Allen, G. (2003) *Roland Barthes* (London & New York, Routledge).

Beck, L. (2000) 'Collective amnesia', *Peace Matters*, 29, available at: http://www.ppu.org.uk/peacematters/pm2000/pm2000_33.html, accessed 6 February 2008.

Barthes, R. (1988 [1964]) 'Semantics of the Object', in *The Semiotic Challenge* [translated by Richard Howard] (Oxford, Basil Blackwell), pp. 179–90.

Barthes, R. (1990 [1973]) *The Pleasure of the Text* [translated by Richard Miller] (Oxford, Basil Blackwell).

Barthes, R. (1997a [1967]) 'Semiology and the urban', in Leach, N. (ed.) (1997) *Rethinking Architecture: A Reader in Cultural Theory* (London, Routledge), pp. 166–172.

Barthes, R. (1997b [1964]) 'The Eiffel Tower', in Leach, N. (ed.) (1997), pp. 172–80.

Burch, S. (2005) 'The texture of heritage: A reading of the 750th anniversary of Stockholm', *International Journal of Heritage Studies*, 11, 3, pp. 211–233.

Burch, S. & Smith, D. J. (2007) 'Empty spaces and the value of symbols: Estonia's "war of monuments" from another angle', *Europe-Asia Studies*, 59, 6, pp. 913–36.

Certeau, M. de (1984) 'Walking in the city', in *The Practice of Everyday Life* [translated by Steven Rendall] (Berkeley, California & London, University of California Press), pp. 91–110.

Coaffee, J. (2000) 'Fortification, fragmentation and the threat of terrorism in the City of London', in Gold, J. R. & Revill, G. E. (eds) (2000), pp. 114–29.

Cobley, P. & Jansz, L. (2004) *Introducing Semiotics* (London, Icon Books).

Connerton, P. (2005) 'Cultural memory', in Tilley, C. *et al.* (eds) (2005), pp. 315–24.

Dean, D. & Rider, P. E. (2005) 'Museums, Nation and Political History in the Australian National Museum and the Canadian Museum of Civilization', *museum and society*, 3, 1, March, pp. 35–50.

Drayton, M. (2007) 'Old world gives way to new as we make a Baltic exchange', Friday 17 August, available at: www.lloydslist.com/ll/news/viewArticle.htm;jsessionid=D2222E4AC7A309631 7F1FDB22EC780D2?articleId=1187276811668, accessed 6 February 2008.

Duncan, J. S. (1990) *The City as Text: The Politics of Landscape Interpretation in the Kandyan Kingdom* (Cambridge, Cambridge University Press).

Earl, J. (1996) 'London government: A record of custodianship', in Hunter, M. (ed.) (1996), pp. 57–76.

Gold, J. R. & Revill, G. E. (eds) (2000) *Landscapes of Defence* (London, Addison Wesley Longman).

Haagensen, M. (2007) *Everlasting Fairytale* [2011 brochure], available at: http://www.tallinn2011.ee/pdf/tallinn2011_eng.pdf, accessed 6 February 2008.

Hallas, K. (ed.) (2000) *20th Century Architecture in Tallinn* (Tallinn, The Museum of Estonian Architecture).

Harris, J. (2007) *Moving Rooms: The Trade in Architectural Salvages* (New Haven & London, Yale University Press).

Hunter, M. (ed.) (1996) *Preserving the Past: The Rise of Heritage in Modern Britain* (Stroud, Alan Sutton).

Kindlam, R. (2007) 'Sakala's last stand', 20 April, *Eesti Elu* (Tartu College Publishing Committee), available at: www.eesti.ca/main.php?op=article&articleid=15989&PHPSESSID=fe0583f91ea1c7c9372a7b947f105971, accessed 6 February 2008.

Kurm, K. (2001) 'Tallinn mayor reveals dark underbelly', *The Baltic Times*, 9 August, available at: www.baltictimes.com/news/articles/5300, accessed 6 February 2008.

Lane, M. (2007) 'Extreme restoration', *BBC News Magazine*, available at: http://news.bbc.co.uk/1/hi/magazine/6230390.stm, accessed 6 February 2008.

Leach, N. (ed.) (1997) *Rethinking Architecture: A Reader in Cultural Theory* (London, Routledge).

Lefebvre, H. (1997 [1974]) *The Production of Space* [translated by D. Nicholson-Smith] (Oxford, Blackwell).

Musil, R. (1995 [1936]) 'Monuments', in *Posthumous Papers of a Living Author* [translated by P. Wortsman] (London, Penguin), pp. 61–4.

Onken, E.-C. (2007) 'The Baltic States and Moscow's 9 May Commemoration: Analysing Memory Politics in Europe', *Europe-Asia Studies*, 59, 1, pp. 23–46.

Orbach, J. (1987) *Victorian Architecture in Britain* (London, A & C Black).

Peterkin, T. (2008) 'Ulster Troubles "could be redefined as a war"', *Daily Telegraph*, 11 January, available at: www.telegraph.co.uk/news/main.jhtml?xml=/news/2008/01/09/nwar109.xml, accessed 6 February 2008.

Powell, K. (2006) *30 St Mary Axe: A Tower for London* (London, Merrell).

Rayment, S. (2007) 'Army forced to move Ulster memorials', *Sunday Telegraph*, 19 February, available at: www.telegraph.co.uk/news/main.jhtml?xml=/news/2007/02/18/ngrave18.xml, accessed 6 February 2008.

Rees, P. W. (2000) *St Helen's Conservation Area Character Summary* (London, Corporation of London).

Saussure, F. de (1966 [1916]) *Course in General Linguistics* [edited by Charles Bally and Albert Sechehaye in collaboration with Albert Riedlinger, translated by Wade Baskin] (New York, McGraw-Hill Book Company).

Tänavsuu, T. (2007) 'Ärimehed toovad Londonist maja Tallinna', *Eesti Ekspress*, available at: www.ekspress.ee/viewdoc/5D0BCDC1138A51B9C22572F00036476D, accessed 14 June 2007.

Tilley, C., Keane, W., Kuechler, S., Rowlands, M. & Spyer, P. (eds) (2005) *Handbook of Material Culture* (London, Sage).

Young, J. E. (1993) *The Texture of Memory: Holocaust Memorials & Meaning* (New Haven & London, Yale University Press).

WHY THE HOLOCAUST DOES NOT MATTER TO ESTONIANS

Anton Weiss-Wendt

This essay examines perceptions of the Holocaust in contemporary Estonia. To comprehend how Estonians have formed their views on the Holocaust is to understand how they conceive of their history. Whereas in Western Europe and North America the Holocaust is perceived as carrying a universalistic message, in Estonia and other East European countries it is ultimately linked to the Jewish minority. Thus, whatever Estonians think of the Jews as a group translates into their perceptions of the Holocaust and vice versa. Therefore it is essentially impossible to discuss what the Holocaust means to Estonians without assessing the levels of anti-Semitism in Estonian society today.

Unlike in neighboring Latvia and Lithuania, the Nazi mass murder of Jews has never become a subject of debate in Estonia. Most Estonians think of the Holocaust as a superimposed discourse that has no direct connection to their country. The lack of interest can be attributed to several factors. As far as Jewish history is concerned, Estonia is a marginal case. The Estonian Jewish community was small and inconspicuous. Even more significantly, in Estonia the Holocaust played out differently than elsewhere in Nazi-occupied Eastern Europe. The implementation of the so-called Final Solution of the Jewish Question in Estonia was less visible than elsewhere and was witnessed by few people. Therefore, the Soviet investigation of war crimes committed in Estonia paid relatively little attention to the plight of the Jews. Even then, both the media and witnesses routinely portrayed Jewish victims as peaceful Soviet citizens murdered by German fascist invaders. These perceptions carried over into the post-1991 period.

Peculiarities of the Holocaust in Estonia

The Estonian case poses a challenge to the generally accepted view of how the Holocaust was carried out in eastern Europe.[1] Unlike in Latvia and Lithuania, there were no anti-Jewish pogroms or ghettos; no death squads staffed and sometime managed by natives, like the Arājs Commando in Latvia or the Hamann Commando in Lithuania. The daylong mass executions of Jews at the Ninth Fort in Kaunas or Rumbuli near Riga did not happen in Estonia until a year later. Due to fierce Soviet resistance, roughly two-thirds of Estonia's Jews managed to escape to Russia during 1941. The remaining 1,000 or so were apprehended by the Estonian Security Police (a semi-independent subsidiary of the German Security Police), which subjected each individual to pseudo-legal investigation. Thus, Estonia was spared the atrocities and public humiliation that accompanied the Nazi mass murder of Jews in other east European countries. Most Estonians, if they bothered to think of it at all, believed that justice had been served and that the executed Jews were punished for a reason.

The two Jewish transports that arrived in Estonia in September 1942 from former Czechoslovakia and Germany respectively had been diverted from Riga. Only a few local people witnessed Jews disembarking at a small railway station not far from Tallinn. Upon arrival, almost 80% of the Jews, a total of 1,650, were executed by a special detachment of the Estonian Security Police. The rest of the prisoners, mainly young women, were later dispatched to Tallinn Battery prison. Finally, in September and October 1943, the Germans deported to Estonia over 9,000 Jews from the dismantled ghettos of Kaunas and Vilnius. While the extermination center at Auschwitz-Birkenau had been working at full capacity, receiving Jews from all corners of occupied Europe, these Polish and Lithuanian Jews sent to Estonia were meant to live. Alongside Soviet prisoners of war, Jews worked in the oil industry and built up defenses in northeastern Estonia. Jews were concentrated in 19 slave labor camps in an otherwise scarcely populated area. Three hundred men from Estonian police battalions 287 and 290 guarded the perimeter of the camps. Otherwise, these were run entirely by the German SS, which, with a few exceptions, carried out the selections, individual killings and mass executions of Jews that occurred during the summer and early fall of 1944. The largest single massacre on the territory of Estonia occurred at Klooga slave labor camp on 19 September 1944, and claimed the lives of 1,634 Jews and 150 Soviet POWs. The total death toll of Jews in Estonia in 1941–1944 could be as high as 8,500, with a death rate of 63%. In Latvia, at the same time, 65% or 61,000 Jews perished. The death rate among Lithuanian Jews was the highest anywhere in Nazi-occupied Europe, 95%, or 195,000.

The Estonian Security Police had a mostly bureaucratic mode of operation, and for this reason it drew only limited attention from the Soviet legal authorities. Furthermore, the commanding echelons of the Security Police and most of its rank-and-file had fled to the West. When interrogating members of the auxiliary police (*Omakaitse*) or police battalions, KGB investigators gave most emphasis to the killing of communists and Soviet paratroopers. In the open war-crimes trials that were staged throughout the Baltic region during the 1960s, however, mass murder of Jews played an important part. The four defendants who stood trial in Tallinn in 1961 (two of them in absentia) were implicated in the mass murder of Jews at Kalevi-Liiva in 1942, whereas the three individuals (of whom only one was present in the courtroom) on trial in Tartu a year later were charged with running a local concentration camp and carrying out mass executions of prisoners. Despite Soviet claims to the contrary, a majority of the Estonian people had never embraced the so-called socialist justice; the ovation with which the audience met the verdict – invariable death sentence – fell short of expectations.

The Nazi mass murder of Jews in Estonia lacks clear markers that would make it easier for common people to grasp. The 963 Estonian Jews murdered in 1941 and 1942 constitute slightly over 10% of the victims of the Holocaust in Estonia. The rest were Polish, Lithuanian, Latvian, Czechoslovakian, German, French, Soviet and Hungarian nationals.[2] The physical space facilitating commemoration is missing in Estonia. One can visit the Maskavas neighborhood in Riga, Slobodka suburb in Kaunas, or the former Jewish quarters in Vilnius to see the places where the Jewish ghettos once used to be. No such place exists in Estonia. The former Tallinn Central prison where many male Jews were incarcerated prior to their execution in September 1941 was until very recently off limits to visitors. Situated between farmlands, swamps and industrial zones, the sites of former Jewish slave labor camps gradually decayed into oblivion. Finally, exhibits – a testimony to the crime in legal jargon – are hard to find in Estonia. Consider the following description of the pogrom that took place in Kaunas on 25 June 1941:

> Women with children on their arms pushed their way to the front rows, while laughter and shouts of 'bravo!' echoed to the sound of the iron rods and wooden clubs used to beat the Jews to death. At intervals, one of the killers struck up the national anthem on his accordion, adding to the festive mood of the day. (Kwiet 1998, p. 14)

And then there are the visual images that can be neither denied nor easily forgotten. One photo depicts a healthy looking, blond Lithuanian with a crowbar posing next to the bodies of Jews whom he just had slain. Another photo shows a somewhat older man with rolled-up sleeves just seconds after he had struck a Jew lying on the ground. This did not happen in Estonia. There is no such striking evidence of the crimes committed. Instead, we can talk about a certain distance between perpetrators and victims. The way the Estonian Security Police handled the Jews more closely resembles the archetype of a desk murderer described in the 1960s by Raul Hilberg: those German bureaucrats who shuffled millions of people on paper, while sitting in the quiet of their Berlin offices (Hilberg 1993, pp. 20–50).

Independent Estonia has lacked well-publicized war crimes cases – such as those against Konrāds Kalējs in Latvia or Aleksandras Lileikis in Lithuania – which have sustained a public discussion on local collaboration in the Holocaust. Attempts to influence the Estonian authorities to prosecute former Estonian policeman Harry Männil, who became a successful businessman in Argentina after the War, failed miserably.[3] Although the deportation of alleged war criminal Karl Linnas to the Soviet Union back in 1987 attracted much attention internationally, it is too distant a case to be remembered in today's Estonia. Furthermore, mainstream Estonian journalists and historians-cum-politicians such as Mart Laar have validated the émigré notion of both KGB war crime investigations and American denaturalization trials as a hoax.[4]

Unsurprisingly, ordinary Estonians tend to share this view too. They dismiss legal investigations of war crimes, arguing that the Soviets had already prosecuted all the individuals suspected of any wrongdoings. Those who evaluate Soviet justice as fair at one time but biased at others obviously do not see the irony in their judgments.

Estonian Historiography of the Holocaust

In marked contrast to Lithuania and Latvia, very little has been published on the Holocaust in Estonia since 1991. The first, and until recently the only, book on the mass murder of Estonian Jews was written in 1994 by the former head of the Estonian Jewish community Eugenia Gurin-Loov. Essentially, it is a collection of documents supplemented by a brief history of Jews in Estonia and their destruction during the German occupation. Gurin-Loov should be credited for discovering the investigation files of the Estonian Security Police, which provide a unique perspective on the extermination of Jews in eastern Europe. At the same time she has unwittingly decontextualized the mass murder of Estonian Jews in 1941 by examining it in isolation from the remaining story of the Holocaust in Estonia. Contrary to expectations, the pioneering study by Gurin-Loov has generated no debate. Financed by the Memorial Foundation for Jewish Culture in New York and the Estonian Jewish community, the book was available in just a handful of bookstores and has remained largely unnoticed. The only review of the book to be published locally appeared in a history journal produced by Tartu University; two more reviews followed in English.[5] Peeter Puide – an Estonian writer living in Sweden – has touched upon the subject of collaboration in the Holocaust by using some of the documents uncovered by Gurin-Loov in his novel published in Stockholm in 1997 (Puide 1997). The novel has attracted considerable attention in Sweden, but not in Estonia.

The Estonian edition of the best-selling book by Stéphane Bruchfeld and Paul Levine, *Tell Your Children About It: A Book About the Holocaust in Europe, 1933–1945* (2003), features a fairly comprehensive chapter on Estonia. Its author, Sulev Valdmaa of the Jaan Tõnisson Institute in Tallinn, did not shy away from discussing the issue of collaboration. Valdmaa addressed this problem from a humanistic point of view, without resorting to moralizing. Numerous quotations from original documents further strengthened his argument. Perhaps the only statement in the book that cannot be corroborated by primary sources is Valdmaa's claim that ordinary Estonians extended substantial support to imperiled local Jews. Tartu University professor Uku Masing, whom Valdmaa mentions, is in fact one of only three Estonians recognized by the Yad Vashem Institute in Jerusalem as a Righteous Among the Nations (Bruchfeld & Levine 2003, pp. 85–93). The official number of individuals who assisted Jews in Lithuania and Latvia is 693 and 103 respectively.

In 2001, the Estonian literary magazine *Vikerkaar* printed a special issue dedicated to the Holocaust. Alongside excerpts from books by renowned authors such as Elie Wiesel, Primo Levi, Victor Klemperer and Raul Hilberg, the magazine featured two articles by Estonian historians. Meelis Maripuu and Riho Västrik provided an overview of the Nazi Final Solution in Estonia, paying particular attention to the problem of local collaboration. An extended version of the articles appeared six years later in

English translation, in a single volume published under the aegis of the Estonian International Commission for the Investigation of Crimes Against Humanity. Incredible as it may sound, the reports of the Commission, printed in 2006 in Tallinn under the title *Estonia, 1940–1945*, represent the first and only scholarly treatment of the Holocaust by Estonian historians (Hiio *et al.* 2006). Any attempt to produce an ultimate collection of knowledge, semi-legal in status and symbolically approved by the international community, poses certain problems. Concerns about the mandate of the Commission and the relation between high politics and history writing, however, have been brushed off as overblown.[6]

The Commission for the Investigation of Crimes Against Humanity

The Commission was convened in 1998, and was the first such body in the Baltic, as has been emphasized. The date is significant, as Estonia was entering into talks with the EU and NATO regarding membership in these two organizations. Brussels and Washington hinted that the chances of east European countries becoming club members would increase if they set their historical record straight, first and foremost with regard to indigenous collaboration in the Nazi mass murder of Jews. This explains why the Commission began immediately to investigate crimes committed in Estonia during the German occupation, leaving the period of Soviet occupation for later. For the same reason, the reports have been translated into English. The full name of the working group – the Estonian *International* Commission for the Investigation of Crimes Against Humanity [italics added] – is somewhat misleading. Of the six international members of the Commission only three were historians, and none of them was an expert on either Soviet or Nazi policies. It was an open secret that they were selected on the basis of their 'friendliness' towards Estonia. Furthermore, all of the research was carried out by a team of Estonian historians, mainly MA and PhD students, who were not officially members of the Commission. Unlike the equivalent commissions in Lithuania and Latvia, which featured a mixture of local, émigré and foreign scholars, the Estonian team consisted solely of Estonian nationals.

The volume looks impressive: 1,357 pages printed on high-quality paper with an excellent selection of photographs, good graphs and maps. Weighing 3.5 kg and containing a total of 69 articles divided into six sections, the book reads as an encyclopedia containing everything that one needs to know about the Soviet and German occupations of Estonia. The historians affiliated with the Commission did a good job of combing through Estonian, German and partially Latvian archives. They provide a fairly comprehensive, factual overview, showing a good command of primary sources. The section entitled 'German Occupation of Estonia' consists of 19 articles over 225 pages. In addition to the articles that deal with Soviet investigations of war crimes, seven articles discuss the various stages of the Holocaust in Estonia. The main authors are Maripuu and Västrik. What is missing in this particular section, and throughout the volume, is analysis and interpretation. The reader is left with a massive body of facts, which are often nothing more than statistics. The issue of motivation, which is central to the whole discussion of local collaboration, is only scantily touched upon. The conclusions are almost stereotypical – brutalization brought about by warfare and the desire to avenge the victims of the Soviet regime (Maripuu 2006, p. 661). To explain this and other lacunae in the Reports one needs to take a closer look at the Commission.

The preamble to the Reports is most instructive, as it explains the *raison d'être* of the Commission. In an opening 'Word of Address' to its members, the then President of Estonia Lennart Meri stated that the Commission would not act as a judicial or prosecutorial body. In this regard, one can observe certain parallels with Truth and Reconciliation Commissions, except that in the Estonian case reconciliation was not on the agenda. The 'Statement' by the Commission that follows Meri's introduction, however, strikes a different line from that of the President. It urges the collection of *all* available documentary evidence and calls for the interviewing of all *possible* witnesses, giving the Reports the appearance of legal proceedings. This contravenes a self-evident fact that history cannot be presented as absolute truth, and hence any history work is incomplete. Unfortunately, the Estonian Commission did not take this into consideration when seeking to present as proof the body of facts that it had collected.

The volume displays a tendency to appropriate history. In the 'Reports' that precede the scholarly part of the Commission's publication, the contributing historians assess the degree of criminal responsibility of particular individuals and agencies. In so doing, they unwittingly capitalize on the Nuremberg model. Much like the German SS and the Security Service at Nuremberg, the B-IV department of the Estonian Security Police is proclaimed to be a criminal organization. Once again, they acquire a judicial rather than an interpretive tone. A verdict – guilty or not – has an apparent legal aspect to it. The 'Reports' also contain awkward sentences such as 'we recognize that Estonia and Estonians were a victim nation', which could have been safely omitted for the benefit of solid research done by historians themselves. Even the use of the word 'Estonian' by the Commission is debatable. By considering citizenship rather than ethnicity as a prime form of identification, it has superimposed modern discourse where it does not apply.

More problems appear when the Commission attempts to define the crimes perpetrated against the Jews and other groups in legal terms. The official title, Estonian International Commission for the Investigation of *Crimes Against Humanity* [italics added], is a misnomer. The Commission contradicts itself by acknowledging that the mass murder of Jews and Roma (Gypsies) constitutes genocide and that the deliberate starvation of Soviet prisoners of war is a war crime. To be on the safe side, the Reports reprint the Rome Statute of the International Criminal Court, in particular the articles that deal with crimes against humanity, genocide and war crimes. In the final analysis, however, the Commission fails to fit their findings into the context of international law. Humble attempts to put Nazi and Soviet crimes in a historical perspective proved to be unsuccessful. This comes as no surprise considering the peculiarities of some of the laws that have been enacted in the Baltic states since 1991.

The Baltic legislation on crimes against humanity, genocide, and work crimes entail peculiar interpretations that would make experts on international law raise their eyebrows. For example, the law on the responsibility for the genocide perpetrated against the inhabitants of Lithuania, enacted in April 1992, interprets the destruction of human beings for any purposes as genocide. Therefore, Soviet mass deportations, according to this law, constitute genocide. In May 1998 the then chairman of the Lithuanian parliament Vytautas Landsbergis signed a resolution that declared mass deportations a war crime displaying characteristics of genocide. Another Lithuanian law from June 1997 combines crimes against humanity and war crimes in a single term, 'war crimes against humankind'. To make the application of these and similar laws easier, in July 1998 the President of Lithuania declared the NKVD and KGB criminal organizations that had committed genocide and war crimes against Lithuanian citizens (Lithuanian Parliament 2000, *passim*). Estonian legislation prescribes the intentional killing of anti-Soviet partisans as a crime against humanity. Several judgments in criminal cases resulting in the conviction of defendants have made use of this interpretation.[7] Such legalistic lapses lead to an absurd situation when, for example, in Lithuania most cases evoking charges of genocide deal with crimes committed during the Soviet rather than the Nazi occupation. Turned upside-down, the law prescribes the indictment of individual Jews for genocide of the Lithuanian people (Krichevsky 1997; Tracevskis 2000).

The larger question is whether the Commission has achieved its objectives and if its work has furthered Holocaust awareness among the Estonian population. The main goal has definitely been attained – to show the Western European and American political establishment that the Baltic governments are ready to submit even the most complex aspects of recent history to critical examination. Ironically, the Reports were published *after* Estonia officially joined the NATO and the EU. After all, setting the historical record straight was not the most important criterion for admission. What about the impact of the volume on the historical consciousness of the Estonians? I do not share the cautious optimism of Matthew Kott, who believes that the publication of the Reports will stimulate innovative Holocaust research in Estonia.[8] The Commission set out to produce a definitive study which was factually accurate and legalistically correct. However, one does not usually question a reference work, particularly if it has been approved for publication by an international body. The Commission failed to resolve a dilemma it had been facing since its inception, namely how to reconcile history and law. The way the Commission treated the Holocaust does not open new vistas but rather reinforces old misconceptions. Estonian scholars compartmentalized the history of the Holocaust by dealing separately with the Estonian, Czech/German, Polish/Lithuanian and French Jews. As we know all too well, the Nazis were exterminating the Jewish people not as Estonian, Lithuanian, French, etc. nationals but as Jews. Finally there is a question of accessibility: how many Estonian readers would be willing to spend 750 Estonian crowns (around one-fifth of the minimum wage) for an encyclopedic volume in English that contains information on both Soviet and Nazi occupations?

The Zuroff Controversy and *Vox Populi*

The treatment of the Holocaust in Estonian historiography suggests certain tendencies. However, the works of historians may not always accurately reflect the views of the general public. Because of the marginality of the Holocaust in Estonia, we do not have any official opinion polls to fall back on. The advance of electronic media, however, has provided us with one other source that makes it easier to examine the so-called *vox populi*. Since the late 1990s, nearly all Estonian newspapers have given their readers the option of commenting on any article of interest. Until very recently, the rules and regulations governing the electronic media in Estonia were not strictly enforced, enabling internet users to exchange extreme views.

I have examined the commentaries submitted by the readers of Estonia's two larger dailies and one weekly. I looked specifically at the Holocaust-related articles that were published between 2001 and 2003 in *Postimees*, *Päevaleht* and *Eesti Ekspress*. The fact that of all east European countries Estonia has the highest number of internet users per thousand inhabitants (after Slovenia) makes it a fairly representative sample of the Estonian population. Altogether I read through some 3,000 electronic submissions. Most of the authors use nicknames or do not disclose their identity at all. Frivolous names refer to the younger cohort, whereas older commentators tend to sign their own names. Some names appear more than once, which attests to their interest in the subject. So what are the issues that trigger discussion? Phrased differently and in different contexts, the problem may be formulated as follows: what is the Estonian share in the Holocaust and what should be done with indigenous collaborators, if anything?

The rise of interest, or I should rather say emotions, towards the subject of the Holocaust in Estonia around the year 2002 is not accidental. A particular individual responsible for this development is Efraim Zuroff, the director of the Israel office of the Simon Wiesenthal Center. Having committed his life to hunting former Nazis and their collaborators, Zuroff accused the Estonian authorities of harboring war criminals. Zuroff has leveled similar accusations against the Latvians and the Lithuanians. In the summer of 2002 the US ambassador in Tallinn further inflamed passions by lamenting Estonia's reluctance to prosecute Nazi collaborators. Frustrated by the failure to influence the Baltic governments to open investigations against certain individuals, Zuroff took an unprecedented step by offering a $10,000 reward to anyone who assisted his office in gathering incriminating evidence leading to a successful prosecution. Zuroff called the campaign that he had launched 'The Last Chance'.

The violent response to Zuroff's demarche would surprise even the most experienced scholars of anti-Semitism. All of the centuries-old stereotypes came to the fore: deicide, ritual murder, the Protocols of the Elders of Zion, etc. A number of readers suggested Zuroff should be gassed, processed into soap, or at least declared *persona non grata*. One *Päevaleht* reader asked: 'why is the Jewish nation hated around the world? Are there any wars that have not been organized at least by a few Jews?' 'Europeans hate the Jews', another reader echoed, while one reader, who wrote under the name 'Anti-Juden', declared that 'Zyklon-B would be a good solution – let us just pour it over Jerusalem, only in the Jewish quarters of course'. The following quotation covers pretty much all of the main themes in anti-Semitic folklore in Estonia: 'The Jews want to make Europeans serve them. This is why they are making a good use of the Holocaust myth. They will not be able to play this trick on Estonians, however. We are not going to fall on our knees, begging forgiveness for the non-existent crimes. The Jews have killed Estonians and other peoples en masse, which cries out for another Nuremberg.' One other commentator tried to prove that the USA is essentially a 'Jewish State': 'in some non-Jewish schools one celebrates Hanukkah instead of Christmas!' What is particularly troubling is the resort to crude ethnic stereotypes. For the first time ever members of the Estonian cultural elite such as Eri Klaas and Eino Baskin were addressed as 'Jews' and not as persons.

Most Estonians deny any responsibility for the crimes committed during the Second World War. According to a legalistic argument, Estonia was an occupied country. This supposedly exempts its citizens from personal responsibility and simultaneously denies the Wiesenthal Center the right to appeal to the Estonian state regarding alleged war criminals. According to the 'humanitarian' argument, it does not make any sense whatsoever to prosecute the old men who are going to die soon anyway. If nothing else could stop Zuroff in pursuit of his mission, several readers suggested just ignoring him.

Another peculiar feature of the Holocaust discussion in Estonia during 2002 was its pronounced anti-Russian character. The line of argumentation was as follows: Jewish claims regarding Estonian accountability for wartime atrocities are part and parcel of a plan to prevent Estonia joining the EU and NATO. Of all the international players, Russia is the most interested in cutting short the Estonian *tour de force*. Thus, it is argued, Efraim Zuroff (Efrem Zurov) must be in conspiracy with the Russian Security Service. One reader even remembered having personally known one of Zuroff's relatives who had allegedly resided in the formerly Estonian province of Pechory. 'It is all about politics,' wrote another: 'first there was the Russian minority-discrimination myth, and now it is the Jewish theme'. Bitter at Russia's refusal to acknowledge crimes committed on Estonian territory, several participants in the exchange tried to challenge Zuroff by suggesting his office should start operations in the Russian Federation. At this point it should be noted that local Russians have for the most part refrained from participating in the discussion. The local Russian press, however, seized the opportunity to stress the plight of the ethnic Russian community (more so in Latvia than in Estonia or Lithuania), referring to the 'innate' anti-Semitism of the Baltic peoples as a proof of malicious intent.

The next stage in the popular discussion, predictably, was to link political discourse with a stereotype of money-greedy Jews. Some people argued that the Wiesenthal Center has been investigating Nazi and not Soviet crimes because there were many Jews among the communists. Many communists have entered Israel amongst the masses of Jewish emigrants from the former Soviet Union. Therefore, it is naive to expect that Jewish organizations would support the search for collaborators with the Soviet regime. Even after the last Nazi criminal has died, it is argued, Zuroff would have to find one in order to keep himself busy, that is, to retain his source of income.

The overwhelmingly negative response is suggestive of a very narrow, *quid pro quo* conception of justice and of a tendency to see history in black-and-white terms. Those who do not resort to juxtaposition, it seems, find refuge in relativism. Normally, this proceeds from the general to particular, stating that Jews are not the only ethnic/religious group in human history that has endured suffering, and that conferring a special status upon the Jews would therefore be unfair with respect to Native Americans, Armenians, Gypsies, etc. Other discussants had an altogether different proposition: 'What is important is to concentrate on all things Estonian, while leaving aside others' problems and suffering. There is simply not enough time, money and energy to share it equally among all.' Many Estonians are eager to engage in a rather unproductive comparative victimization contest. In the course of the heated online exchange it was claimed, among other things, that the Estonian nation, which was arguably subjected to genocide, had in fact endured the most suffering in the history of humankind. In this regard, it was predictable that Judeo-Bolshevism should become the next subject for discussion, with claims that the Jews had played a prominent role in dismantling the Estonian State in 1940. By way of illustration, some newspaper readers 'pasted in' extensive excerpts about this or that Soviet official who happened to be Jewish. Finally, the contributors displayed a tendency – widespread in today's Europe – to attack Israel for its policies vis-à-vis the Palestinians. The message could be translated as follows: you, the Jews, have no moral right to judge us!

However vague the idea of justice held by many ordinary Estonians, Zuroff's approach appears to have been equally misguided. According to Zuroff, he pursued a threefold objective when he first came to Estonia: to press for legal investigation in the case of one particular individual; to launch an educational program; and to have justice run its course. Unfortunately, the tactics adopted by Zuroff rendered his efforts futile. What should rightly have become the subject of investigation by legal experts was presented to the general public by Zuroff as a definite proof. In doing this he ignored one of the basic principles of justice – the presumption of innocence. (Zuroff told journalists that he would publicly apologize if his allegations were proved false.) Several discussants pointed out the factual errors in his statements. By offering money in exchange for information, Zuroff also unwittingly invoked the much-despised idea of denunciation, which had been introduced in Estonia mainly by the Soviets. The few sober voices emerging from an otherwise militant public debate hinted that Zuroff might have gained more support if he had chosen a 'more elegant' form of language.

The contribution of Estonian intellectuals to the discussion was at best disappointing. Unable to provide a viable analysis, most newspaper articles and editorials simply ridiculed Zuroff's statements. The authors have failed to find the right language to address the audience and therefore preferred to follow the mainstream. Perhaps the only Estonian intellectual who has made a genuine attempt to reach deep into the Estonian collective memory is Jaan Kaplinski. He has chosen the language of metaphor and hyperbole to deliver his annihilating commentary on Holocaust revisionism, and he does not have any inhibitions when discussing bigotry in contemporary Estonian society. He argues that in order to be able to put national history into perspective, the Estonians have first to remove certain ideological barriers.[9] The problem is that the kind of people who usually read Kaplinksi's writings do not need to be convinced. Those who tend to think in black-and-white categories, however, refuse to listen. As one *Delfi* reader commented in May 2007: 'Kaplinski has never thought of Estonians, but only appealed on behalf of the Jews and the Russians'.

The Estonian Jewish Community

The Estonian Jewish community has remained for the most part passive when it comes to the examination of the most tragic period in its history. Less than 5,000 strong, the local Jewish community stood at the forefront of the minority movement in Estonia in the late 1980s and early 1990s. Alongside Swedish, German, Belorussian, Tartar and other numerically insignificant ethnic groups, the Jews have been viewed by the government as a loyal minority, in contrast to the large Russian minority, which has maintained links to Russia. The minority legislation that has been enacted in independent Estonia caters mainly to the former group, addressing in the first place their cultural needs. Although predominantly Russian-speaking, the Estonian Jews have been careful to distance themselves from any forms of separatism arising from within the local Russian community. At the same time, they have not developed their own agenda for the study and teaching of Jewish history in Estonia, including the Holocaust. In comparison, the Lithuanian Jewish community, which is only marginally larger than its Estonian counterpart, has, since the late 1980s, maintained its own museum with a permanent exhibition on the Holocaust in Lithuania.

The lack of a well-defined position on issues of history (which in eastern Europe tends to be interwoven with politics) came back to haunt Estonia's Jews during the Zuroff controversy, when the community found itself caught between the hammer and the anvil. Zuroff emphasized that he was working in close cooperation with the local Jewish community, and gave the phone number of a Jewish organization in the advertisement that his office had published in newspapers. This elicited a negative response within public opinion, which sought to imply that the local Jewish community was responsible for anything Zuroff had said. Unable to withstand the pressure, the head of the community, Cilja Laud, made a 'gesture of reconciliation', arguing that the Soviet practice of banning Jewish language and culture had amounted to a *cultural Holocaust*. Next, Laud assured the Estonian majority that she personally did not believe that any collaborators in the Holocaust were still alive. Finally, referring to the results of a linguistic study that was commissioned specifically for the purpose, she announced in the name of the Estonian Jewish community that she did not consider the publication of the advertisement by the Wiesenthal Center altogether appropriate. This action definitely improved the image of 'our Jews' in the eyes of some Estonian commentators, but put the semi-independent status of minorities in Estonia in question. If anything, the nature of the discussion suggested that the titular population did not consider the Jews a part of Estonian history.

In this respect, it is notable that a recent initiative to memorialize the sites of Jewish slave labor camps in Estonia originated not in Estonia but in the USA.[10] It was neither the Estonian government nor the local Jewish community but the US Commission for the Preservation of America's Heritage Abroad that had decided to erect markers at these sites, pursuant to a bilateral agreement between Estonia and the USA signed in January 2003. The Commission was established in 1985 with the purpose of preserving the cultural heritage of American citizens of east and central European descent, first and foremost the Holocaust sites. Since the collapse of the Soviet Union in 1991, the Commission has been pursuing a secondary objective of helping those nations aspiring to membership of NATO and the EU to raise the standards of treatment of ethnic and religious minorities. As of 2004, the Commission has identified 5,000 sites in 11 countries (US Commission for the Preservation of America's Heritage Abroad 2004). While striving for historical accuracy, the Commission has not chosen the most efficient mode of operation. When it comes to Holocaust sites, the Commission has established a practice of using local Jewish communities as proxies, including in Estonia. The Jewish communal leaders are expected to collect additional evidence from survivors and their relatives. The problem is that as of 2005 there were only 15 Holocaust survivors in Estonia. Most, if not all, of them had moved to Estonia after the Second World War from other parts of the Soviet Union, and therefore can be of little help when it comes to establishing the facts. At the same time, the invaluable data collected by local enthusiasts such as Boris Lipkin in Sillamäe have remained unutilized.[11] Acting on behalf of the US Commission, the Estonian Jewish community relied on the Estonian International Commission for the Investigation of Crimes Against Humanity for information, without trying to engage with other historians working on the subject. In short, one would expect a more rigorous approach on the part of the US Commission for the Preservation of America's Heritage Abroad in pursuit of its objectives.

Without knowing the context, one might be surprised to hear the explanation of Alexander Dusman, the head of the Jewish communities in East Viru Province, regarding the delay in erecting cenotaphs at the sites of the slave labor camps. He said, among other things, that it was not the best time and that there were some political aspects involved. Otherwise, one would think that the only issue at stake was that of historical memory. Dusman was apparently referring to the controversy surrounding the monument to Estonians who had fought in the ranks of the German Waffen-SS, which was erected at Lihula in August of 2004. The monument was established at the initiative of the local mayor, the notorious nationalist and ardent anti-Semite Tiit Madisson. The then Estonian Prime Minister, apprehensive of negative reactions abroad, ordered the dismantling of the monument, causing a public outcry and a minor government crisis. Nationalist sentiments, peppered by occasional anti-Semitic remarks, flared. Ironically, in October 2005 the monument was re-erected in the grounds of a privately owned museum at Lagedi near Tallinn, without attracting much public attention.[12] The sociologist Andrus Saar warned that in the ideologically charged environment created by the Lihula affair, the erection of new memorials could strain interethnic relations.[13] What both Dusman and Saar meant was that the radical elements in Estonian society would object to the commemoration of Jewish victimhood while the true Estonian patriots, as they see them, are not being acknowledged by their own government. The memory of the Holocaust has prompted a bitter reaction from some Estonians who feel robbed of their status as a victim. The ill-conceived balance theory has also extended into commemoration: if communist crimes were as gruesome as Nazi crimes, then the perpetrators of the latter can only be punished if the perpetrators of the former are put into the dock.

When making a connection between the Holocaust and Estonian history, ordinary Estonians, local politicians, amateur historians and homegrown revisionists tend to speak the same language. The leader of a political party answered the question of why the Holocaust has never become a subject of discussion in Estonia as follows: 'For fifty years the Estonians have been occupied and persecuted by the Soviet power. The West did not help us when Estonians were deported to Siberia. Back then no one protested.... Therefore only few people [in Estonia today] are concerned about the crimes committed during the period of German occupation, however horrible they were' (Kubu 2000, p. 44). A majority of online readers reacted negatively to the introduction of the Holocaust Memorial Day in 2003. The commentators stuck to the 'all-suffered' argument, while alluding to the past experience of official Soviet holidays that had been observed only insincerely. The Estonian officials echoed these sentiments in their statements. In October 2000 the then Minister of Education, Tõnis Lukas, declared that he did not see the need to study the Holocaust or to mark Auschwitz Day in schools. His successor Toivo Maimets three years later suggested linking the commemoration of Holocaust Memorial Day in schools with events marking the mass deportation of Estonians in 1941 and 1949 (The Stephen Roth Institute 2004, 2005). In January 2002 the Jewish community in Tallinn hosted a traveling exhibition about the life of Anne Frank. All of the local Russian schools visited the exhibition, but not a single Estonian school.[14]

Holocaust Denial

Popular attitudes towards the Holocaust and its commemoration in Estonia often carry over into the historical profession. For example, a local historian, Ivika Maidre, argued against what she called 'double marking' of the sites of former Jewish slave labor camps in Estonia. Maidre appears both arrogant and cynical in her argumentation. 'I would understand if those monuments had been put up by some kind of UFOs, but they were actually erected by people', she said about the Soviet-era memorials marking some of the camp sites. According to Maidre, the memorial stone at Vaivara that was erected by the Jewish community in 1994 'had a Star of David and even a piece of barbed wire engraved on it. In other words, everything is already there'. As far as the main camp at Vaivara is concerned, Maidre believes that 'many have an impression that it had been something horrible'. She backs her argument by referring to the fact that the former head of Vaivara camp, Helmut Schnabel, had been sentenced to 16 years of jail, but served only six: 'since he had not been incriminated in anything much after the war, it appears that things were not actually that bad'.[15]

Holocaust denial began making inroads in Estonia in the late 1990s, and has been firmly established since then. The publication of the Estonian translation of Jürgen Graf's infamous *Der Holocaust Schwindel* in 2001 helped to spread the message and to secure a following. In November 2002 the Swiss 'revisionist' made a blitz visit to the Estonian capital and even received an hour on Estonian state TV. The undeserved attention that Graf received in Estonia made some of the participants in the discussion embrace the pseudo-scientific theories that he has been promoting as an authoritative source, though it is mainly Graf's image as a martyr rather than his poorly constructed arguments that appeals to some nationalist Estonians. In 2005 the Estonian revisionists received an institutional cover in the form of a website called

Sõltumatu Infokeskus (Independent Information Center). The Independent Information Center is a reincarnation of an organization established under the same name in 1988, except that it no longer adheres to the guiding principle of 'not promoting ideas that incite violence, racism, and chauvinism'.[16] In the best tradition of the California-based Institute for Historical Review, the Independent Information Center nominally promotes free speech but actually engages with conspiracy theories of various kinds, including 'the Holocaust myth'.[17]

Remarkably, the two best known anti-Semites and Holocaust deniers in Estonia, Jüri Lina (b. 1949) and Tiit Madisson (b. 1950), are former dissidents who at one point were forced to emigrate (Madisson also served a six-year prison sentence). With the Soviet Union gone for good, they have discovered for themselves new enemies in the form of Jews and Freemasons. Lina and Madisson have contributed to the body of revisionist literature by each authoring several books of an anti-Semitic nature. Lina's *Under the Sign of the Scorpion: The Rise and Fall of Soviet Power* (2003) and Madisson's *The New World Order: Secret Activities of the Judaists and Freemasons to Subjugate Nations and States* (2004) and *The Holocaust: The Most Dispiriting Zionist Lie of the 20th Century* (2006) offer the usual mélange of insinuations and untruths from the repertoire of Holocaust deniers. According to Madisson, Hitler's *Mein Kampf* did not contain calls to destroy the Jews; the *Kristallnacht* pogrom of 1938 was a Zionist provocation; the Wannsee Conference had nothing to do with the mass murder of Jews; no Jews were gassed at Auschwitz-Birkenau; and the Nuremberg Tribunal was a hoax; etc. Most of his sources, predictably, come from the internet. Madisson urges his readers to stop cringing before Zionists, as they did in the past before communists, and to break away from the 'Holocaust industry' (referring to the term coined by Norman Finkelstein). Why do Estonians have to commemorate Auschwitz Day and learn about the Holocaust in schools, he asks, while the mass deportation of Estonians has not been attached a universal significance. 'Perhaps because our pain does not matter to the world', Madisson speculates.[18] The latest opus by Madisson – which is designated as 'a book for those who think' – became a bestseller in the bookstore chain *Rahva Raamat* and received several positive reviews.[19] Lina and Madisson appear to be the only east Europeans to enter the pantheon of Holocaust deniers. They have the dubious honor of being listed in an informal top-20 alongside Jean-Marie Le Pen, Mahmoud Ahmadinejad, Ernst Zündel and David Irving.

Holocaust denial is not criminalized in Estonia. Legal mechanisms that would effectively prevent the distribution of this kind of literature are missing (Poleshchuk 2006). The government refuses to interfere, referring to freedom of the press. In spring 1993, bookstores in the Estonian capital received a shipment of anti-Semitic pamphlets called *The Program of Jewish World Conquest* (a reprint from a publication banned in Estonia in 1933). The Justice Ministry had just one suggestion of how to address this issue – to file a court case. In the end, the store managers yielded to the request of a member of the local Jewish community to remove the pamphlet from the shelves. Two months later, however, the same lampoon was printed in Tartu under the title *The Protocols of the Elders of Zion*. The publisher ended up in court; the court of first instance in Tartu dismissed the case, but the court of second instance prohibited the circulation (Saks 2003).

Anti-Semitism in Estonia: Aberration or Tendency?

How far has anti-Semitism permeated the fabric of Estonian society? The reluctance to reopen war crime cases, the rise of Holocaust denial, the lack of comprehensive historical studies and the failure to see the long-term benefits of Holocaust education can all be viewed as part of a larger phenomenon. As always, it is most difficult to make generalizations about the so-called 'ordinary people', the 'common folk', or simply the 'masses'. The aggressive response to Zuroff's campaign might be circumstantial, and the anti-Russian attitudes might be caused by anxiety on the eve of joining the EU, as some newspaper readers did indeed suggest. To check whether this explanation holds water, I chose at random an article on a relevant topic a few years down the line. My eye caught an article with a provocative title, 'Are the Estonians Judeophobes?', which appeared on 3 March 2005, on the *Delfi* internet portal. By that time Estonia had already become an EU member, the Zuroff controversy no longer received prime-time coverage, and the Lihula affair was almost a year old. In other words, there was nothing that could spark immediate reaction. The article itself was less instructive than the responses it had generated – to be precise 422 commentaries at the time of reading – which shows a profound interest on the part of the readers.

The article was written by Aavo Savitsch, who signed in using the pseudonym 'person interested in history' (*ajaloohuviline*). Since the time of writing Savitsch has developed into a full-fledged Holocaust denier. Although Savitsch does not directly address the question he has posed, the arguments used suggest a positive answer. The arguments are old: Jews suffered but so did other nations, including the Estonians; individual Jews who served in the NKVD tortured Estonians; the more we hear about the six million victims of the Holocaust, the more exaggerated that number appears; so many decades have elapsed since the end of World War Two that we should let the dead rest in peace and not work them into the foundation of a certain state (Savitsch 2005).

The commentaries can be divided by major themes, which are as easily identifiable as they are predictable. Judging by the number of messages that attack Zuroff, he has left a lasting impression on the Estonians. The readers prove quite imaginative, fantasizing about tortures to which they want to subject Zuroff. 'Thank you, Efroim, for having taught us to hate Jews!' concludes one contributor. Jews supposedly hate all other nations, and also themselves. What is even worse, 'a few among the Jews who mistreated Estonians are certainly still around'.

Some of the discussants suggest a 'final solution to the Jewish problem' either in the form of emigration or physical violence. A reader who identified himself as 'Liberty' exclaimed: 'the article gets ten points, and all the Zionists get the hell out of here!' 'SS' puts it more eloquently: 'Every Jew is a moving advertisement for the next Holocaust!' Attempts to appeal to well-known historical facts prompt even more hostile reactions. Thus, 'Gabriel' wrote that thousands of Jews had been murdered in Estonia with the help of the locals, and that Estonia was the first country in Europe proclaimed *judenfrei*. In response, someone threatens: 'we will kill even more [of them] if you do not shut up!'

Particularly striking is the inability to sustain a dialog. Those who share the views expressed in the article (an overwhelming majority) rarely cross swords with opponents. Inattentive to what the other side is saying, discussants immediately propose to put their antagonists against the wall. A certain Aleksandrov, writing entirely in capital letters, praises the French law on Holocaust denial and laments the negative effects of freedom of speech in Estonia, claiming that those individuals who maintain that the Nazis did not seek the annihilation of Jews should be fined, jailed or even executed. In response, someone suggests killing off people like Aleksandrov who 'promote the Holocaust myth'. Another contributor, meanwhile, threatens to start 'hanging all the damn NKVD people' who insist that Estonians are Judeophobes.

Although homophobic attitudes do not transpire in the discussion surrounding the Holocaust and anti-Semitism, anti-Russian sentiments feature prominently. One contributor, for instance, wonders where anti-Semitism came from: 'Ten years ago there was no other hostility but hostility towards the Russians. Jews should probably blame themselves for that'. Another states plainly that, 'Estonians [only] hate Russians. Jews do not belong under discussion'. Several readers believe that anti-Semitism has been deliberately promoted in Estonia by the Russian security service in an attempt 'to spread hostile information about Estonians' and 'to pitch Jews and Israel against Estonia and vice versa'. As often happens, those who preach anti-Semitism also tend to be xenophobic. The way 'Rgu' and 'Ma' write about Africans refers to the same phenomenon. 'Rgu': 'I like Arabs even less. Even Negroes are ok'; 'Ma': 'False political correctness is when you cannot tell a Negro he is a Negro, since it is considered offensive . . . . I used to have a positive attitude towards the Jews. Now, however, my blood pressure rises when I hear the word "Jew". In no time I have turned into a Jew-hater'.

Those among the Estonians who have been unable to face the Holocaust are employing the usual set of arguments to negate it. The most predictable is denial. For a particular individual Savitsch's article was a revelation: 'I am very glad that someone has dared to describe also the other side, and not what Jews have been telling [us]'. Many readers are eager to engage in the number-game: 'The figure, six million Jews, has been falsified. In reality, the Nazis killed a few thousand communists, whom Estonians would have cleansed sooner or later anyway'. The ongoing conflict in the Middle East provides a further excuse for ignorance: 'The number of Jewish victims in Germany is bluff, chutzpah'. '[E]in Mensch' went further than any other commentator-denier, by praising Hitler and his policies: 'Such extraordinary individuals like Hitler get born once in hundreds of thousands of years. Hitler sacrificed his country and himself to save Europe from destruction. If it had not been for him, we would not be speaking Estonian now. Hitler was aware what he did when he adopted his racial laws. It was simply a question of survival. If it had not been for Hitler, the Jews would have seized power in Germany, and history would have turned bloodier . . .' Remarkably, 'ein Mensch' has drawn some criticism from his pen pals, not because of his bigotry, though, but rather because of his adoration of all things German.

The most potent conduit of Holocaust denial in Estonia is, however, historical relativism. A majority of Estonians have used the recent history of their country, the Soviet period in particular, as a measuring stick of human suffering/cruelty. This attitude was spelled out in a sentence by one of the contributors: 'As if we had not suffered!' The online readers keep repeating the same argument over and over again: 'Believe me, Estonians suffered more than the Jews during the war and the subsequent Soviet occupation'; 'Estonians did not have it easy either. We have been terrorized for long fifty years, but carry on living and do not whimper much. You better shut up, Jews!' One can often encounter the following exposition: 'What is so special about the Jews, that the international media is talking about them and their problems all the time? Why not other nations and their problems? For example, why have those who murdered Estonians not been prosecuted in Russia?' The idea of Estonia as a victim nation makes commemoration of the Holocaust redundant. As one of the *Delfi* discussants stated: 'True Estonians will never lower their heads before Jewish suffering because we have endured even worse suffering. Americans and Jews do not understand that!' One after another, commentators discard the Holocaust and its commemoration as something that allegedly belittles the Estonians' trauma and provokes resentment. The discussion stalls when someone suggests: 'Commemorate your Holocaust – why should we be bothered – but do not expect us to howl along!' Some argued that, 'the time has come to close this chapter and carry on with one's life'. The older generation of internet users not only reject the need for Holocaust education but also assert their right to impose this view on their offspring. 'Capone' sides with Holocaust deniers when he exclaims: 'And why should my children study . . . this shit, which is apparently exaggerated and sometimes built directly on lies?'

It would be erroneous to conclude that anti-Semitism and Holocaust denial in Estonia is nothing but a result of the collective trauma inflicted by the Stalinist USSR. Even if we decide for a moment to overlook the most extreme views, popular opinion superimposes the notion that Jews do not belong to Estonian history. The following commentary by one of the *Delfi* contributors is fairly representative of that mindset: 'For some reason, the discussion as to whether Estonians are anti-Semites reoccurs when we commemorate our history and suffering. Jews do not respect other peoples' history. Otherwise why do they consider themselves the chosen people?' Commentaries such as 'I do not believe that this problem will disappear until after the last Jew has vanished from planet earth' sound almost weird in the Estonian context. The Estonian Jewish community has shrunk by more than 50% (from 4,613 to 1,818) over the past 18 years, becoming virtually invisible. At the same time, many online readers argue that their attitudes towards the Jews started changing for the worse only recently. The irony is that as soon as Jews attempted to assert their identity – of which the Holocaust is an essential part – emerging from the rubble of the 'family of Soviet peoples' myth, they made many of their former 'relatives' feel uncomfortable. The numbers do not actually matter. Jean-Paul Sartre had pointedly described this phenomenon in his essay, 'Anti-Semite and Jew' (1948). Circumstances and names change but the emotional response stays the same. The name of this negative emotion is anti-Semitism, and there are many people in Estonia who harbor it.

Naturally, not all of the individuals who express their opinion on the internet are hostile towards the Jews. The minority of voices that are not sound depressed and pessimistic: 'Just read those commentaries. Hostility is definitely there. Do Estonians themselves not like [discussing] the theme of deportation and suffering? Continually! All the time! Do you not get tired of it?' Someone had followed the discussion very closely: 'At the moment we have got 387 commentaries, 95 percent of which condemn the Zionist cult of Holocaust as pseudoscientific, among them school kids and people with somewhat better writing skills'. One other reader went even further in his or her conclusions: 'Most (perhaps 99 percent) commentators who have been bashing Jews in Delfi.ee have not acquired even basic norms of ethics and behavior. It is unfortunate that people of the older generation harbor hatred and hostility. I think that one should be blaming one's parents, not the Jews'. The saddest part is that during the entire discussion only one individual was able to explain what makes the Holocaust different from other forms of mass violence: 'You should understand that whether Jews were killed on a lesser or larger scale than the others does not matter. What matters is that were killed because of their ETHNICITY!'

Conclusions

Not without reason, anti-Semitism has been described as a litmus test for any given nation. The perceptions of the Holocaust in Estonia thus project the views of ordinary Estonians with regard to their history. The Estonians seem to be engrossed in their past. Age difference appears to play no role in the popular perception of communism as a quintessential evil. The reflections on recent history, unexpectedly, have given a boost to latent anti-Semitism. Peculiar to Estonia, Stars of David (along with friendly advice to leave for Israel) that occasionally appear on the walls of buildings in larger cities sometimes contain swastikas, at other times a hammer and a sickle. The discussion on the Holocaust in Estonia has also revealed certain insecurities about regained independence. One internet commentator argued that altogether the Estonians have an inferiority complex. Many Estonians are afraid to acknowledge that some of their countrymen committed crimes against the Jews because they believe that by so doing they would stain the reputation of the new democracy. In effect, this makes it even harder to get out of the state of denial and to face the challenges posed by modernity.

The Holocaust runs counter to the Estonian (read: Baltic) national narrative. The Jews, who had been marginalized as a minority, appear to have claimed a victim status reserved for the titular population. This has served to revive old stereotypes, from deicide and treachery to greed and behind-the-scenes manipulation. In the current political context, the myth of Judeo-Bolshevism has been replaced (or rather augmented) by a similar myth of the Russo-Jewish conspiracy. Some Estonians suspect the hand of Moscow behind the calls of the Simon Wiesenthal Center to prosecute the few surviving Nazi collaborators. Ironically, the upsurge of anti-Semitism occurred in the run-up to EU ascension. The peculiarity of anti-Jewish sentiment in Estonia, marked by the references to the Soviet occupation period, adds value to Sartre's analysis of 'anti-Semitism without Jews'. No matter what the primary cause, latent anti-Semitism may come to the fore when and where we least expect it. Unfortunately, the Estonian case teaches us exactly that.

We should thus abandon the fiction that Estonia and Estonians are somehow unique in the context of eastern Europe, and immune to the bacillus of anti-Semitism. The references to the benevolent treatment of the Jewish minority and low levels of anti-Semitism in interwar Estonia obscure rather than help to explain the reasons why some Estonians decided to collaborate in the Nazi mass murder of Jews. The figures of economic growth, high computer literacy, political stability and journalistic transparency cannot, and should not, deflect attention from the problems intrinsically connected to recent Estonian history and its interpretations. One needs simply to scratch the surface in order to find lurking behind it banal, blatant, inexplicable anti-Semitism. At the same time I acknowledge the limitations of my analysis. What cannot be answered with certainty is whether Estonians are more anti-Semitic now than they were, say, 15 years ago. One can only speculate what the electronic media could have revealed if it were as advanced in 1991 as it is in 2007.

In the face of rising anti-Semitism in Estonia, the position adopted by the representatives of the local Jewish community leaves one puzzled. The head of the Estonian Jewish community keeps pronouncing from high tribunes that the Estonian government has condemned anti-Semitism in Estonia, that the Jewish community is highly regarded in Estonia, and that the Estonians are learning how to appreciate the suffering of other peoples. Simultaneously, she has emphasized that one cannot learn only from negative examples, encouraging her audiences not to base their conclusions about the level of anti-Semitism in Estonia on 'single negative incidents'.[20] It appears almost as if the leadership of the Jewish community has bought into the popular anti-Semitic discourse. As one internet user urged: 'Estonian Jews: do not submit yourself to Zuroff's provocations, but continue living your life in peace. Zuroffs do not care about you or the Holocaust. They are using the Holocaust as their last chance to squeeze money from other nations'. I cannot help wondering whether this is blindness, self-deception or a deliberate attempt to pass over a problem in silence.

The greatest challenge is to explain to Estonians, Latvians and Lithuanians the difference between Auschwitz and Kolyma, without rushing to emphasize the 'uniqueness' of the Holocaust. The context is everything. There is a strong need to put the Holocaust, as it played out in the Baltic, into the general history of the Nazi Final Solution. In other words, the Baltic scholarly community has to help the critical mass of citizens to break through the narrow confines of national history. Only then may ordinary Estonians, Latvians and Lithuanians be able to face the issue of collaboration and the lasting consequences of denial *sine ira et studio*. Although the new status of EU member state has not performed miracles in this respect, it may prove beneficial in the long run. It is also clear that due to latent anti-Semitism anything coming from Jewish groups will be considered biased in Estonia. This automatically increases the role of local agencies – historians, intellectuals, politicians, NGOs, etc. An emphasis on the rule of law and constructive debate, macro thinking and universal justice would make Estonia's entry into the era of globalization smoother. And who said that history is not part of the globalization process?

Notes

1 The facts are derived from my forthcoming book, *Murder Without Hatred: Estonians and the Holocaust* (Syracuse University Press).

2 Eight Jews were deported to Estonia from Finland in November 1942, but none of these held Finnish citizenship. Upon arrival, all of them were executed.

3 Männil was one of several deserters from the Red Army hidden by a Jewish woman, Miriam Lepp, in the summer of 1941. She was executed on 13 July 1942. One can only speculate whether Männil as a policeman was aware of her arrest and whether he did anything to save her from death.

4 See, for example: Lepassalu (1998, pp. 1–2); Kaldre (1998, pp. 1–7); Jõgeda (2000). Laar wrote that Tallinn Police Prefect Evald Mikson was not guilty (*Miksonil ei ole süüd*). In December 1941 the German Security Police arrested Mikson on charges of torturing prisoners and misappropriating their valuables. He was not released until two years later. The Estonian State Archives in Tallinn contain several documents from August and September 1941 with Mikson's signature authorizing the execution of individual Jews.

5 Weiss-Wendt (1997, pp. 53–5); Levin (1997, pp. 297–300); Weiss-Wendt (1998, pp. 193–95).

6 See the exchange between A. Weiss-Wendt and T. Hiio in *Vikerkaar* (Weiss-Wendt & Hiio 2001).

7 A. Jaarma, 'Nõukogude okupatsiooni poolt 1940–1950-ndail aastail Eestis toime pandud sõja- ja inimsusevastaste kuritegude uurimine ja inimsusevastaste kuritegude eest vastutusele võtmine', lecture delivered at the Estonian National Library in Tallinn on 24 April 2001.

8 See Kott's book review in *Holocaust and Genocide Studies* (2007, p. 323). Eva-Clarita Onken, who evaluated the volume as part of a recent review article in *Journal of Baltic Studies*, is also pessimistic about its ability to encourage debate and critical reflection (Onken 2007, p. 112).

9 See Kaplinski's exposé, for example, in *Vikerkaar* (2001, pp. 214–19).

10 There were 19 such camps in Estonia (going from east to west): Narva, Narva-Jõesuu, Auvere, Putke, Vaivara, Viivikonna, Soska, Kuremäe, Jõhvi, Ereda, Kohtla, Saka, Kiviõli, Sonda, Aseri, Kunda, Jägala, Lagedi and Klooga. Jägala and Lagedi were not, strictly speaking, 'labor camps'. Larger camps such as Viivikonna, Kiviõli and Ereda were effectively subdivided into two sections; hence the disparity in numbers of Jewish slave labor camps in Estonia as they appear in various accounts. In addition, the Germans operated five smaller camps in northwestern Russia, southern Estonia and northern Latvia, which were in existence for only a brief period.

11 Starting from the late 1980s Lipkin, who is not affiliated with the Jewish community, began mapping the former sites of Jewish slave labor camps at Viivikonna and Vaivara and interviewing farmers who had lived in the vicinity of the camps. The material thus collected has been published in a local newspaper and is available at a local museum.

12 Between 29 July and 18 September 1944, Lagedi was the site of a makeshift Jewish camp. The camp was located across from the train station and housed 2,050 Jewish prisoners from Ereda who were awaiting a further deportation to Stutthof concentration camp. On 18 September an estimated 426 Jews who had been previously transferred to Lagedi from Klooga were executed in a nearby forest.

13 *Põhjarannik*, 18 September 2004; *Postimees*, 10 September 2004.

14 The Round Table meeting on minority issues by the Estonian President (2002) minutes, 10 June, available at: http://vp2001-2006.vpk.ee/et/institutsioonid/ymarlaud.php?gid=24080, accessed 5 July 2007. This does not imply that ethnic Russians on the whole are less prone to anti-Semitism than Estonians.

In March 2004, two individuals were detained in Sillamäe – a city with a predominantly Russian-speaking population – for painting anti-Semitic slogans and swastikas on the walls of a building.

15 *Põhjarannik*, 18 September 2004. Schnabel had been part of the Nazi camp administration since 1934, first at Sulza in Thuringia and then at Buchenwald. Many Holocaust survivors have identified Schnabel as the individual who had carried out selections at Vaivara. He was implicated in homicide at Viivikonna and Narva camps and oversaw the liquidation of Ereda camp.

16 http://si.kongress.ee/?a=page&page=43e129325acc205ba5ece&subpage=42f293855c1750876fbc, accessed 2 August 2007.

17 See organization website at: http://si.kongress.ee/. According to the website, the organization was founded in response to the parliament's decision to drop the territorial claims to Russia (based on the Tartu Peace Treaty of 1920). The unilateral decision of the Estonian President to seek membership in the EU was cited as another unlawful act that warranted intervention.

18 Lina (2003); Madisson (2004, 2006). See also Lina's article in *Eesti Aeg*, 8 April 1992. In his first book Madisson blamed the Jews for masterminding both World Wars and the Bolshevik Revolution, financing Hitler, and planning a conspiracy to rule the world.

19 See, for example, Piirisild (2006) and A. Savitsch's review on the website of the Independent Information Center, 1 August 2007, available at: http://si.kongress.ee/?a=page&page=42e12d241a164247355b6&subpage=45016c51ddfee722755eb, accessed 1 August 2007.

20 'Statement by the President of the Estonian Jewish Community Mrs. Cilja Laud', delivered on her behalf at the OSCE Conference on Anti-Semitism in Cordoba on 8 June 2005, available at: http://www.osce.org/documents/cio/2005/06/15052_en.pdf+Statement+by+the+President+of+the+Estonian+Jewish+Community+Mrs.+Cilja+Land%E2%80%90,&hl=no&ct=clnk&cd=1&gl=ee, accessed 30 July 2007.

References

Bruchfeld, S. & Levine, P. (2003) *Jutustage sellest oma lastele: Raamat holokaustist Euroopas aastatel 1933–1945* (Tartu, Israeli Sõbrad), pp. 85–93.

Hiio, T., *et al.* (2006) *Estonia, 1940–1945: Reports of the Estonian International Commission for the Investigation of Crimes Against Humanity* (Tallinn, Tallinn Publishing House).

Hilberg, R. (1993) *Perpetrators, Victims, Bystanders: The Jewish Catastrophe, 1933–1945* (London, Lime Tree).

Jõgeda, T. (2000) 'Kuidas Tartu koonduslaagri ülemast Karl Linnasest nõukogude sõjatrofee tehti', *Kes/Kus*, May.

Kaldre, P. (1998) 'Wiesenthali vendeta', *Luup*, 12, June, pp. 1–7.

Kaplinski, J. (2001) 'Mida need juudid ometi tahavad?', *Vikerkaar*, 15, 8–9, August–September, pp. 214–19.

Kott, M. (2007) 'Book review (*Estonia 1940–1945: Reports of the Estonian International Commission for the Investigation of Crimes Against Humanity* (Tallinn: Tallinn Publishing House, 2006)', *Holocaust and Genocide Studies*, 21, 2, Fall, p. 323.

Krichevsky, L. (1997) 'Lithuania May Indict Jews for Genocide', *Jewish News of Greater Phoenix*, 50, 11, December.

Kubu, M. (2000) *Sverige og Estland/Rootsi ja Eesti* (Trelleborg, The Swedish Institute), p. 44.

Kwiet, K. (1998) 'Rehearsing for Murder: The Beginning of the Final Solution in Lithuania in June 1941', *Holocaust and Genocide Studies*, 12, 1, Spring, p. 14.

Lepassalu, V. (1998) 'Kas eestlased olid massimõrvarid?', *Luup*, 9, May, pp. 1–2.

Levin, D. (1997) 'Book Review, The Holocaust of the Estonian Jews, 1941', in Frankel, J. (ed.) (1997) *The Fate of the European Jews, 1939–45: Continuity or Contingency?* (New York & Oxford, Oxford University Press), pp. 297–300.

Lina, J. (2003) *Skorpioni märgi all: Nõukogude võimu tõus ja langus* (Stockholm, Referent).

Lithuanian Parliament (2000) *Foreign Power: Excerpts from Lithuanian Laws on Communism, Occupation, Resistance* (Vilnius, Lithuanian Parliament).

Madisson, T. (2004) *Maailma uus kord: Judaiistide ja vabamüürlaste varjatud tegevus rahvaste ning riikide allutamisel* (Lihula, Ohvrikivi).

Madisson, T. (2006) *Holokaust: XX sajandi masendavaim sionistlik vale* (Lihula, Ohvrikivi).

Maripuu, M. (2006) 'Execution of Estonian Jews in Local Detention Institutions in 1941–42', in Hiio, T. *et al.* (2006), p. 661.

Onken, E.-C. (2007) 'The Politics of Finding Historical Truth: Reviewing Baltic History Commissions and their Work', *Journal of Baltic Studies*, 38, 1, March, p. 112.

Piirisild. J. (2006) 'Tiit Madisson juutide vandenõust', *Pärnu Postimees,* 19 April.

Poleshchuk, V. (2006) *Estonian Minority Population and Non-Discrimination*, Report (Tallinn, Legal Information Center for Human Rights), p. 21f, available at: http://www.lichr.ee/docs/cerd-final.pdf, accessed 1 August 2007.

Puide, P. (1997) *Samuil Braschinskys försvunna vrede. Dokumentärroman* (Stockholm, Norstedts).

Saks, E. (2003) *Kes on juudid ja mis on Holokaust?* (Tallinn, Sild), p. 147.

Savitsch, A. (2005) 'Kas eestlased on juudivaenulikud? 3 March, available at: http://www.delfi.ee/archives/print.php?id=9888280, accessed 29 July 2007.

The Stephen Roth Institute for the Study of Contemporary Anti-Semitism and Racism at Tel Aviv University (2004, 2005) *Annual Report: Baltic States*, available at: http://www.tau.ac.il/Anti-Semitism/; http://www.tau.ac.il/Anti-Semitism/asw2005/baltics.htm, accessed 2 August 2007.

Tracevskis, M. (2000) 'Law Opens Way for Genocide Home Trials', *The Baltic Times*, 16–22 March.

US Commission for the Preservation of America's Heritage Abroad (2004) *Report to the Congress and the President of the United States of America*, 2–7, 20–21, available at: http://www.heritageabroad.gov./reports/doc/2004_Report.pdf, accessed 7 July 2007.

Weiss-Wendt, A. (1997) 'Eestlased, lätlased ja Holocaust', *Kleio*, 19, 1, pp. 53–5.

Weiss-Wendt, A. (1998) 'Book review (Eugenia Gurin-Loov, *Suur Häving: Eesti juutide katastroof/The Holocaust of the Estonian Jews*)', *Holocaust and Genocide Studies*, 12, 1, Spring, pp. 193–5.

Weiss-Wendt, A. (2009) *Murder Without Hatred: Estonians and the Holocaust* (Syracuse, NY, Syracuse University Press).

Weiss-Wendt, A. & Hiio, T (2001) 'Inimsusevastaste Kuritegude Uurimise Eesti Rahvusvahelise Komisjoni tööst', *Vikerkaar*, 15, 8–9, August–September, pp. 220–24.

HISTORY AS CULTURAL MEMORY: MNEMOHISTORY AND THE CONSTRUCTION OF THE ESTONIAN NATION

Marek Tamm

The question I want to address in this essay is a quite simple one, if not simplistic: what do Estonians remember of their past? More specifically, my intention is to analyse how the memories of different groups that make up the Estonian nation 'are conveyed and sustained' (Connerton 1989, p. 1). For this, I will focus mostly on the origins and nature of the narrative logic which enables one to pull a set of events from a nation's past together into a coherent whole. However, before addressing this question, I would like to discuss the conceptual framework of my approach. In the last few decades, the theoretical language of collective memory has become increasingly important to historical and sociological research on how societies construct and understand what went before.[1] This orientation to the study of how collectivities make sense of their own present through recourse to reconstructed narratives of their past also offers important insights to scholars of national identity.

History, Memory and Mnemohistory

It is widely known that the concept of memory was introduced to current debates by way of its opposition to history. Although I would rather not open a Pandora's Box by starting a discussion about the relationship between the two, one cannot skip this problem entirely. I do not subscribe to the view that history and memory are more or less the same thing and that distinguishing between them is a useless exercise. At the same time, as Klein (2000, p. 127) has observed, 'the declaration that history and memory are not really opposites has become one of the clichés of our new memory discourse'. In exploring this complex interrelationship, first, we have to remind ourselves that the notion of history and memory as distinguishable from each other is a recent invention.[2] It is a cultural construction which came about at a certain moment in time and which is linked to general changes in Western historical culture at the end of the eighteenth and the beginning of the nineteenth century (Assmann, A. 2006, p. 44; 2008, pp. 58–61). At that time, the idea of the past began to lose its exemplary meaning, and the concepts of the past and the present were divided. Equally importantly, historical writing became more and more the preserve of a small scholarly circle (Koselleck 2004). The juxtaposition of history with memory gained theoretical legitimacy at the beginning of the twentieth century, when Maurice Halbwachs in particular defined the concept of 'collective memory' by way of contrast to history (Halbwachs 1997, pp. 131–5).

Secondly, I find that history and memory are not equal concepts to contrast. The forced opposition between them seems to derive from an urge to validate a new historical discipline, rather than being a reflection of their actual relationship; it 'is a matter of disciplinary power rather than of epistemological privilege' (Olick & Robbins 1998, p. 110). To my mind, it is much more appropriate to treat *history as a mode of remembering*, as a mnemonic practice (e.g. Assmann, A. 2003, pp. 133–4; Olick 2007, p. 10; Olick & Robbins 1998; Suleiman 2006, p. 48). From this perspective, history is first of all a subcategory of memory. This approach was formulated best by Peter Burke in his article first published in 1989, '*History as Social Memory*'. Burke states that the 'traditional account of the relation between memory and written history, in which memory reflects what actually happened and history reflects memory, now seems much too simple' (1997, pp. 43–4). He continues by arguing that, 'many recent studies of the history of historical writing treat it much as Halbwachs treated memory, as the product of social groups such as Roman senators, Chinese mandarins, Benedictine monks, university professors and so on' (p. 45). Following Burke, but relying on concepts introduced by Jan and Aleida Assmann, I would like to argue that the most fruitful way to comprehend history is to consider it as a particular form of cultural memory.

What does the notion of 'cultural memory' mean? Jan Assmann has proposed a fourfold typology of collective memory: material memory, based on objects; mimetic memory, based on imitation; communicative memory, based on oral discussion; and cultural memory, based on written and visual carriers of information (Assmann 1999). In terms of history, the distinction between communicative and cultural memory is especially useful. While the former corresponds to the earliest phase when multiple narratives by eyewitnesses circulate and compete with each other, the latter corresponds to a much longer phase when all participants have died out, and a society has only traces and stories left as a reminder of past experience (Assmann 1999, pp. 48–65; Assmann 2006, p. 27; Rigney 2005, p. 14). Cultural memory, in Assmann's definition, 'comprises that body of reusable texts, images, and rituals specific to each society in each epoch, whose "cultivation" serves to stabilize and convey that society's self-image' (Assmann 1995, p. 132).

Cultural memory helps us to understand the formation of national identity and the role of representations of the past in that identity. Assmann writes: 'Cultural memory preserves the store of knowledge from which a group derives an awareness of its unity and peculiarity. The objective manifestations of cultural memory are defined through a kind of identificatory determination in a positive ("We are this") or in a negative ("That's our opposite") sense' (Assmann 1995, p. 130). Historical writing is therefore inseparable from cultural memory. Cultural memory determines the general framework within which the past acquires a meaning and history becomes possible. Concurrently, cultural memory determines the events to be recorded and passed on. Or, in Assmann's words: 'Cultural memory has its fixed point; its horizon does not change with the passing of time. These fixed points are fateful events of the past, whose memory is maintained through cultural formation (texts, rites, monuments) and institutional communication (recitation, practice, observance)' (Assmann 1995, p. 129).

However, it is important to take into account that cultural memory is not so much a reservoir in which traces of the past are gradually deposited by some ongoing spontaneous process. Instead, it is the historical product of cultural mnemotechniques and mnemotechnologies, which range from commemorative rituals to history writing (Rigney 2004, p. 366). Yurii Lotman, one of the initiators of the 'cultural memory' concept, had already emphasized in 1985 that 'memory is not for the culture a passive depository, but part of its mechanism of textual creation' (Lotman 2000, p. 676).[3] Cultural memory is governed by a logic of relevance that gives priority to certain aspects of the past and sidelines others. Therefore, cultural memory studies have to focus on the multiple ways in which images of the past are communicated to and shared among the members of a community, highlighting the importance of remembering certain parts of the past and forgetting or ignoring others.

In order to analyse the workings of cultural memory, the ongoing process of shaping an identity by reconstructing its past, Jan Assmann has proposed the concept of mnemohistory. 'Unlike history proper, mnemohistory is concerned not with the past as such, but only with the past as it is remembered' (Assmann 1997, p. 9). Mnemohistory relinquishes a positivistic investigation of the past in favour of a research into the actuality, not into the factuality of the past. 'Mnemohistory is reception theory applied to history', writes Assmann, 'but "reception" is not to be understood here merely in the narrow sense of transmitting and receiving. The past is not simply "received" by the present. The present is "haunted" by the past and the past is modelled, invented, reinvented, and reconstructed by the present' (Assmann 1997, p. 9). This new research agenda had already been formulated by Pierre Nora some years earlier in his preface to the third volume of the famous *Les lieux de mémoire*:

> The road is open for a totally different history: instead of determinants, their effects; instead of actions remembered or commemorated, the marks they have left and the games of commemoration; not events for their own sake, but their construction in time, the gradual disappearance and reappearance of their significances; instead of the past as it was, its constant re-exploitation, utilization and manipulation; not the tradition itself, but the way it was constituted and transmitted. (Nora 1992, p. 24)

A philosophical formulation of the same kind of approach can also be found in the work of Hans-Georg Gadamer. Gadamer argues that whenever we seek to understand a historical phenomenon we are always already subject to the effects of what he calls 'effective history' (*Wirkungsgeschichte*). By effective history Gadamer means the history of the event or other item as understood and interpreted. In understanding a historical phenomenon, our understanding, whether we are aware of it or not, is conditioned by the history of its interpretation. Gadamer stresses also that the history of the interpretations of an event is not something external to the event but constitutes the self-unfolding of the event itself (Gadamer 2004, pp. 299–306).[4]

Narrating the Nation: Stories we Live by

As argued previously, cultural memory entails constant shaping of the past, during which it is determined what should be preserved and what should be forgotten. Several people engage in this memory work, particularly the 'six P's', as they are wittily called by Reinhart Koselleck: priests, professors, PR specialists, politicians, poets and publicists (Tamm 2007, p. 115). In modern times, it is historians who have probably been the most influential in shaping the nation's representation of the past, trading places with poets and publicists of earlier times. Jörn Rüsen notes aptly that 'modern states use academic history in order to prepare specialists for the shaping and legitimization of historic identity' (Rüsen 1989, p. 60).

But although many individuals are actively engaged in this memory work, an equally important role is played by cultural tools, such as narrative (Brockmeier 2002; Wertsch 1998, 2002, 2004, 2008). As I argue below in my analysis of the remembrance of Estonian past, narrative is one of the most influential shapers of cultural memory. A nation can be viewed not just as a 'mnemonic community' (Booth 2006; Zerubavel 2003), but also as a 'narrative community'. The narrative defines a boundary between members who share the common past and those who do not (Seixas 2003, p. 6). National identity is, to a large extent, based on 'stories we live by'.[5] More precisely, the identity is based on narrative templates, which give coherence to a nation's past. Coherence is one of the cornerstones of collective identity: repetition and consistency constitute the two most important attributes of a nation's historical consciousness (Assmann, A. 1993, pp. 52–7). The narrative form allows the nation to be imagined as continuous, and for discrete events to be interlinked into a meaningful history, rather than letting them appear as one odd thing after another. Consequently, different historical events come to acquire meaning when included as part of a general narrative template.[6]

As noted by James Wertsch (2002, p. 62), a particular set of these narrative templates form what David Lowenthal calls a 'textual heritage'. This concept suggests that rather than learning a long list of specific narratives about the past as separate items, there is a tendency to construct the means used in textual mediation out of a few basic building blocks. Wertsch argues that these schematic narrative templates are not some sort of universal archetype, but belong instead to particular cultural and narrative traditions (Wertsch 2002, p. 62). These narrative templates do not spring from the past itself but are to be constructed only in the framework of cultural memory. Thus, in the next part of my essay, I shall address the cultural memory work in Estonia and one of the main narrative templates which underlies the remembrance of the Estonian past.

Memory Work and Nation-building in Estonia

One can make a distinction between more active and more passive periods in the history of memory work. In the case of Estonia we can, for the sake of simplicity, distinguish three principal phases. The first is the period between the 1860s and 1890s, when, across the whole of Europe, the process of shaping the 'genealogy of nations' (Smith 1986, pp. 209–26) was at its most intensive. The cultural memory of Estonians was formed in the context of a radical re-writing of history, of writing Estonians into history as a nation. Another pivotal period of memory work was the two decades of independence between the two World Wars, when Estonian historical memory finally acquired a thematic backbone, which remained unbreakable even during the subsequent Soviet period. A third key moment of memory work occurred during the re-establishment of Estonian independence at the end of the 1980s and the beginning of the 1990s, and was characterized by a yearning to return to pre-war memory templates.

The first shapers of Estonian cultural memory were Baltic German Estophiles at the end of the eighteenth and the beginning of the nineteenth century (August Wilhelm Hupel, Garlieb Helwig Merkel etc.), with the Estonians taking the initiative in the memory work during the 1860s. This was the time when the so-called St. Petersburg patriots, i.e. Estonian intellectuals living in St. Petersburg, reached the conclusion that there was a need for a compiled Estonian history. Artist Johann Köler (1826–1899) wrote to pastor Jakob Hurt in 1863 that: 'In order to awaken the spirit of the nation a bit, four people (Karell, Russow, Berendhoff and myself) have come to an understanding that the history of our homeland is what is needed most' (quoted in Põldmäe 1988, p. 103). Actually, a similar sentiment was voiced a quarter of a century earlier, when Baltic German scholar Georg Julius von Schultz-Bertram declared in his speech before the Learned Estonian Society in October 1839: 'Let us give the people an epic and history, and everything is won!' However, this initiative of the St. Petersburg intellectuals did not immediately bear fruit. The first prominent outcome of Köler's initiative was the 'First Fatherland Speech' given by a young pedagogue and cleric, Carl Robert Jakobson (1841–1882), in October 1868 in Tartu. Jakobson initiated a fundamental re-periodization of Estonian history by changing the positives of Baltic German historiography into negatives: whereas in earlier debates the period before the arrival of German missionaries and crusaders in the thirteenth century was viewed as a harsh and barbarous time, according to Jakobson Estonia was experiencing an 'age of light', followed, after the conquest by Germans, by several centuries of 'the age of darkness' which was only now changing into 'the age of dawn' – the new era of freedom. This new, ternary structure of history proposed by Jakobson started to shape Estonian history with unexpected effectiveness, maintaining some of its influence even today.

At the same time as Jakobson, Lutheran pastor Jakob Hurt (1839–1907) also directed his attention to Estonian history, undoubtedly spurred on by a desire to complement and elaborate on the work of his younger and fiercer colleague. The completed manuscript, entitled *Mõni pilt isamaa sündinud asjost* [A Few Impressions of the Fatherland's History], was published by Hurt in 1871 in the form of periodical articles in a supplement of the newspaper *Eesti Postimees*, of which he himself was the editor. The book version was published as much as eight years later. This publication, proposing the first coherent survey of Estonian national history, gives a good summary of the objective of early historical writing: 'Past times and events should teach and caution us all about what we should do and what we should leave undone. That is the reason they are told of in our time' (Hurt 1879, p. 76).

During the subsequent period of the Estonian Republic, historian Hans Kruus (1891–1976) became the most persistent promoter of national historiography (Hackmann 2005, p. 128–135; Kivimäe & Kivimäe 1995). In 1930 he identified, based on the legacy of Jakobson and Hurt, 'three categorical imperatives' of Estonian historical research, which fittingly summarize the fundamental issue of memory work at that time: '(1) In learning the past of our homeland we must focus on the history of the Estonian nation. (2) The current discourse of the homeland's history has to be re-evaluated in the past orientation of the Estonian nation. (3) The homeland's history must educate the people' (Kruus 2005, p. 127). His view reflected the general opinion of the first generation of professional Estonian historians, which was summed up by Otto Liiv in 1938: 'Estonian history is foremost the history of the Estonian nation and its living space', and should 'serve Estonian interests' (Liiv 1938, pp. 300, 303). The task of early professional historians was the production of national collective memory, a memory which succeeded in achieving striking degrees of continuity over temporal distances.

After the *coup d'état* staged by Konstantin Päts and Johan Laidoner in 1934, one can observe a rise in state-controlled history politics, as evidenced by numerous monuments, new commemorations, state jubilees etc. The heroization of the Estonian past gained new importance and negative historical discourse was rejected (Karjahärm & Sirk 2001, p. 292). This new concept of history politics is exemplified by the 1938 speech given by Johan Laidoner, Commander in Chief of the Estonian Armed Forces, entitled 'History and the Current Moment', which stressed the far greater role of Estonians in the past than had hitherto been accepted. Laidoner claimed that Estonians had been a state-based nation even under the rule of the Teutonic Order, when they promoted statehood as vigorously as they were now doing in the context of the Estonian Republic (Laidoner 1995). A similar school of thought was represented by politician and legal historian Jüri Uluots, who formulated 'the theory of national legal history', according to which the Estonian state – in its central elements as a political system – reaches back to the pre-thirteenth-century period. Uluots remarks: 'Therefore, the Estonian state is not young, it is not a recent result of passing events, but a societal-political construction spanning from a primeval age to the present time through numerous historical formations' (Uluots 1940, p. 54).

The national heroization of the Estonian past was abruptly ended by World War II and Estonia's annexation to the Soviet Union. Although the Soviet period should not be underestimated in terms of memory work, surprisingly little of it has influenced the patterns of national historical memory. A new surge in the promotion of nationalistic history occurred at the end of the 1980s and the beginning of the 1990s, when, in parallel with the restoration of statehood, an active reconstruction of pre-war historical memory took place. With little exaggeration, the re-establishment of the Estonian Republic can be described as the construction of 'the Republic of Historians' (Tamm 2006, see also Hackmann 2003). A great many founders and leaders of the newly independent republic had received their education from the Department of History at the University of Tartu, and first garnered recognition as historical publicists. At the beginning of the 1990s, Estonia experienced a unique situation where almost all prominent positions of the state, including the president and the prime minister,[7] were occupied by historians. 'The Republic of Historians' started to crumble only in 1994, with the end of Mart Laar's first term as prime minister. The whole of the period in question was characterized by the idea of restoration, at both the political and the cultural level: the ideal was to re-establish pre-war Estonian society, including laws, pre-war ownership rights, and also monuments and interpretation of history. This brought about the restoration of one of the most prominent narrative templates of Estonian history, first formulated in the 1930s.

Constructing the National Narrative: 'The Great Battle for Freedom'

As I have already noted, narrative is the essential device for containing cultural memory and for guaranteeing the coherence of different events of the past. Narrative binds the elements stored in cultural memory into one meaningful sequence, giving us a small collection of narrative templates, which, in a sense, remember for the nation. Estonia's national historical narrative is inseparable from the concept of independence. Estonian national history has always, starting from the very first endeavors in this area, been analysed from the perspective of losing and gaining liberty. The history of Estonians begins with the age of 'ancient freedom', which precedes the thirteenth-century German–Danish conquest. This in turn is followed by the '700-year night of slavery' (a popular image from the mid-nineteenth century); then, from 1918 to 1939, new independence in the form of the republic, followed by foreign occupation that only came to an end with the re-establishment of independence in 1991. This articulation of history is supported by narrative constructed with the aim of binding different battles and uprisings into one great struggle. We can conditionally call this schematic narrative template 'The Great Battle for Freedom', where Estonian history is characterized by centuries of struggle for liberty and against the Germans. Indeed, it is not surprising, since historical consciousness is usually closely associated with victory (or, more rarely, defeat) in battle. Military historian Michael Howard sums this up neatly when he writes that: 'as nations came to define themselves and trace their origins, the history of their conflicts with one another became a central part of this process of definition, and the concept of the "nation" became inseparably associated with the wars it had fought' (Howard 1991, p. 40).

The narrative of 'The Great Battle for Freedom' combines into one coherent plot all of the prominent conflicts with Germans that Estonians have preserved in their cultural memory, from the crusades of the thirteenth century to the so-called War of

Independence of 1918–1920. The latter was fought against the Bolshevik Red Army, but Estonian cultural memory has given prominence to the battle against the *Landeswehr* near Võnnu (Lat. Cēsis) in the summer of 1919. In this narrative template, all previous uprisings against the Germans had marked a temporary defeat for the Estonians, but Võnnu became the final victory of The Great Battle for Freedom. This narrative template is open in its nature, which means that it can accommodate a number of different conflicts. From the standpoint of Estonian cultural memory, five of these stand out the most: the Battle of St. Matthew's Day, where Estonian forces were defeated by German crusaders (1217), the St. George's Night uprising, where an Estonian insurgency was quelled by the Teutonic Order (1343), the so-called Mahtra War, where peasants revolting against the landlords were suppressed by Tsarist penal squads (1858) and, finally, Võnnu in 1919.

The narrative of 'The Great Battle for Freedom' took shape gradually following the establishment of the Estonian Republic. This provides a necessary endpoint, which, in turn, allows for a retrospective alignment of past events into one thematic thread. The tone is set on 24 February 1918, in Tallinn, with the 'Manifesto to all peoples of Estonia' by the Committee of Elders of the Land Council, the declaration of which marks the birth of the Estonian Republic. The manifesto opens with the following words:

> Throughout centuries, the Estonian people have not lost their desire for independence. Generation after generation, they have preserved a secret hope that despite the dark night of slavery and violent foreign rule, there will be a time in Estonia 'when all spills, at both their ends, will burst forth into flame' and 'then the Son of Kalev [*Kalevipoeg*] will come home, to bring his children happiness'. Now is that time.[8]

The manifesto, relying on the national epic *Kalevipoeg*, declares that, with newly gained independence, Estonian history has reached its logical conclusion and that the true meaning of the events of previous centuries has finally become clear.

The national narrative template achieved its final form in the 1930s. This is when the state endorsed the notion that the battles of the Ancient Struggle for Freedom were continued in the glow of St. George's Night fires, flared up again in the unrest of Mahtra and reached their victorious conclusion in the Battle of Võnnu. This construction was given official status in 1934, when the anniversary of the Battle of Võnnu was declared a national holiday. A brochure published a year later detailed official guidelines for the celebration of the new holiday and stated unequivocally that:

> On the Victory Day of June 23rd, we celebrate the realization of the determined aspirations and dreams that Estonian people have nourished for dozens of generations. . . . The never-ending struggle for the continued existence and political freedom of the Estonian people which was started during the days of Lembitu [early thirteenth century], has lasted through centuries, through occupations by the Teutonic Order, Swedes and Russians, and blazed in the fires of St. George's Night, in the horrors of St. Thomas' Day, in the uprisings of Pühajärve, Mahtra and Anija. (*II Võidupüha 1935*)

The same phrasing, word by word, is used by President Konstantin Päts in his address on the Third Victory Day in 1936: 'Today, on June 23rd, the Victory Day, we celebrate the realization of the determined aspirations and dreams of dozens of generations of Estonian people' (Päts 1936, p. 2). There was even a desire to transform the new national holiday into a cornerstone of a civil religion, as evidenced by the following extract from the 1935 brochure:

> It is not enough that the victory at Võnnu has become a national holiday celebrated across the country. *Its meaning*, the historical disaster remedied and the ultimate attainment of freedom, *has to be made as comprehensible to every person, to every child even, as the meaning of Christmas*. On the basis of this understanding, the youth must be raised to courageous deeds similar to those of their forefathers in their long struggle for freedom and to those of our soldiers in the War of Independence, which all culminated near Võnnu. (*II Võidupüha* . . . 1935, pp. 19–20, emphasis in original)

In the 1930s discourse, the Battle of Võnnu marked the end of a centuries-long struggle for freedom against the Germans. This struggle, however, was later prolonged during World War II, through the work of Estonian historians and publicists working on and behind the Soviet front. The most passionate defender of this concept was Hans Kruus, a newly converted communist, whose countless speeches and writings during the first half of the 1940s were motivated by a need to link contemporaneous battles to the heroics of Lembitu and the insurgents of St. George's Night. In a speech given on 6 September 1942 in Moscow, and quite tellingly bearing the title of 'The ancient struggle of Estonian people against the German invaders is continued in Great Patriotic War', Kruus praised the bravery of Estonians in their fight against German knights and asserted that this struggle

> has stayed with the Estonian people in fiery letters throughout generations, vital, encouraging and inciting; it has stayed, because the enemy stayed; the same enemy, who was led here by the robber knight at the start of the thirteenth century, the same atrocious and violent destroyer and enslaver, as is his current descendant who bears the iron cross. (Kruus 1943, p. 27)

The same idea is equally and vividly expressed in a brochure published on the occasion of the 600th anniversary of St. George's Night: 'Our fight continues the struggles of our strong and valorous forefathers from the time when the soil of our homeland was violated by the vile foot of the first German invader bringing destruction, humiliation and enslavement' (Kruus 1943, p. 3). The anniversary of St. George's Night awakened deeper layers of national historical memory with amazing effectiveness and allowed the projection of contemporary struggles on the universal background of ancient events.

It has to be stressed, however, that the most influential constructors of 'The Great Battle for Freedom' narrative were not historians or politicians, but writers. The most famous episodes of this narrative template – the Ancient Struggle for Freedom (i.e. battles with thirteenth-century crusaders), the uprising of St. George's Night and the Mahtra War – were thus etched into cultural memory by the works of belletrists. In addition to numerous novels and stories on the different episodes of the Ancient Struggle for Freedom, St. George's Night in particular owes its prominent place in Estonian cultural memory to Eduard Bornhöhe's (1862–1923) historic story *Tasuja*

[*The Avenger*] (1880) which, for the first time, presented the 1343 peasant uprising in the Estonian language. Bornhöhe soon found many followers and the uprising of St. George's Night became one of the most popular themes of Estonian historic fiction (Tamm 1998). The unrest in Mahtra during the spring and summer of 1858 was just one incident in a wider peasant movement which started from Vaivara parish in present-day Latvia at the end of April, spread to several Estonian regions during the summer and, in some manors of the Estonian Province, lasted until the end of September. Still, the events of Mahtra claim special significance in Estonian cultural memory. There is little doubt that the reason behind this is Eduard Vilde's famed novel *Mahtra sõda* [*The Mahtra War*], which was published as a feuilleton in the newspaper *Teataja* in 1902 and has become part of the school curriculum. Nor can one underestimate the role of writers in the heroization of the War of Independence. Among the large body of fiction, a novel *Nimed marmortahvlil* [*Names in Marble*] (1936) by Albert Kivikas stands out, its current relevance being demonstrated by a popular feature film adaptation in 2002 (dir. Elmo Nüganen).

Also notable is the fact that nationalistic historic fiction was one of the principal supporters of the Battle of Võnnu, understood as the last episode of the mythic struggle for freedom. This was the first battle where, by virtue of fictional idols, Estonians were aware of their historic mission and where they tried to remedy their past defeats. Politician Jaan Tõnisson had no qualms about labelling the Mahtra War as the pre-battle of the War of Independence. The war against the *Landeswehr* was equally enthusiastically linked to the example of Bornhöhe's story. Jaan Roos (1888–1965) admits tellingly that:

> In me personally, *Tasuja* aroused feelings of heroism and nationalism in the form of anger against the unjust oppressors of our people. The effect of the book was especially emphasized by illustrations. Later, upon reading *Mahtra sõda*, the anger grew even deeper. One has to admit that historic fiction has had an enormous influence on our people as it has awakened the hitherto latent sense of injustice. The participants of the war against the *Landeswehr* describe the primal thrill and excitement with which they fought, the ferocious release of centuries of fury. This primal excitement and anger whipped up by historic fiction was a deciding factor in the defeat of the *Landeswehr*. A man from my home parish died in the Battle of Võnnu with a copy of *Tasuja* in his pocket. This is symbolic. (Palm 1935, p. 171)[9]

Using Heinrich Heine's famous dictum one might conclude that *Tasuja* has indeed become a 'portable fatherland' for Estonians.

Performing the National Narrative

'Cultural memory works by reconstructing,' writes Jan Assmann (1995, p. 130), 'that is, it always relates its knowledge to an actual and contemporary situation'. But cultural memory, as noted by Rudy Koshar (2000, p. 8) among others, is also ritualistic and performative. It derives its motive force not only from constant 'construction' and 'invention', but also from the repetition of culturally specific bodily practices associated with commemorations, demonstrations and other ritual activities. Also, Paul Connerton has pointed out that a nation's master narrative is 'more than a story told and reflected on; it is a cult enacted. An image of the past, even in the form of a master narrative, is conveyed and sustained by ritual performances' (Connerton 1989, p. 70, see also Burke 2005 and Burke forthcoming). Estonian master narrative soon became performative in nature due to different commemorations and rituals. A most crucial change was undoubtedly the turning of the Battle of Võnnu into a national Victory Day in 1934. This took place just weeks before the *coup d'état* of Päts and Laidoner, who became active promoters of the new holiday and its rituals. In 1936, President Päts declared in his Victory Day address:

> The fight for independence has been the largest shared act of Estonian nation. On 23rd of June, on Victory Day, we celebrate the unification of Estonian people into a nation, the return of our shared resolve and the moral reformation of Estonian people which all started with the War of Independence. (Päts 1936, p. 2)

Victory Day, which very conveniently preceded Midsummer Day, became thus part of a traditional Estonian summer holiday, an effect strengthened further by a ritual of lighting the Torch of Victory, which was then carried across the country and used for lighting the pyres of Midsummer Day. This was carried out in the hope of establishing a new national ritual, as Leo Kalmet, one of the organizers of Victory Day, admitted in 1937: 'The ancient custom of Midsummer pyres and the new ceremony of lighting the Torch of Victory are practically destined to fuse into a great, beautiful and all-inclusive national tradition' (Kalmet 1937, p. 23). As evidenced earlier, the new public holiday and its rituals were viewed as major future inciters and shapers of the historical awareness of the younger generation. General Aleksander Tõnisson placed a special emphasis on this aspect in a speech given in Tartu on 23 June 1934: 'It is important to remind people of great battles so that we can raise the upcoming generation in the spirit of courageousness. For that purpose we now have a special day – Victory Day. Let this public anniversary deepen our faith in our glorious future' (*Postimees*, 24 June 1934, quoted by Brüggemann 2003, p. 139).

However, even before the establishment of Victory Day there had been a public debate about commemorating the uprising of St. George's Night as a national holiday. The first rallies and speeches commemorating the uprising of St. George's Night were organized at the end of the 1920s, and they quickly developed into a drive to establish the event in question in the official commemorative calendar. This ignited a journalistic debate in which one side viewed the uprising as a 'day of great trouncing' and the celebration of a Christian St. George's Day as ill-suited, while the other side saw it as the Estonians' heroic revolt against the German oppressors, which, although unsuccessful at the time, came to fruition hundreds of years later. The latter view is succinctly summarized by a 1929 article published in the newspaper *Vaba Maa* (10 May): 'No-one denies the fact that the post-St. George's Night battles failed to yield *immediate* results for Estonians. The victory came as much as 576 years later, when it was realized in the historic Battle of Võnnu, magnificently started by *our* ancestors *at St. George's Night*' (emphasis in original).

A brochure commissioned by the Inter-Organizational Committee for Organizing the 1931 St. George's Night Celebrations in Tallinn strongly emphasizes this point, treating the War of Independence as directly contingent on the uprising of

St. George's Night. The same publication also posits in no uncertain terms the performative signification of the St. George's Night narrative: 'The fact that the glow of the fires of St. George's Night unites us all – that is the real reason for celebrating the Night of Our Great Struggle – that is what unites us into a nation willing to continue its battle for independence' (*Jüriöö* . . . 1931, p. 24). Nevertheless, the supporters of St. George's Night were unsuccessful and the holiday was not marked into the official calendar. Regular commemoration of the St. George's Night uprising did not lose momentum, however, with the memory of the event being highly esteemed even today as evidenced by the Park of St. George's Night in Tallinn, the building of which started in 1935, and which frequently hosts a symbolic fire as well as various public events. Commemorative rituals also extend to other episodes of the 'Great Battle for Freedom': 1933 saw the formal opening of a major monument commemorating the Mahtra War, followed by the establishment of the Mahtra War Museum in 1969, which, albeit under the new name of Mahtra Peasantry Museum, operates to this day. There has also been a decades-long tradition of conferences and other public events commemorating the Mahtra War, especially in the context of various anniversaries.

Conclusions

As recently noted by Alon Confino, the birth of the historical discipline in nineteenth-century Europe took place just as nationhood was becoming a fundamental creed of political sovereignty and group identity (Confino 2006, p. 3, see also Berger, Donovan & Passmore 1999; Pearson 1999). Nation building and history writing became closely intertwined. This connection was, however, masked by the scientific jargon of the new discipline, which opposed history to all other representations of the past. Now we are more and more aware that history is first and foremost a highly specialized form of collective memory. History does not simply reproduce facts; rather, it constructs their meaning by framing them within a cultural memory (Zampony 1998, p. 423). This is not to undermine the scientific claims and professional skills of historians; I do agree with David Lowenthal (1985, p. 213) that 'history and memory are distinguishable less as types of knowledge than in attitudes toward that knowledge'. Therefore, I do not believe that considered as a specific mode of cultural memory, history will lose its unique epistemological status. Rather, taking this approach helps us to understand more properly and more precisely the function of historiography among other social mnemonic practices.

While it is very important to study historical events for their own sake, we also need to pay more attention to how these events are interpreted and appropriated later on. In other words, I consider the study of mnemohistory to be one of the major challenges facing contemporary historical research. The notion of mnemohistory allows one to move past the otherwise often unresolveable questions of 'what really happened' to questions of how particular ways of construing the past enable later communities to constitute and sustain themselves.

In this process of memory work the narrative plays a crucial role. Every community, including the nation, is based on 'stories we live by', on narrative templates which give coherence to a community's past. In this way, the nation is depicted as an outgrowth of earlier periods of the community's history, establishing itself as its lineal descendant through different times (Papadakis 2003, p. 254; Smith 1997, p. 50). The nation is indeed, as Homi Bhabha has pointedly put it, 'a narrative strategy' (Bhabha 1990, p. 292).

The Estonian nation has remembered itself very much as a product of historical and literary imagination.[10] There is a clear tendency in Estonian national historiography to reduce all the major political events to a narrative template which could be called 'The Great Battle for Freedom'. This narrative template is one of the main underlying stories of the Estonian cultural memory, and its significance has endured up to the present day. It forms a basic plot for representing several of the most important events in the Estonian history, from the early thirteenth-century crusades to the Second World War.

Acknowledgements

This essay is based on a paper presented at the 6th International Conference on History and Culture in North Eastern Europe on 'Places of Commemoration in North Eastern Europe: National – Transnational – European?', held on 20–23 September 2007 at Tallinn Town Archives. The research was supported by Estonian Ministry of Research and Education (targeted financed project SF0402739s06) and by the Estonian Science Foundation (grant no. 7129). I am grateful to Peter Burke, Linda Kaljundi and Siobhan Kattago for their comments.

Notes

1 For some recent overviews of the rapidly growing field, see Winter and Sivan (1999), Radstone (2000), Winter (2001), Müller (2002), Hodgkin and Radstone (2003), Lebow, Kansteiner and Fogu (2006). See also the first issue of the new journal *Memory Studies* (Volume 1, issue 1, 2008) and the recent special issue on collective memory and collective identity of *Social Research* (Volume 75, issue 1, 2008).

2 Although we can find in Greek mythology a distinction between two goddesses: Clio, the Muse of history, is the daughter of Mnemosyne, the Titan goddess of memory.

3 The same aspect is underlined by Michel de Certeau: 'Far from being the reliquary or trash can of the past, memory sustains itself by *believing* in the existence of possibilities and by vigilantly awaiting them, constantly on the watch for their appearance' (Certeau 1984, p. 87, italics in original).

4 In similar terms, Michel de Certeau has stated that 'event is not what we can see or know about, but what it becomes later (first of all for us)' (Certeau 1994, p. 51).

5 The expression was introduced in different context by Dan P. McAdams (1993). Also W. L. Randall speaks in similar terms about 'stories we are', arguing for the concept of 'narrative identity' which consists of 'stories we tell to ourselves about ourselves and the stories we or others tell to others, or stories that are told to others about ourselves – all the stories in which we are included'

(Randall 1995, pp. 54–6). See also classical statements on 'the narrative construction of reality' by Jerome Bruner (1991, 2005) and Marc Augé's interesting reflections on 'life as story' (2001, pp. 39–74).

6 See also Straub (2005, p. 64, italics in original): 'Historical narrative and reflection do not simply shape subjects cognitively. Narratives, especially historical narratives formulated from the perspective of the present, are unique articulations of a continuity that creates and maintains *coherence*. This coherence is generally perceived as a meaning-structured unity of events, occurrences, and acts'

7 Respectively, Lennart Meri (president in 1992–2001) and Mart Laar (prime minister in 1992–1994, and again in 1999–2002).

8 'Kalevipoeg' (Son of Kalev) by Fr. R. Kreutzwald (1853). The manifesto quotes the last lines of the poem (canto XX, lines 1047–1050, 1053–1055).

9 See also a vivid testimony in the very influential Estonian novel *Kevade* [*Spring*] (1913) by Oskar Luts: 'Tõnisson has read only one book on the battles and subsequent slavery of ancient Estonians, but this one has had such an impact on him that he had became an implacable enemy of Germans' (Luts 1982, p. 43). Luts probably had Bornhöhe's *Tasuja* in mind.

10 However, one should not forget the importance of artistic imagination, although the role of visual culture in the construction of the Estonian nation has been less important than in many other eastern and central European countries. For a comparative survey of the visual history of nation building in Europe, see Flacke (1998).

References

II Võidupüha 23. juunil 1935. Kava, põhimõtteid, materjale (1935) (Tallinn, Võidupüha Pühitsemist Korraldav Komitee).

Assmann, A. (1993) *Arbeit am nationalen Gedächtnis. Eine kurze Geschichte der deutschen Bildungsidee* (Frankfurt am Main, Campus).

Assmann, A. (2003) *Erinnerungsräume. Formen und Wandlungen des kulturellen Gedächtnisses* (Munich, C.H. Beck).

Assmann, A. (2006) *Der lange Schatten der Vergangenheit. Erinnerungskultur und Geschichtspolitik* (Munich, C.H. Beck).

Assmann, A. (2008) 'Transformations between History and Memory', *Social Research*, 75, 1, pp. 49–72.

Assmann, J. (1995) 'Collective Memory and Cultural Identity', *New German Critique*, 65, pp. 125–33.

Assmann, J. (1997) *Moses the Egyptian. The Memory of Egypt in Western Monotheism* (Cambridge, MA & London, Harvard University Press).

Assmann, J. (1999) *Das kulturelle Gedächtnis: Schrift, Erinnerung und politische Identität in frühen Hochkulturen* (Munich, C.H. Beck).

Assmann, J. (2006) *Religion and Cultural Memory* (Stanford, Stanford University Press).

Augé, M. (2001) *Les Formes de l'oubli* (Paris, Payot).

Berger, S., Donovan, M. & Passmore, K. (eds) (1999) *Writing National Histories. Western Europe since 1800* (London & New York, Routledge).

Bhabha, H. K. (1990) 'DissemiNation: Time, Narrative, and the Margins of Modern Nation', in Bhabha, H. K. (ed.) (1990) *Nation and Narration* (London & New York, Routledge), pp. 291–322.

Booth, W. J. (2006) *Communities of Memory. On Witness, Identity, and Justice* (Ithaca & London, Cornell University Press).

Brockmeier, J. (2002) 'Remembering and Forgetting: Narrative as Cultural Memory', *Culture & Psychology*, 8, 1, pp. 15–43.

Brüggemann, K. (2003) 'Võidupüha. Võnnu lahing kui Eesti rahvusliku ajaloo kulminatsioon', *Vikerkaar*, 10–11, pp. 131–42.

Bruner, J. (1991) 'The Narrative Construction of Reality', *Critical Inquiry*, 18, 1, pp. 1–21.

Bruner, J. S. (2005) 'Past and Present as Narrative Constructions', in Straub, J. (ed.) (2005), pp. 23–43.

Burke, P. (1997) 'History as Social Memory', in Burke, P. (1997) *Varieties of Cultural History* (Cambridge, Polity Press), pp. 43–59.

Burke, P. (2005) 'Performing History: The Importance of Occasions', *Rethinking History*, 9, 1, pp. 35–52.

Burke, P. (forthcoming) 'Co-memorations: Performing the Past', in Tilmans, K. & Winter J. (eds.) *Performing Memory*.

Certeau, M. de (1988) *The Practice of Everyday Life* (Berkeley & Los Angeles, University of California Press).

Certeau, M. de (1994) *La prise de parole et autres écrits politiques* (Paris, Seuil).

Confino, A. (2006) *Germany as a Culture of Remembrance. Promises and Limits of Writing History* (Chaper Hill, The University of North Carolina Press).

Connerton, P. (1989) *How Societies Remember?* (Cambridge, Cambridge University Press).

Flacke, M. (ed.) (1998) *Mythen der Nationen. Ein europäisches Panorama* (Berlin, Koehle & Amelang).

Fogu, C. & Kansteiner, W. (2006) 'The Politics of Memory and the Poetics of History', in Lebow, R. N., Kansteiner, W. & Fogu, C. (eds) (2006), pp. 284–310.

Gadamer, H.-G. (2004) *Truth and Method,* 2nd edition (London & New York, Continuum).

Hackmann, J. (2003) 'Past Politics in North-Eastern Europe: The Role of History in Post-Cold War Identity Politics', in Lehti, M. & Smith, D. J. (eds) (2003) *Post-Cold War Identity Politics. Northern and Baltic Experiences* (London & Portland, Frank Cass), pp. 78–100.

Hackmann, J. (2005) '"Historians as Nation-Builders". Historiographie und Nation in Estland von Hans Kruus bis Mart Laar', in Krzoska, M. & Maner, H.-Ch. (eds) (2005) *Beruf und Berufung. Geschichtswissenschaft und Nationsbildung in Ostmittel- und Südosteuropa im 19. und 20. Jahrhundert* (Münster, Lit), pp. 125–42.

Halbwachs, M. (1997) *La mémoire colléctive*. Edition critique établie par Gérard Namer (Paris, Albin Michel).

Hodgkin, K. & Radstone, S. (eds) (2003) *Contested Pasts. The Politics of Memory* (London & New York, Routledge), pp. 1–21.

Howard, M. (1991) *The Lessons of History* (Oxford, Clarendon Press).

Jüriöö 1343 (1931) (Tallinn, Kalevlaste Ühing).

Kalmet, L. (1937) 'Võidupüha sisustamisest', in *Võidupüha pidustused Tallinnas 1937* (Tallinn, Tallinna Võidupüha Korraldav Komitee).

Karjahärm, T. & Sirk, V. (2001) *Vaim ja võim. Eesti haritlaskond 1917–1940* (Tallinn, Argo).

Kivimäe, J. & Kivimäe, S. (1995) 'Hans Kruus und die deutsch–estnische Kontroverse', in Garleff, M. (ed.) (1995) *Zwischen Konfrontation und Kompromiß. Oldenburger Symposium: 'Interethnische Beziehungen in Ostmitteleuropa als historiographisches Problem der 1930er/1940er Jahre* (München, R. Oldenburg Verlag), pp. 155–70.

Klein, K. L. (2000) 'On the Emergence of *Memory* in Historical Discourse', *Representations*, 69, pp. 127–50.

Koselleck, R. (2004) *Futures Past. On the Semantics of Historical Time* (New York, Columbia University Press).

Koshar, R. (2000) *From Monuments to Traces. Artifacts of German Memory 1870–1990* (Berkeley, University of California Press).

Kruus, H. (1943) *Eesti ajalugu saksa fašismi vastu* (Moscow, Iskra revoljutsii).

Kruus, H. (2005) 'Ärkamisaja pärandus Eesti ajaloo uurimisele', in Kruus, H. (2005), *Eesti küsimus* (Tartu, Ilmamaa), pp. 122–33.

Laidoner, J. (1995) 'Ajalugu ja praegune silmapilk. Johan Laidoneri kõne Tartumaa rahvus- ja noortepäeval 6.1.1938', in Valge, J. & Pajur, A. (eds) (1995) *Poliitilise mõtte ajaloost Eestis aastatel 1930–1940. Dokumente ja materjale* (Tallinn, Jaan Tõnissoni Instituut), pp. 154–9.

Lebow, R. N., Kansteiner, W. & Fogu, C. (eds) (2006) *The Politics of Memory in Postwar Europe* (Durham & London, Duke University Press).

Liiv, O. (1938) 'Eesti ajalooouurimise sihist ja sisust', *Akadeemia*, 5, pp. 299–303.

Lotman, Yu. (2000) 'Pamyat' v kulturologicheskom osveshchenii', in Lotman, Yu. (2000) *Semiosfera* (Sankt-Petersburg, Iskusstvo-SPB), pp. 673–6.

Lowenthal, D. (1985) *The Past is a Foreign Country* (Cambridge, Cambridge University Press).

Luts, O. (1982) *Kevade. Pildikesi koolipõlvest I ja II* (Tallinn, Perioodika).

McAdams, D. P. (1993) *The Stories We Live By. Personal Myth and the Making of Self* (New York, The Guilford Press).

Müller, J.-W. (ed.) (2002) *Memory and Power in Post-War Europe. Studies in the Presence of the Past* (Cambridge, Cambridge University Press).

Nora, P. (1992) 'Comment écrire l'histoire de France?', in Nora, P. (ed.) (1992) *Les lieux de mémoire, III: Les France, 1: Conflits et partages* (Paris, Gallimard), pp. 11–32.

Olick, J. K. (2007) *The Politics of Regret. On Collective Memory and Historical Responsibility* (New York & London, Routledge).

Olick, J. K. & Robbins, J. (1998) 'Social Memory Studies. From "Collective Memory" to the Historical Sociology of Mnemonic Practices', *Annual Review of Sociology*, 24, pp. 105–40.

Palm, A. (1935) 'Ärkamisaja olustiku- ja ideeproosa ning ajalooliste jutustiste osatähtsus rahva elus', in *Raamatu osa Eesti arengus* (Tartu, Eesti Kirjanduse Selts).

Pearson, R. (1999) 'History and historians in the service of nation-building', in Branch, M. (ed.) (1999) *National History and Identity. Approaches to the Writing of National History in the North-East Baltic Region. Nineteenth and Twentieth Centuries* (Helsinki, Finnish Literature Society), pp. 63–77.

Päts, K. (1936) 'Riigivanema läkituskiri III Võidupühaks', in *Koguteos Võidupüha* (Tallinn, Eesti Lipu toimkond).

Papadakis, Y. (2003) 'Nation, Narrative and Commemoration: Political Ritual in Divided Cyprus', *History and Anthropology*, 14, 3, pp. 253–70.

Põldmäe, R. (1988) *Noor Jakob Hurt* (Tallinn, Eesti Raamat).

Radstone, S. (2000) 'Working with Memory: an Introduction', in Radstone, S. (ed.) (2000) *Memory and Methodology* (Oxford & New York, Berg), pp. 1–22.

Randall, W. L. (1995) *The Stories We Are: An Essay on Self-Creation* (Toronto, University of Toronto Press).

Rigney, A. (2004) 'Portable Monuments: Literature, Cultural Memory and the Case of Jeanie Deans', *Poetics Today*, 25, 2, pp. 361–96.

Rigney, A. (2005) 'Plenitude, Scarcity and the Circulation of Cultural Memory', *Journal of European Studies*, 35, 1, pp. 11–28.

Rüsen, J. (1989) 'Strukturen historischer Sinnbildung', in Weidenfeld, W. (ed.) (1989) *Geschichtsbewusstsein der Deutschen. Materialien zur Spurensuche einer Nation* (Köln, Wissenschaft und Politik), pp. 52–64.

Seixas, P. (2004) 'Introduction', in Seixas, P. (ed.) (2004), pp. 3–20.

Seixas, P. (ed.) (2004) *Theorizing Historical Consciousness* (Toronto, Buffalo & London, University of Toronto Press).

Smith, A. D. (1986) *The Ethnic Origins of Nations* (Oxford, Blackwell).

Smith, A. D. (1997) 'The "Golden Age" and National Renewal', in Hosking, G. & Schöpflin, G. (eds) (1997) *Myths and Nationhood* (London, Hurst & Company), pp. 36–59.

Straub, J. (2005) 'Telling Stories, Making History. Toward a Narrative Psychology of the Historical Construction of Meaning', in Straub, J. (ed.) (2005), pp. 44–98.

Straub, J. (ed.) (2005) *Narration, Identity, and Historical Consciousness* (New York & Oxford, Berghahn Books).

Suleiman, S. R. (2006) *Crises of Memory and the Second World War* (Cambridge, MA & London, Harvard University Press).

Tamm, M. (1998) 'Jüriöö-tekst eesti kultuuris', *Looming*, 3, pp. 401–11.

Tamm, M. (2006) '"Vikerkaare ajalugu"? Märkmeid üleminekuaja Eesti ajalookultuurist', *Vikerkaar*, 7–8, pp. 136–43.

Tamm, M. (2007) 'Intervjuu Reinhart Koselleckiga', in Tamm, M. (2007) *Kuidas kirjutatakse ajalugu? Intervjuuraamat* (Tallinn, Varrak), pp. 109–24.

Uluots, J. (1940) 'Eesti riik ajalooliselt vaatepunktilt', *ERK*, 2, pp. 49–54.

Wertsch, J. V. (1997) 'Narrative Tools of History and Identity', *Culture and Psychology*, 3, 5, pp. 5–20.

Wertsch, J. V. (2002) *Voices of Collective Remembering* (Cambridge, Cambridge University Press).

Wertsch, J. V. (2004) 'Specific Narratives and Schematic Narrative Templates', in Seixas P. (ed.) (2004), pp. 49–61.

Wertsch, J. V. (2008) 'Collective Memory and Narrative Templates', *Social Research*, 75, 1, pp. 133–56.

Winter, J. (2001) 'The Memory Boom in Contemporary Historical Studies', *Raritan*, 21, 1, pp. 52–66.

Winter, J. & Sivan, E. (eds.) (1999) *War and Remembrance in the Twentieth Century* (Cambridge, Cambridge University Press).

Zampony, S. F. (1998) 'Of Storytellers and Master Narratives. Modernity, Memory, and History in Fascist Italy', *Social Science History*, 22, 4, pp. 415–44.

Zerubavel, E. (2003) *Time Maps: Collective Memory and the Social Shape of the Past* (Chicago, Chicago University Press).

REMEMBERING AND FORGETTING: CREATING A SOVIET LITHUANIAN CAPITAL. VILNIUS 1944–1949

Theodore R. Weeks

Ernest Renan remarked in his famous essay 'What is a Nation?' that while remembering was crucial in forming national identity and consciousness, no less important was forgetting. Indeed, the writing of history as a patriotic enterprise proves this statement time and again, with the patriot-historian emphasizing the glorious and admirable deeds of his (nearly always 'his') nation and passing less agreeable – or more complex – realities unmentioned.

One may observe the same phenomenon of selective memory in certain policies of the Lithuanian communist leadership in the post-World War II period. While men such as long-time party leader Antanas Sniečkus were certainly communist believers (and loyal Stalinists), they were also Lithuanians. More importantly, they needed to rule a mainly hostile Lithuanian population that regarded communism as a foreign import. While they certainly did not shrink from terror and intimidation to push through their unpopular programs, at the same time they also did not shy away from using Lithuanian national symbols – *lieux de mémoire* – giving them, one might say, a rosy hue. They also attempted to re-define 'Lithuanian' by stressing the secular, cultural and linguistic aspects and downplaying the religious.

In this essay I would like to look at rhetoric, policies and city building (sometimes the three elements coincide) used by the Lithuanian communists in establishing Vilnius[1] as the 'Soviet Lithuanian Capital' in the years immediately after World War II. The communists held one very important trump card: the Red Army had seized Vilnius from the Poles in 1939 and it was from Stalin's hands that the Lithuanians received the city some weeks thereafter. Ironically this long-desired goal of the 'nationalist' and 'bourgeois' interwar governments (to use Soviet rhetoric) was only realized by the Lithuanian communists. Another long-standing goal of Lithuanian patriots was to lithuanize (or, to use their rhetoric, 're-lithuanize') the city. When the city was taken by the Red Army in July 1944, very few members of Vilnius' large and distinguished Jewish community remained alive. The communists encouraged (to put it mildly) the exodus of Poles so that by 1949 the city, while very far from purely Lithuanian, had a larger percentage of ethnic Lithuanian inhabitants than for many previous generations. And the city would grow steadily more Lithuanian throughout the Soviet years.

The Lithuanian communists also attempted a full-scale redefining of Lithuanian identity by stressing a new and modern interpretation, based on 'progressive' political views, a growing industrial working class, high culture (schools, university, Academy of Sciences, publishing), and friendship with the other nations of the USSR. While most Lithuanians would, no doubt, have interpreted the closing of churches in Vilnius as an anti-Lithuanian policy, communists dismissed such claims either by pointing to Polish influences among Catholic clergy or by simply dismissing religion as a personal (and rather retrograde) matter.

At the same time, forgetting was very important for creating a Soviet Lithuanian capital (and republic). More generally, Lithuanians were called on to remember the interwar republic in entirely negative terms as bourgeois and nationalist, ineffective in defending and expanding Lithuanian culture. In Vilnius, the city's multiethnic past was actively forgotten, both rhetorically (e.g., by obliging Polish publications to use the term 'Wilnius' instead of the normal 'Wilno' to refer to the city) and physically (most egregiously, by the express 'erasing' of Jewish sites such as the old Jewish cemetery in Snipiškės and what remained of the Jewish quarter, including the damaged, but still standing in 1944, Old Synagogue). Another policy of forgetting was more general: a very selective memory of World War II which condemned a narrow stratum of Lithuanians as collaborators and 'bourgeois nationalists' while remaining silent on Lithuanian participation in the Holocaust.

Multiethnic Vilna-Wilno-Vilnius to 1944

Throughout its modern history, the population of Vilnius has been made up of a variety of ethnicities. Looking at the city's Christian population in the second half of the seventeenth century, David Frick has remarked on the presence of Calvinists, Eastern Orthodox and Uniates among the majority Catholics in the city (Frick 2003, pp. 23–59). Aside from Christians, among the town's inhabitants one could find Muslim Tatars, Karaites (a sect of Judaism), and of course Jews. Jews had resided in Vilnius since the fifteenth century, but the Jewish community gained importance (and underwent various attacks, expulsions and returns to the city) during the sixteenth century (Klausner 1988, pp. 3–6). The Great Synagogue in the Jewish quarter dates from the final years of the sixteenth century; it was destroyed during anti-Jewish riots in 1592 but thereafter reconstructed (Jankevičienė 1996).

When the Russians extended their power over Vilnius in 1795, the bulk of the town's population consisted of Poles and Jews, with significant Lithuanian, Belarusian and Russian minorities. The population of Vilna before 1897 – when the first scientific census of the Russian Empire was carried out – can only be estimated. Around 1800 the population was said to be around 20,000. This figure was challenged, however, as too low by Michał Baliński in the most detailed statistical work on Vilna of this period. Using more precise official statistics of the early 1830s, Baliński set the city's population at a minimum of 35,922 (and a maximum of 50,000). By 'estate' (*stan*) Jews formed the majority – nearly two thirds – of the city's population. The second largest estate, remarkably, was not townspeople (*mieszczanie*, ca. 5,000) but nobles (*szlachta*), numbering nearly 6,600. Over 700 persons in Vilna belonged to the clerical caste and around 300 serfs made the city their home. The exact figures were: clericals 523 men and 188 women, *szlachta* 3,289 and 3,369, *mieszczanie* 2,424 and 2,506, serfs 152 and 167, Jews 10,040 and 10,606 (Baliński 1835, pp. 59–61, 153). Even among the non-Jewish minority, Vilnius was a religiously and ethnically diverse city. To be sure, the majority (nearly two-thirds) of the city's Christians were Roman Catholics, but almost 3,000 Orthodox believers lived in Vilna, along with Uniates, Lutherans, Calvinists and almost certainly a few Muslims and Karaites who do not, however, appear among Baliński's figures (Baliński 1835, p. 64).

It is exceedingly difficult to state with any precision just how many Lithuanians resided in Vilnius before the twentieth century. During the nineteenth century Lithuanians were a mainly peasant people, the Lithuanian nobles of earlier centuries having been thoroughly Polonized, in most cases for several generations before 1800. According to the census of 1897, Lithuanians made up only 2.1% of the total population (3,238 of 154,532) but many commentators at the time and later pointed out that this figure is almost certainly too low (Jurginis 1968, p. 304). As Catholics, Lithuanians tended to be counted with Poles; as servants, peasants and manual workers they were not always particularly interested in pressing the issue of national identification with census workers. In any case, however, it is clear that the Lithuanian minority in Vilnius before 1914 was small, almost certainly between one-tenth and one-twentieth of the city's inhabitants.

After the First World War Vilnius was fought over by Polish, Soviet and Lithuanian troops, with the Poles finally capturing the city in October 1920 and holding it until the Soviet invasion of September 1939 (Senn 1966; Łossowski 1966). The Lithuanians, however, refused to concede the city to Poland, proclaiming it their capital and Kaunas only the 'provisional capital'. This intransigence over the Polish occupation (from their point of view) of Vilnius translated into a total lack of diplomatic relations between Lithuania and Poland throughout nearly the entire interwar period.

In the late 1930s Vilnius was a provincial city with a university in the extreme northeast of the Polish republic with a population of just over 200,000. According to the late pre-war figures we have on nationalities in the city (1931), Poles made up 66% of the total city population, followed by Jews (28%), Russians (nearly 4%), and Lithuanians (under 1%).[2] To be sure, the Polish authorities tended to do what they could to exaggerate the percentage of Poles among this region's population, but these figures seem at least roughly correct. These official statistics almost certainly underestimated the number of Lithuanians in the city but their numbers were probably at most a few thousand (though no doubt higher than the 1579 total officially counted).

The Red Army entered Vilnius on 19 September 1939, having invaded Poland from the east two days earlier in accordance with the secret provisions of the Molotov–Ribbentrop Pact. The Soviet occupation lasted just over a month and on 28 October the Red Army relinquished control of the city to the Lithuanian authorities (Manelis & Samavičius 2003, pp. 434–450). Thus, the later Lithuanian communist leadership could boast plausibly that without the help of the Soviet Union, Lithuania would never have achieved its goal of regaining its capital city.

Vilnius in 1944

The period 1939–1944 was an immensely painful one for all inhabitants of Vilnius. To be sure, Poles and Jews suffered more than Lithuanians, and Jews suffered far more than anyone else. When the Red Army once again entered the city in mid-July 1944, many of the city's buildings were in ruins and nearly all of its Jewish inhabitants were dead (Arad 1982; Lewandowska 2004; Weeks 2006). The only Jews left in the city emerged from hiding in the next few days, and as concentration camps were liberated further west some hundreds made their way back to the city in the next few months (Bak 2001, pp. 362–381). Few Jews remained in the city, especially as local Soviet authorities were increasingly hostile to Jewish memories of the war, as the destruction in 1952 of the first Ponary (Lith.: Paneriai) monument (where thousands of Vilnius Jews had been murdered) showed. According to NKVD figures, at the end of 1944 84,990 Poles and 7,958 Lithuanians lived in the city (which had a total population of 106,500 – less than half its population in 1939) (Lewandowska 1997, p. 326).

While the percentage of Lithuanians in the city had increased during the war, Vilnius remained in 1944 a mainly Polish city by ethnicity – and this was a major problem and challenge for the new Lithuanian Soviet regime. It was, to say the least, problematic to have a Polish majority in the city which had been proclaimed the capital of Soviet Lithuania.[3] A solution was rapidly found. On 22 September 1944 an agreement was reached between representatives of the Lithuanian SSR and the Polish Committee of National Salvation (the so-called 'Lublin Poles', a pro-communist government formed under Stalin's auspices) for the voluntary evacuation of Poles from the LSSR and Lithuanians from Poland.[4] According to this agreement, transportation would be provided for anyone wishing to leave, and the evacuations would take place from December 1944 to June 1945. Evacuees would be allowed to take personal effects with them, with some exceptions (no automobiles, motorcycles or furniture). Peasants could take tools, small livestock and the like, and would have land restored to them on the other side.[5]

Immediately upon the arrival of the Red Army, Poles were given many indications that their days in Vilnius were numbered. One such 'hint' was the spelling of the city in the Polish-language communist newspaper, *Prawda Wileńska*, in its first issue on 17 July 1944 – the paper wrote of 'Wilnius' (a form never used in Polish, simply the transliteration of the Lithuanian form) and greeted the liberation of the city and spoke of fraternal relations with the Lithuanians (*Gazeta Wileńska*, 17 July 1944). The subtext could not have been clearer: Poles were now tolerated by the benevolence of the new masters, the Lithuanians, and could continue to live in 'Wilnius', the capital of the Lithuanian Soviet Socialist Republic (LSSR) only under those terms. Only with the signing of the 22 September 1944 accord was it made clear that the Poles were expected to leave their native town and evacuate to Poland.

The first mention of the signing of the accord was published in *Prawda Wileńska* on 26 September with a short informational notice. Over a week later a longer article interpreted and evaluated the agreement in entirely positive terms, calling it a 'new historical phase' that would help wipe out 'any kind of misunderstandings between Lithuanians and Poles'. Rather than living as a minority in the other's country, now Lithuanians and Poles would join their national brethren in the two nation states. No doubt anticipating an obvious objection and uncomfortable comparison, the article declared that this agreement was 'the diametrical opposite' of Hitlerian policies of destroying nations and letting one rule over another. Now, rather, members of each nation would live among their own kind; in this way both the countries and individuals would quickly be able to develop normal and positive relations. As for the practical matter of moving thousands of people (numbers are never mentioned), the 'extremely favorable conditions for evacuees' was stressed several times. While the tone of the article was relentlessly upbeat and optimistic, it left no doubt that Poles were expected to leave Vilnius (*Gazeta Wileńska*, 5 October 1944).

In late 1944 and early 1945 arrests of Poles were also stepped up. To be sure, this was a rather grim period for anyone living in the LSSR but Poles in Vilnius had the additional disability of being considered 'foreign', middle-class, and quite possibly connected with the Polish underground that was being rooted out by the NKVD at that time (Niwiński 1999). By the end of 1944, over 2,000 Poles had been arrested in Vilnius, and Polish residents, remembering the previous Soviet occupation of 1940–1941, had reason to fear worse. Different Polish historians cite figures of between 10,000 and 20,000 arrests from July 1944 to early 1945 (Mikłaszewicz 2002, p. 245; Lewandowska 2007, pp. 55–7). Whatever the exact figures, one thing was clear: the end for Polish Vilnius was approaching. Perhaps not realizing that the NKVD would be reading their letters (report [*Spetssoobshchenie*] of 27 February 1945), Poles expressed their fears that they would soon have to leave home. Anna Anasowicz (Vilnius, ul. Sadovskaia 3–3) wrote sadly, 'We will have to abandon our beloved Wilno . . . for Soviet power has given over Wilno to the Lithuanians and we Poles, like it or not, will be forced to leave'. Around the same time Galja Dmitrowicz (Vilnius) wrote 'they're giving out new passports, but only Russian and Lithuanians get them, not Poles, so they will be forced to leave for Poland. . . . We Poles don't want to leave for Poland'.[6]

Taking into consideration the enormous energy lavished on the evacuation effort by the Soviet authorities, it seems impossible not to agree with a Polish historian's assessment that 'the Soviet authorities aimed at the quickest possible, most radical de-polonization of Vilnius'. However, the second part of this same sentence seems quite incorrect: 'and to give it the character of a Russian city' (Lewandowska 1997, p. 330). On the contrary, the Soviet authorities wished to give the city a *Soviet* and *Lithuanian* character. While Russian specialists did arrive in Vilnius in large numbers after World War II, even larger number of Lithuanians migrated to the city. From the late 1940s to the end of the century, the percentage of Russians among the Vilnius population declined steadily.

Making Vilnius Lithuanian and Soviet

The most pressing single task for the Lithuanian communists upon liberating Vilnius was to rid the town of its Polish population. As we have seen, the 22 September 1944 agreement between the Lithuanian SSR (*nota bene*: **not** the USSR) and the Lublin Polish committee cleared the way for just such a population transfer. I do not wish to suggest, of course, that the Lithuanian communists were acting on their own or that the LSSR was a sovereign state. The expulsion of Poles from the LSSR was part of a larger program to expel ethnic Poles from the USSR's (newly acquired in World War II) western borderlands. What I *do* wish to stress is that the Lithuanian communists used this all-Soviet program for their own ends, in particular to empty Vilnius of Poles while being much less concerned about Poles living on the countryside. As I have argued in some detail elsewhere, the clearing of Vilnius of its former Polish population was a matter of primary importance for the new Lithuanian rulers (Weeks 2007). Indeed, in a secret letter signed by high Soviet officials A. Vyshinskii and A. Pavlov to Foreign Minister V. M. Molotov the fact that the 'Lithuanians are primarily interested in evacuating Poles living in Vilnius (Vil'no)' was noted.[7]

The evacuation was carried out by two separate sets of bureaucrats, Polish and Lithuanian, with frequent stresses and (verbal) clashes between them. The Poles were fundamentally interested in evacuating anyone who wanted to leave; the Lithuanians led by later Minister of Education of the LSSR A. Knyva consistently demanded a closer scrutiny of evacuees' nationality to prevent Lithuanians from emigrating. Of course nationality was not easy to ascertain in many cases, a fact tacitly acknowledged by the Poles' more lenient approach.[8] The Lithuanian side also pressed for the evacuation of Vilnius but devoted far less attention to rural areas populated by Poles. In the end, nearly all Poles in Vilnius left for Poland. Of the 171,168 individuals who evacuated from the LSSR to Poland, over half (89,596) were from the Vilnius region (we have no figures for the city proper, but the city made up the bulk of the population in the '*rajonas*'). The disparity from other regions is even more striking when one compares numbers of those who registered to leave and the actual number of evacuees. In Vilnius region over 80% of those who registered actually left (89,596 of 111,341). In the other regions put together, fewer than one-quarter of those who registered actually evacuated (Srebrakowski 2001, p. 98; Original source: AAN, Akta Gł. Pełnomocnika d/s Ewakuacji . . . , sygn. 167). In short, the ejection of Poles from the Lithuanian SSR amounted to 'ethnic cleansing' only for the city of Vilnius. To be sure, in time many Poles from nearby rural areas would come to Vilnius but their presence did not challenge the primary objective of creating a Soviet Lithuanian city. After 1947 the predominance of Lithuanian culture in Vilnius would never again be challenged by Poles.

A Soviet Lithuanian capital must obviously have appropriately named streets. Street names had already been Lithuanized in late 1939, the Polish names replaced by translated or entirely new designations (e.g., Mickiewicza became Gedimino).

During the first Soviet occupation (that is, 1940–1941) efforts were under way to remove inappropriate names (with religious connotations or referring to the interwar Lithuanian Republic). With few exceptions, however, proposed name changes did not feature Russian socialist heroes (the exceptions are predictable enough: Stalin, Lenin, Gorkii, Voroshilov, Sverdlov, Kirov, Maiakovskii). On 9 May 1941 the Vilnius City Executive Committee and the presidium of the LSSR Supreme Soviet approved over 100 name changes of streets and squares. Thus 'Archangel Way' was to become 'The People's Way' (Liaudies), Church Street – Citizens Street (Baznyčios – Piliečių), Martyrs Street – Fighters Street (Aukų – Kovotojų), Muhammedan Street – Uzbek Street (Mahometanų – Uzbekų), St. Peter and Paul – Tractorists (Šv. Petro ir Povilo – Traktorininkų), and Good Hope Street was to become Industry Street (Gerosios Vilties – Pramonės). Streets bearing the names of distinguished local Jews (Strašūno, Dr. Šabado, Gaono) were to receive the names of other distinguished non-local Jews (Mendelės, Š. Aleichem, M. Antokolskio).[9] The great men Engels and Marx were also to be honored (Vokiečių and Domininkonų-Šv. Jono-Trakų, respectively).

The German invasion six weeks later probably prevented any of these name changes from being carried out. Discussions in 1944–1947 continued to mention the 1940 names (such as St. Stephen, Gaon, and the like). Lithuanian historian (and later co-author of the most comprehensive city history to this day) Juozas Jurginis addressed a letter to the Vilnius City Committee dated 16 May 1947 urging that a number of local notables be honored by having streets named after them. Among the names Jurginis put forward were the writer Žemaitė, poet Kazys Binkis, Vilnius resident and 'historian of Lithuania' Joachim Lelewel (his Polish nationality left unsaid), 'anti-tsarist Vilnius worker' [Hirsh] Lekert (his Jewish nationality and obviously Jewish first name left unmentioned), and others. In many cases these recommendations were accepted by the town council.[10] Remarkably, the main downtown street Gedimino retained its Lithuanian name until 1952, when it was – for a few short years – renamed Stalino. Thus street names were to reflect both the international and socialist nature of the city, but also its past (though without specific reference to non-Lithuanian nationality, including the spelling of names in the Lithuanian manner). The city was also to undergo significant reconstruction to make it a suitable site for a capital of a Soviet republic. In the plans for urban transformation, the specific national element is seldom emphasized but could be taken for granted. In early 1941 a detailed report (in Russian) set down basic principles for the transformation of the city. First of all, all institutions of the capital city (many of which continued to function in Kaunas) needed to be brought to Vilnius as one means of sweeping away its present condition as a 'provincial city of bourgeois Poland [Panskoi Pol'shi] which continues to preserve its half-feudal character and a chaotic building muddle'. The goal was to create a 'well-built socialist city'. Mincing no words, the report stated baldly that insisting on '"conservation" [*konservatsiia*] of the old city' was 'entirely incorrect from the point of view of socialist city planning'.

Denouncing the Polish city planners who apparently planned to circumvent rather than modernize the old town, it was concluded that the old town needed a thorough and radical reconstruction. The idea of leaving the inhabitants of the old town 'and in particular of the former Jewish "ghetto" [sic]' in the terrible existing hygienic and transportation circumstances as 'a peculiar museum exhibit' was unacceptable in a modern Stalinist world (or, 'in light of Stalinist concerns': '*v svete Stalinskoi zaboty*'). In particular, city traffic should be modernized by the extension of Gedimino across Cathedral Square to the east (which, presumably, would have involved the destruction of the cathedral itself), linking Vilnius Street directly with the Green Bridge to the north and plowing a 'magistral' (a favorite word in this report) to the railroad station. The report also bewailed the lack of proper open spaces for demonstrations and called for the opening up of such large squares. All of these plans would have involved a considerable destruction of the Old City and it is interesting that none of these ambitious projects was taken up again after the war.[11]

The most immediate considerations after the war were practical. According to the later city architect of Vilnius, some 40% of living space and 30% of industry in the city had been destroyed under the German occupation (Mikučianis 2001, p. 64). This impression is borne out by photographs and drawings taken of major streets of the city, showing numerous burned out and destroyed buildings.[12] The area of the former Jewish ghettos in the middle of the city had been left in a state of almost total waste after the final liquidation of the Vilnius ghetto in September 1943 (Ran 1974, pp. 515–22). Despite the devastation, the principal monuments of non-Jewish Vilnius still stood (mainly, of course, churches). But the Soviet leadership had grand plans for the city.

According to architect Vladislovas Mikučianis, who came to Vilnius in 1945, three basic principles were followed in drawing up a general city plan: (1) to open up the 'picturesque Neris river scene' which previous architectural plans had neglected; (2) 'retain the rich silhouette of architectural monuments' found within the Old City; (3) in developing the city, to preserve its natural setting (hills and surrounding forests) (Mikučianis 2001, p. 69). At the same time, Mikučianis and his colleagues wanted to develop the city's industry further, improve its profile as a Soviet capital with various prestigious architectural projects, and repair housing, infrastructure and communications. One of the earliest Soviet monuments to mark the downtown was the monument to Ivan Cherniakhovskii, the Soviet general who had liberated Vilnius and was killed in action shortly thereafter. The general's remains were interred and topped with a large obelisk in the downtown square that had previously borne Polish writer Eliza Orzeszkowa's name (Mikučianis 2001, pp. 75–7). The temporary monument was already in place for the 1 May 1945 holiday. In this way one relic of the Polish past was erased and replaced with a Soviet (though not ethnically Lithuanian) site.

Other major construction projects of the early post-war included the '"academicians" house' (*mokslininkų namas*) constructed on the banks of the Neris River. This building was to be in a sense Vilnius' answer to the famous 'house on the embankment' in Moscow, but in this case not specifically for party higher-ups but for scientists. The impressive structure, topped with a pompous Stalinist tower, contained 50 apartments of five rooms with 120 square meters each and even including a small room for 'home workers' (servants). The completion of this building in 1950 was a major event for Vilnius (Mikučianis 2001, pp. 78–9; *Vilnius 1900–2005* (2005), G 1). Around the same time, the 'Green Bridge' over the Neris River was rebuilt and opened, adorned with four impressive statues representing students, the Red Army, industry and agriculture. The Railroad Station, devastated in World War II, was reconstructed in a pompous neoclassical/Stalinist style, and the 'Victory' Cinema in the same style was opened downtown (*Vilnius 1900–2005*, 2005, G2-G6). These major architectural projects emphasized Vilnius' status as a republic capital of the USSR, but can hardly be termed 'Lithuanian'. Rather, their architecture stressed the break with the past and Vilnius' present status within the USSR.

Vilnius as a Center of Soviet Lithuanian Culture

While new architectural forms did not stress the national side of the Lithuanian Soviet capital, the uses of some new buildings did. For example, the Vilnius Pedagogical Institute (built across the river from the 'Scientists' House' and completed in 1955) considerably expanded the possibilities for young Lithuanians to gain a university education. Vilnius University, too, was built up as a center for Lithuanian learning. Vilnius University had operated under Nazi rule for nearly two years until it was shut down in March 1943 (*Naujoji Lietuva*, 18 March 1943; *Tiesa*, 28 October 1944, p. 2). M. Biržiška continued on as rector until that date but – perhaps not surprisingly – ends his university war memoirs with the German invasion, noting that the Germans discovered a (Soviet) list with the names of many university officials (including the rector) who were to be evacuated to the Russian interior (Biržiška 1948, p. 58; Merkys *et al.* 1979, pp. 27–44). During the war years Lithuanian culture had, on the whole, developed normally – at least compared to Polish or Jewish. The Lithuanian press, literature and theater in Vilnius expanded in the early 1940s (Linčiuvienė 1999).

The communists did not, however, emphasize such continuities but preferred instead to dwell on the considerable damage that the Nazis had done to Lithuanian scholarship. The Communist Party daily *Tiesa* published an article entitled 'How the Occupiers Destroyed Vilnius State University' in late October 1944, the week after classes had begun at the newly reopened university. Headed by a Lithuanian rector (Professor Bieliukas), the university was already enrolling several hundred students in fall 1944 (*Tiesa*, 19 October 1944; 28 October 1944; 11 November 1944). The destruction of the war years, combined with the large numbers of arrests, deaths and emigration since 1940 meant that in many ways the university had to be recreated from scratch. It should also not be forgotten that the Lithuanian Vilnius University had only existed since the end of 1939 when the Polish professors at what was then called Uniwersytet Stefana Batorego (USB) had been unceremoniously fired and replaced by Lithuanians (Łossowski 1991). While many specialists had fled Lithuania from 1940 on, the university was nonetheless reopened with overwhelmingly Lithuanian personnel, the language of instruction was Lithuanian, and the student body was predominantly Lithuanian (Manelis & Samavičius, 2003, p. 590). Indeed, Lithuanians were often obliged to come to Vilnius to study (or work) because of the post-war 'downsizing' of many faculties at the former Vytautas the Great University in Kaunas (Merkys *et al.* 1979, pp. 45–6).

Re-opening Vilnius University as a Lithuanian institution was extremely important both as a symbolic act and as a means of ensuring the training of proper Soviet Lithuanian specialists and scholars for the future. Equally important as both a matter of prestige and a method of tying the Lithuanian Republic into the Soviet system of research and scholarship was the founding of the Academy of Sciences of the Lithuanian SSR, which began work in October 1944 (*Tiesa* 31 October 1944). By institutionalizing Lithuanian scholarship within the framework of the multinational USSR, the Academy of Sciences served to strengthen both the Lithuanian and the Soviet elements in Vilnius (Šadžius *et al.* 1972, pp. 268–75). The party organ *Tiesa* repeatedly made this point by pointing out the flourishing of Lithuanian learning and culture since its liberation by the Red Army and arguing that for a small nation such as Lithuania, the best way for its security and cultural development to be ensured was the guarantee provided by being part of the powerful multinational USSR (*Tiesa* 17 March 1945, 27 March 1945).

Forgetting

In their attempts to fashion a new Soviet Lithuanian capital in Vilnius, the Lithuanian communists also had to forget – and seek to blot out, at least rhetorically – many aspects of the city's past and present. The city's rich religious heritage, for example, was ignored or actively opposed as sites of religious practice or memory were transformed into secular uses, altered in appearance, or simply swept away. In Vilnius, religion and nationality had always gone hand in hand. Now the city's long multiethnic history (and the relatively small role played in it by ethnic Lithuanians since the eighteenth century at least) was also actively ignored or glossed over. While the friendship of nations within the USSR was trumpeted, mention of the now-absent Polish and Jewish inhabitants of Vilnius might call into question the now unquestioned dominance of ethnic Lithuanians in the Soviet capital. In another attempt to create a kind of new Soviet Lithuanian patriotism, the post-war authorities also fashioned a one-sided and Manichean 'memory' of Lithuanians' experience in World War II.

For centuries, Vilnius had been an outpost of Catholicism in the east. But Catholicism had no role to play in the new Soviet Lithuanian patriotism. Catholic churches were shut down, though seldom actually destroyed. The cathedral became a picture gallery and had statues and its enormous cross removed from its façade (Pšibilskis 1995). The Three Crosses monument, associated with the Polish 1830 Rebellion against Moscow, located on a hill next to the downtown Castle Hill was destroyed in the middle of the night on 30 May 1950. Less dramatically, dozens of other churches were closed in the late 1940s. City architect Mikučianis (who despite his Lithuanian name barely knew Lithuanian and spoke Russian as his native tongue and had only come to Vilnius after the war) recalled that after the 'repatriation' of Poles it was argued that there were 'too many churches' in the city (ignoring the inconvenient fact that most Lithuanian immigrants were just as Catholic as the Poles had been). Mikučianis also noted that the high Lithuanian communist official E. Ozarskis constantly complained that the church of St. Jacob clashed with the statue of Lenin on Lukiškių Square and should be destroyed (happily the church has outlived the statue) (Mikučianis 2002, pp. 86–8). Following normal Soviet practice, one of these (St. Kazimierz/Kazimieras) was converted into the Museum of Atheism in 1961. Other churches were turned into storehouses, offices and in one case (the former Basilian Monastery near Ostra Brama) into a Technical Institute.

The timing of these repressions of religious 'monuments' is interesting. No major church was closed or destroyed (few were, in any case, actually destroyed) before 1948. In other words, the first order of business was to establish Soviet power (including putting the apparatus of repression in place) (Truska *et al.* 1999), expel the Poles (completed by 18 September 1946),[13] and ensure the basic stability of the new Soviet order. It is surely no coincidence that the closing of churches came at the same time as the collectivization of Lithuanian agriculture (1948–1952).

Memory of Vilnius' multiethnic past was also a victim of the postwar remaking of Soviet Lithuania. Reading any of the three main party newspapers of the LSSR, *Tiesa*, *Prawda Wileńska* or *Sovetskaia Litva*, in these years, one is struck by the almost complete lack of mention of non-Russian and non-Lithuanians in the city and region. To be sure, *Prawda Wileńska* did mention the opening of a Jewish museum in the city (at Strašuno 6) by 'comrades Markelsówna and Sz. Kaczergiński' (Bagrowska 1945), but the same paper was capable of devoting an article to the 'cruel past' of the Vilnius suburb Paneriai (where the majority of Vilnius' Jews had been murdered) – without mentioning Jews at all (*Prawda Wileńska*, 25 August 1944). Even in that Polish-language daily, one finds enthusiastic articles extolling the great things being done by the USSR for 'our Lithuanian nation' ('*nasz naród litewski*') and its 'capital Vilnius' (using the Lithuanian spelling in Polish) (*PW*, 10 February1945). In the late 1940s *Sovetskaia Litva* devoted remarkably little room to anything Lithuanian at all, addressing more frequently the Belarusian population (though using the Russian language). However, one article in March 1949 did breathlessly describe the forward 'rapid rebuilding of the capital of Soviet Lithuania', with much about new buildings, landscaping and decisions of the Soviet of Ministers of the USSR, and not a word about the actual inhabitants of the town (*Sovetskaia Litva*, 20 March 1949).

Not surprisingly, the most enthusiastic reports about the new Lithuanian Soviet capital appeared in the Lithuanian-language *Tiesa*. Here Lithuanian patriotism was inextricably intertwined with enthusiasm for Soviet construction, as in the article 'Attention! Vilnius Speaking!' about the opening of radio broadcasts in Lithuanian from the city, already in 1940 and once again in 1944 after the Germans had been defeated (*Tiesa*, 9 January 1945). A campaign in April 1945 called specifically on Lithuanians to move to Vilnius and repopulate the city, even calling it their patriotic duty (*Tiesa*, 4 April 1945, 8 April 1945). At the same time the newspaper was full of articles about the 'eternal friendship' between the Lithuanian and Russian peoples, enthusiastic *subbotniki* (*sekmadienio talka*) to clear rubble and rebuild, and of course on the great benevolence and interest of the USSR in general and Stalin in particular for the prosperity and cultural development of the Lithuanian people.

In the late 1940s Poles are seldom mentioned as inhabitants (past or present) of Vilnius in the Lithuanian Soviet press, except in the context of their 'repatriation'. Similarly missing from press accounts is any mention of Vilnius' once large Jewish community. Given the Nazi obsession with Jews and their unspeakable crimes against this nation, one might have expected the Soviets to emphasize these black deeds of their adversaries. In fact, however, the murderous deeds are discussed but often without any mention of the main target of these mass murders. We have already seen an article on Paneriai which failed to mention that over 90% of the tens of thousands of people murdered there were Jews. Perhaps even more egregiously, an article in

Prawda Wileńska in early November 1944 mentions the death camp at Auschwitz (Oświęcim) but mentions Jews only in passing, as 'one of the nationalities' murdered there (*Prawda Wileńska*, 1 November 1944). Four months later another article on Auschwitz lacked any mention of Jews whatsoever (*Prawda Wileńska*, 25 February 1945).

Perhaps a few hundred Vilnius Jews had managed to survive to July 1944 in hiding. Once they emerged, however, they found that neither the general population nor the Soviet leadership had much interest in them or their story. Within weeks of the Soviet liberation of Vilnius, the Yiddish poets Abraham Sutzkever and Shmerke Kaczerginski had founded in their apartment at Gedimino 15a the 'Museum for Jewish Art and Culture' and called on all survivors to contribute any documents or artifacts they had that related to Jewish Vilnius (Fishman 1998, pp. 23–31), In a short time they had collected hundreds of documents only a few of which, unfortunately, have come down to us.[14] The two poets who had survived as partisans also wrote their own accounts of the last days of Jewish Vilnius; Sutzkever's was published first in 1946 in Paris and Moscow (later also in Buenos Aires); Kaczerginski's appeared in 1947 in New York (Sutzkever 1946; Kaczerginski 1947).

By early 1945 the Jewish Museum had moved to Strašuno 6 (the previous location of the 'paper brigade' employed by the Germans in ghetto times to sift through Jewish-language materials) but suffered from the unwillingness of the Lithuanian Soviet authorities to provide it with basic funding, office supplies and furniture. Kaczerginski went to Moscow in March 1945 to complain about this neglect (to use a mild word) and there found out that 30 tons of material from the YIVO-Institute library and archives seized by the Nazi *Amt für Müllabfuhr* had miraculously survived the war. But despite all of Kaczerginski's impassioned efforts, the material not destroyed by the Nazis was pulped by the Soviet authorities.

By mid-1945 the Jewish Museum was officially registered with three paid employees and the Moscow Yiddish journal *Einikayt* published an article on 2 October 1945 praising Kaczerginski and Sutzkever's efforts. The museum, however, was forbidden to lend out any books without specific permission from *Glavlit* (censorship). The poets had had enough of the disinterest and even hostility of the Soviet authorities and left Vilnius in July 1946 for Paris. The Jewish Museum survived two more years before being shut down by the KGB in 1949 (Ran 1974, p. 524; Atamukas 2001).

The fate of other Jewish sites in Vilnius was similar. The area of the two Jewish ghettos set up by the Nazis (in the middle of the city) was a site of almost total ruin in 1944. (Agranovskii & Guzenberg 1992, p. 49). The city architect Mikučianis recalled that despite the destruction, the walls of the Great Synagogue were intact and only the roof had been destroyed (Mikučianis 2001, pp. 90–1). The surrounding buildings were damaged, but not gravely, and could have been repaired without enormous expense. In the end, however, the synagogue and surrounding buildings were razed and the entire former Jewish quarter essentially reconstructed, eliminating most of the small alleys which, admittedly, had long presented a problem for hygiene and sanitation. 'German Street' (Nemetskaia, Vokiečių) in the middle of the former ghetto area was widened and a small park constructed in the middle of the street (rather like a boulevard, but with the promenade in the middle rather than on the sides). The street was also renamed 'Muzejaus' (referring to the former town hall at its southern end, in Soviet times an art museum); 'Jewish' street (Žydų, Evreiskaia) was essentially eliminated by considering it merely an extension of Stiklių (Glasier) Street (Agranovskii & Guzenberg 1992, pp. 69–70). In this way the Jewish quarter of Vilnius, now devoid of Jews, also had most of its specifically Jewish character and sites of memory erased.

Perhaps the most egregious destruction of a Jewish site was the paving over of the old Jewish cemetery just across the Neris River from downtown. Amazingly, this cemetery had survived the Nazi occupation almost intact (Ran 1974, vol. II, p. 532). Mikučianis mentions laconically that already before the war the Polish authorities had planned to develop this site (it is, to be sure, a very central location). In 1950 certain historically important graves (such as that of the Vilna Gaon) were transferred to a new Jewish cemetery and the cemetery was razed to make way for a sports complex, pool and athletic fields (Mikučianis 2001, p. 108; and Guzenberg 1992, pp. 64–66). While such facilities may well have been welcomed by the residents of Vilnius, given other available plots in the vicinity it seems clear that the old Jewish cemetery was destroyed not primarily for practical reasons but to blot out an inconvenient memory of a population that no longer existed in the city.

Actions taken by the Soviet leadership in Vilnius at the memorial site of Paneriai, where most of Vilnius' Jewish population had been murdered, also demonstrate this desire to remove Jewish traces. Soon after liberation a monument was erected at the site which proclaimed in Yiddish and Russian eternal memory for the Jews of Vilnius and elsewhere murdered here. This monument was put up by Jewish survivors in 1945. Seven years later it was dynamited and replaced with a more modest obelisk without any Yiddish inscription and that spoke (in Lithuanian and Russian) only of 'Victims of Fascism' (Ran 1974, pp. 533–4). The fact that Jews had been singled out for extermination and indeed had been treated vastly worse by 'Fascism' than ethnic Lithuanians was conveniently forgotten.

The Lithuanian communists knew well that they lacked popularity among the Lithuanian people and that they ruled only with the support of Moscow. At the same time, they made special efforts not to antagonize Lithuanian sensibilities. In particular the sensitive issue of Lithuanian collaboration with the Nazi occupiers was portrayed in a highly simplistic manner. *Tiesa* repeatedly denounced, for example, 'Lithuanian-German Nationalists' as the 'Mortal Enemies of the Lithuanian people' (*Tiesa*, 13 January 1945). But by portraying these Lithuanian nationalists as monstrous stooges of the Nazis (and, conveniently, as individuals who had fled to the West and/or had become anti-Soviet partisans), the Soviet Lithuanian officials both justified their brutal crushing of any anti-Soviet resistance and at the same time exculpated the vast majority of the Lithuanian population. Essentially a tacit agreement was reached: we Lithuanian communists will not examine the actual events and perpetrators of 1941–1944 too carefully (unless they were and are explicitly anti-Soviet). Thus even when volumes were published (often first in Russian) on the anti-Jewish massacres of the war period, the impression was given that only a very few despicable 'Lithuanian-German nationalists' (to use the above nomenclature) played any part, while the vast majority of the Lithuanian population actively attempted to help their Jewish neighbors (Kaplanas 1962; *Masinės žudynės* 1965, 1973). In fact, of course, initial mass murders of Lithuanian Jews in summer 1941 were carried out almost entirely by

Lithuanians, not Germans, though of course the Germans were quite happy to let the Lithuanians do their dirty work (Eidintas 2003; Kwiet 1998; MacQueen 1998; Stang 1996). The issue of 'collaboration' is obviously a painful and complicated one, but it is also a matter of crucial importance for understanding the history of the twentieth century (Tauber 2006).

In the decade after 1944, the Lithuanian communists attempted to create a new Vilnius: the Soviet Lithuanian capital. To do this, they used a variety of means, combining repression, cultural policies and rhetoric. They essentially emptied the city of its Polish population and worked to bring in ethnic Lithuanians. On the rhetorical front, the Lithuanian communists harked back to historical figures (among them, Grand Duke Gediminas) and repressed more recent historical events and memories, in particular of the Polish and Jewish past in the city. They also worked to build up Vilnius as the center of Lithuanian culture and scholarship while making it a modern, industrial Soviet city.

In many respects the Lithuanian communists helped pave the way for the predominantly Lithuanian city of today. We, too, should be wary of 'partial memory' and 'intended forgetting' as perhaps understandable psychological mechanisms for wiping away uncomfortable and unattractive historical facts. Rather, by honestly and openly facing the multi-faceted and complex past, including Vilnius' multiethnic population and the not-always-benevolent relations between Lithuanians and others, we fulfill our duty as historians and true patriots.

Notes

1 Throughout this essay I will use the Lithuanian name for the city, 'Vilnius', for the sake of clarity.

2 *Rocznik statystyczny Wilna 1937* (Wilno, Skład Główny w centralnym biurze statystycznym m. Wilna, 1939), p. 9.

3 Recently the Lithuanian historian Česlovas Laurinavičius suggested that the Soviet authorities may have considered forming a Lithuanian SSR without Vilnius. However, I find this argument rather speculative and contradicted by policies followed from July 1944 in the city (Anušauskas & Laurinavičius 2007, pp. 181–7).

4 'Podpisanie Układu', *Prawda Wileńska*, 26 September 1944, p. 1. It is remarkable that after this front-page announcement of the signing of this agreement, the planned evacuations are not again mentioned until the very end of the year. ('Zawiadomienie do Polaków i byłych obywateli polskich narodowości żydowskiej, zamieszkałych w Litewskiej SRR,' in *Prawda Wileńska* 135, (397), 27 December 1944, p. 1).

5 Lietuvos Centrinis Valstybės Archyvas, Vilnius (LCVA), f. R-841, ap. 10, b. 9.

6 LCVA, f. R754, ap. 13, b. 40, ll. 20–24; 88–91. The excerpts from letters, in Russian translation (with the remark 'translated from Polish'), formed part of frequent NKVD *Spetssoobshcheniia*.

7 LCVA, f. R841, ap. 10, b. 27, l. 64.

8 For correspondence regarding individuals of 'doubtful' nationality, see LCVA, f. R841, ap. 10, b. 37.

9 This proposed name change is rather perplexing, though the desire to get rid of the famous religious leader of the late eighteenth and early nineteenth century, the Gaon ('genius'), is readily understandable. Samuel Strashun, who died in 1872, was also a well-known local Talmudist (who left a rich library of religious works to the city) and for that reason was probably unpalatable to communists. Dr. Shabad had been a distinguished physician and community leader who had only died in 1935. Mark Antokolskii was, of course, born in Vilnius but made his career in St. Petersburg and Paris. As a Russified (at least by language) and non-religious Jew he was probably less offensive to communist sensibilities.

10 Vilniaus Apskrities Archyvas (VAA), f. 761, ap. 9, b. 71. The documents in this file are a remarkable mixture of Lithuanian and Russian texts, including one (ll. 72–3) pointing out that the Russian versions of street names should not simply be a transliteration of the Lithuanian but should follow Russian grammar (e.g., not 'Antokol'skio' in Russian but Antokol'skogo). This suggestion was not, however, consistently adopted in Soviet times.

11 VAA, f. 761, ap. 4, b. 135.

12 VAA, f. 5, b. 1014; and f. 5, b. 598 contain dozens of pictures of the devastated city in late 1944 and early 1945.

13 For a final (Soviet) report on the carrying out of the evacuations of Poles, see LCVA, f. R841, ap. 10, b. 27, ll. 94–101. A somewhat different report covering the same events was published in Kołodziej (1997).

14 See the several dozen files in LCVA, f. R1390. These files are available in microfilm at the United State Holocaust Memorial Museum, General Directorate of Lithuania Archives collection, 1998. A. 0073, reel 52. Unfortunately in many cases we do not have the artifacts or documents themselves, only lists of material which was later lost.

References

Agranovskii, G. & Guzenberg, I. (1992) *Litovskii Ierusalim: Kratkii putevoditel' po pamyatnym mestam evreiskoi istorii i kul'tury v Vil'niuse* (Vilnius, Lituanus).

Anušauskas, A. & Laurinavičius, Č. (eds) (2007) *Lietuva antrajame pasauliniame kare* (Vilnius, LII).

Arad, Y. (1982) *Ghetto in Flames: the Struggle and Destruction of the Jews in Vilna in the Holocaust* (New York, Holocaust Library).

Atamukas, S. (2001) *Lietuvos žydų kelias. Nuo XIV amžiaus iki XX a. pabaigos* (Vilnius, alma littera).

Bagrowska, L. (1945) 'Muzeum żydowskie w Vilnius' [sic], *Prawda Wileńska*, 4 March, p. 2.

Bak, S. (2001) *Painted in Words – A Memoir* (Bloomington, Indiana University Press).

Baliński, M. (1835) *Opisanie statystyczne miasta Wilna* (Wilno, Józef Zawadzki własnym nakładem).

Biržiška, M. (1948) *Vilniaus universiteto, 1940–1941 m* (Memmingen, 'Mintis').

Eidintas, A. (2003) *Jews, Lithuanians and the Holocaust* (Vilnius, Versus Aureus).

Fishman, D. (1998) *Dem Feuer entrissen: Die Rettung jüdischer Kulturschätze in Wilna* (Hannover, Laurentius).

Frick, D. (2003) 'The Bells of Vilnius: Keeping Time in a City of Many Calendars', in Burger, G. (ed.) (2003) *Making Contact: Maps, Identity and Travel* (Edmonton, University of Alberta Press).
Jankevičienė, A. (1996) *Vilniaus Didžiojo Sinagoga/Great Synagogue of Vilnius* (Vilnius, Savastis).
Jurginis, J., Merkys, V. & Tautavičius, A. (1968) *Vilniaus miesto istorija nuo seniausių laikų iki Spalio revoliucijos* (Vilnius, Mintis).
Kaczerginski, S. (1947) *Khurbn vilne* (New York, Bikher-farlag).
Kaplanas, O. (1962) *Devtasis Fortas kaltina* (Vilnius, Valstybinės politinės ir mokslinės literatūros leidykla).
Klausner, I. (1988) *Vilna, yerushalayim deLita. Dorot rishonim 1495–1881* (Tel Aviv, Beth lohmei ha'ghettaoth).
Kołodziej, E. (1997) 'Sprawozdania Głównego Pełnomocnika Rządu RP do spraw Ewakuacji Ludności Polskiej z Litewskiej SRR w Wilnie z przebiegu zbiorowej repatriacji w latach 1945–1946', *Teki Archiwalne*, 2, 24, pp. 167–94.
Kwiet, K. (1998) 'Rehearsing for Murder: The Beginning of the Final Solution in Lithuania in June 1941', *Holocaust and Genocide Studies*, 12, 1, Spring, pp. 3–26.
Lewandowska, S. (1997) *Życie codzienne Wilna w latach II wojny światowy* (Warsaw, Neriton).
Lewandowska, S. (2004) *Losy wilnian. Zapis rzeczywistości okupacyjnej. Ludzie, fakty, wydarzenia 1939–1945* (Warsaw, Wydawnictwo Neriton IH PAN).
Lewandowska, S. (2007) *Wilno 1944–1945: Oczekiwania i nastroje* (Warsaw, Neriton).
Linčiuvienė, D. (ed.) (1999) *Kultūrinis Vilniaus gyvenimas 1939–1945* (Vilnius, Lietuvių literatūros ir tautosakos institutas).
Łossowski, P. (1991) *Likwidacja Uniwersytetu Stefana Bartorego przez władze litewskie w grudniu 1939 r. Dokumenty i materiały* (Warsaw, 'Interlibro').
Łossowski, P. (1966) *Stosunki polsko-litewskie w latach 1918–1920* (Warsaw, Książka I Wiedza).
MacQueen, M. (1998) 'The Context of Mass Destruction: Agents and Prerequisites of the Holocaust in Lithuania', *Holocaust and Genocide Studies*, 12, 1, Spring, pp. 27–48.
Manelis, E. & Samavičius, R. (eds) (2001) *Vilniaus miesto istorijos skaitiniai* (Vilnius, Vilniaus knyga).
Manelis, E. & Samavičius, R. (eds) (2003) *Vilniaus miesto istorijos dokumentai* (Vilnius, Vilniaus knyga).
Masinės žudynės (1965, 1973) *Masinės žudynės Lietuvoje (1941–1944). Dokumentų rinkinys* (Vilnius, Mintis), Vol. 2.
Merkys, V., *et al.* (1979) *Vilniaus universiteto istorija (1940–1979)* (Vilnius, Mokslas), Vol. 3.
Mikłaszewicz, I. (2002) 'Postawa biskupów wobec próby przeciwstania interesów katolików, Polaków, i Litwinów w Wilnie w latach 1944–1953', in Feliksiak, E. & Leś, M. (eds) (2002) *Wilno i świat. Dzieje środowiska intelektualnego*, (Białystok, Towarzystwo Literackie im. Adama Mickiewicza) vol. 2.
Mikučianis, V. (2001) *Norėjau dirbti Lietuvoje* (Vilnius, Vilniaus dailė akademijos leidykla).
Misius, K. (2001) 'Bažnyčių uždarinėjimas Vilniuje pokario metais', in Manelis, E. & Samavičius, R. (eds) (2001), pp. 812–5.
Niwiński, P. (1999) *Okręg Wileński AK w latach 1944–1948* (Warsaw, Oficyna Wydawnicza Volumen).
Pšibilskis, V. (1995) 'Byla dėl Vilniaus Arkikatedros: 1949–1956', *Kultūros barai*, 5, May, pp. 66–72.

Ran, L. (1974) *Yerushalayim de Lita = Jerusalem of Lithuania* (New York, Laureate Press).
Šadžius, H., *et al.* (1972) *Vilniaus miesto istorija nuo Spalio revoliucijos iki dabartinių metų* (Vilnius, 'Mintis').
Senn, A. (1966) *The Great Powers, Lithuania and the Vilna Question 1920–1928* (Leiden, Brill).
Srebrakowski, A. (2001) *Polacy w Litewskiej SSR, 1944–1989* (Toruń, Adam Marszałek).
Stang, K. (1996) *Kollaboration und Massenmord. Die litauische Hilfspolizei, das Rollkommando Hamann und die Ermordung der litauischen Juden* (Frankfurt am Main, Peter Lang).
Sutzkever, A. (1946) *Fun vilner geto* (Moscow, 'Der emes').
Tauber, J. (ed.) (2006) *'Kollaboration' in Nordosteuropa. Erscheinungsformen und Deutungen im 20. Jahrhundert* (Wiesbaden, Harrassowitz Verlag).
Truska, L., Anušauskas, A. & Petravičiūtė, I. (1999) *Sovietinis saugumas Lietuvoje 1940–1953 metais* (Vilnius, Lietuvos gyventojų genocido ir rezistencijos tyrimo centras).
Vilnius 1900–2005 (2005) *Vilnius 1900–2005: A Guide to Modern Architecture* (Vilnius, Architektūros fondas).
Weeks, T. (2006) 'A Multi-Ethnic City in Transition: Vilnius's Stormy Decade, 1939–1949', *Eurasian Geography and Economics*, 47, 2, pp. 153–175.
Weeks, T. (2007) 'Population Politics in Vilnius 1944–1947: A Case Study of Socialist-Sponsored Ethnic Cleansing', *Post-Soviet Affairs*, 23, 1, pp. 76–95.

INDEX

Page numbers in *Italics* represent tables.
Page numbers in **Bold** represent figures.

For Product Safety Concerns and Information please contact our EU representative GPSR@taylorandfrancis.com
Taylor & Francis Verlag GmbH, Kaufingerstraße 24, 80331 München, Germany

www.ingramcontent.com/pod-product-compliance
Lightning Source LLC
Chambersburg PA
CBHW050717280326
41926CB00088B/3081
9780415846776